PLATINUM EDITION

D0071188

Series Director: Diane Larsen-Freeman

GRAMMAR DIMENSIONS

FORM, MEANING, and USE

Victoria Badalamenti
LaGuardia Community College

Carolyn Henner Stanchina
Queens College

City University of New York

Listening Activities in this text were developed by the editorial team at Heinle & Heinle.

THOMSON

✦

HEINLE

Australia • Canada • Denmark • Japan • Mexico • New Zealand
Philippines • Puerto Rico • Singapore • Spain • United Kingdom • United States

THOMSON

HEINLE

Grammar Dimensions 1
Platinum Edition
Victoria Badalamenti and Carolyn Henner-Stanchina
Series Director: Diane Larsen-Freeman

Acquisitions Editor: *Eric Bredenberg*
Senior Developmental Editor: *Amy Lawler*
Production Editor: *Michael Burggren*
Senior Marketing Manager: *Charlotte Sturdy*
Manufacturing Coordinator: *Mary Beth Hennebury*
Composition/Project Management: *The PRD Group, Inc.*
Text Design: *Sue Gerould, Perspectives*
Cover Design: *Hannus Design Associates*

Printed in Canada
5 6 7 8 9 10   07 06 05 04 03

For more information contact Heinle, 25 Thomson Place, Boston, MA 02210 USA,
or you can visit our Internet site at http://www.heinle.com

ISBN: 0-8384-0260-7

TOEFL® is a registered trademark of Educational Testing Service (ETS). This product is not
endorsed or approved by ETS.

A Special Thanks

The series director, authors, and publisher would like to thank the following individuals who offered many helpful insights and suggestions for change throughout the development of *Grammar Dimensions*.

Jane Berger
Solano Community College, California
Mary Bottega
San Jose State University
Mary Brooks
Eastern Washington University
Christina Broucqsault
California State Polytechnic University
José Carmona
Hudson Community College
Susan Carnell
University of Texas at Arlington
Susana Christie
San Diego State University
Diana Christopher
Georgetown University
Gwendolyn Cooper
Rutgers University
Sue Cozzarelli
EF International, San Diego
Catherine Crystal
Laney College, California
Kevin Cross
University of San Francisco
Julie Damron
Interlink at Valparaiso University, Indiana
Glen Deckert
Eastern Michigan University
Eric Dwyer
University of Texas at Austin
Ann Eubank
Jefferson Community College
Alice Fine
UCLA Extension
Alicia Going
The English Language Study Center, Oregon
Molly Gould
University of Delaware
Maren M. Hargis
San Diego Mesa College
Mary Herbert
University of California, Davis Extension

Jane Hilbert
ELS Language Center, Florida International University
Eli Hinkel
Xavier University
Kathy Hitchcox
International English Institute, Fresno
Joyce Hutchings
Georgetown University
Heather Jeddy
Northern Virginia Community College
Judi Keen
University of California, Davis, and Sacramento City College
Karli Kelber
American Language Institute, New York University
Sherwin Kizner
LaGuardia Community College
Anne Kornfeld
LaGuardia Community College
Kay Longmire
Interlink at Valparaiso University, Indiana
Roberta Martin
Queens College
Bernadette McGlynn
ELS Language Center, St. Joseph's University
Billy McGowan
Aspect International, Boston
Margaret Mehran
Queens College
Richard Moore
University of Washington
Karen Moreno
Teikyo Post University, Connecticut
Gino Muzzetti
Santa Rosa Junior College, California
Mary Nance-Tager
LaGuardia Community College
Karen O'Neill
San Jose State University
Mary O'Neal
Northern Virginia Community College

Nancy Pagliara
Northern Virginia Community College
Keith Pharis
Southern Illinois University
Amy Parker
ELS Language Center, San Francisco
Margene Petersen
ELS Language Center, Philadelphia
Nancy Pfingstag
University of North Carolina, Charlotte
Sally Prieto
Grand Rapids Community College
India Plough
Michigan State University
Mostafa Rahbar
University of Tennessee at Knoxville
Dudley Reynolds
Indiana University
Ann Salzman
University of Illinois at Urbana-Champaign
Jennifer Schmidt
San Francisco State University
Cynthia Schuemann
Miami-Dade Community College
Jennifer Schultz
Golden Gate University
Mary Beth Selbo
Wright College, City Colleges of Chicago
Stephen Sheeran
Bishop's University, Lenoxville, Quebec
Kathy Sherak
San Francisco State University
Keith Smith
ELS Language Center, San Francisco
Helen Solorzano
Northeastern University
Brad Waltman
LaGuardia Community College
Warren Wilson
Queens College

Contents

Unit 4 | Nouns
Count and Noncount Nouns, *Be* + Adjective + Noun   46

Unit 5 | The Verb *Have*
Affirmative and Negative Statements, Questions and Short Answers, *Some/Any*   64

Unit 6 | *This/That/These/Those* and Possessives   80

A Word from Diane Larsen-Freeman, Series Director

Before *Grammar Dimensions* was published, teachers would always ask me, "What is the role of grammar in a communicative approach?" These teachers recognized the importance of teaching grammar, but they associated grammar with form and communication with meaning, and thus could not see how the two easily fit together. *Grammar Dimensions* was created to help teachers and students appreciate the fact that grammar is not just about form. While grammar does indeed involve form, in order to communicate, language users also need to know the meaning of the forms and when to use them appropriately. In fact, it is sometimes not the form, but the *meaning* or *appropriate use* of a grammatical structure that represents the greatest long-term learning challenge for students. For instance, learning when it is appropriate to use the present perfect tense instead of the past tense, or being able to use two-word or phrasal verbs meaningfully, represent formidable challenges for ESL students.

The three dimensions of form, meaning, and use can be depicted in a pie chart with their interrelationship illustrated by the three arrows:

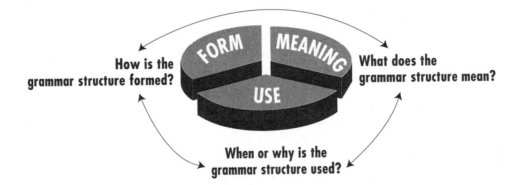

Helping students learn to use grammatical structures accurately, meaningfully, and appropriately is the fundamental goal of *Grammar Dimensions.* It is consistent with the goal of helping students to communicate meaningfully in English, and one that recognizes the undeniable interdependence of grammar and communication.

Enjoy the Platinum Edition!

To learn more about form, meaning, and use, read *The Grammar Book: An ESL/EFL Teacher's Course,* Second Edition, by Marianne Celce-Murcia and Diane Larsen-Freeman, also from Heinle & Heinle. It helps both prospective and practicing teachers of ESL/EFL enhance their understanding of English grammar, expand their skills in linguistic analysis, and develop a pedagogical approach to teaching English grammar that builds on the three dimensions. ISBN: 0-8384-4725-2.

Welcome to Grammar Dimensions, Platinum Edition!
The most comprehensive communicative grammar series available.

Updated and revised, *Grammar Dimensions, Platinum Edition,* makes teaching grammar easy and more effective than ever. Clear grammar explanations, a wealth of exercises, lively communicative activities, and fully annotated Teacher's Editions help both beginning and experienced teachers give their students the practice and skills they need to communicate accurately, meaningfully, and appropriately.

Grammar Dimensions, Platinum Edition, is:

Communicative	• Students practice the **form, meaning,** and **use** of each grammar structure.
	• **Improved! A variety of communicative activities** helps students practice grammar and communication in tandem, eliciting self-expression and personalized practice.
	• Students learn to communicate accurately, meaningfully, and appropriately.
Comprehensive	• **Improved!** Grammar is presented in **clear charts.**
	• **A wealth of exercises** helps students practice and master their new language.
	• **The Workbook** provides extra practice and helps students prepare for the TOEFL® Test.
	• **Engaging listening activities** on audiocassette further reinforce the target structure.
Clear	• **Improved! Simplified grammar explanations** help both students and teachers easily understand and comprehend each language structure.
	• **Improved! A fresh new design** makes each activity engaging.
	• **New! Communicative activities** ("the Purple Pages") are now labeled with the skill being practiced.
	• **New!** The Teacher's Edition has **page references** for the Student Book and Workbook, minimizing extra preparation time.

User-Friendly for Students	• **Contextualized grammar explanations and examples** help students understand the target language.
	• **New! Goals** at the beginning of each unit focus students' attention on the learning they will do.
	• **Sample phrases and sentences** model the appropriate use of the structure.
User-Friendly for Teachers	• **New!** Teacher's Edition now contains answers, tests, tape scripts, and complete, **step-by-step teaching suggestions** for every activity.
	• **New!** "Purple Page" activities are now labeled with the skill.
	• **Improved! A tight integration** among the Student Book, the Workbook and the Teacher's Edition make extension activities easy to do.
Flexible	• Instructors can use the units in order or as set by their curriculum.
	• Exercises can be used in order or as needed by the students.
	• "Purple Page" activities can be used at the end of the unit or interspersed throughout the unit.
Effective	Students who learn the form, meaning, and use of each grammar structure will be able to communicate more accurately, meaningfully, and appropriately.

Grammar Dimensions, Platinum Edition

With *Grammar Dimensions, Platinum Edition,* students progress from the sentence level to the discourse level, and learn to communicate appropriately at all levels.

Grammar Dimensions Book 1   Grammar Dimensions Book 2   Grammar Dimensions Book 3   Grammar Dimensions Book 4

Sentence level   Discourse level

	Grammar Dimensions, Book 1	Grammar Dimensions, Book 2	Grammar Dimensions, Book 3	Grammar Dimensions, Book 4
Level	High beginning	Intermediate	High intermediate	Advanced
Grammar level	Sentence and subsentence level	Sentence and subsentence level	Discourse level	Discourse level
Primary language and communication focus	Semantic notions such as *time* and *place*	Social functions, such as *making requests* and *seeking permission*	Cohesion and coherence at the discourse level	Academic and technical discourse
Major skill focus	Listening and speaking	Listening and speaking	Reading and writing	Reading and writing
Outcome	Students form accurate, meaningful, and appropriate structures at the sentence level.	Students form accurate, meaningful, and appropriate structures at the sentence level.	Students learn how accurate, meaningful, and appropriate grammatical structures contribute to the organization of language above the simple sentence.	Students learn how accurate, meaningful, and appropriate grammatical structures contribute to the organization of language above the simple sentence.

Unit Organization

Used with or without the Workbook and the *Grammar 3D* CD-ROM, *Grammar Dimensions* Student Book units are designed to be clear, comprehensive, flexible, and communicative.

Goals	• **Focus students' attention** on the learning they will do in each unit.
Opening Task	• **Contextualizes** the target grammatical structure. • **Enables teachers to diagnose** their students' performance and identify the aspect of the structure with which their students have the most difficulty. • **Provides a roadmap** for the grammar points students need to work on in that chapter.
Focus Boxes	• **Present the form, meaning,** or **use** of a particular grammatical structure. • **Focus students' attention** to a particular feature of the target structure. Each rule or explanation is preceded by examples, so teachers can have students work inductively to try to discover the rule on their own.
Exercises	• Provide a wealth of opportunity to **practice** the form and meaning of the grammar structures. • Help students develop the skill of **"grammaring"**—the ability to use structures accurately, meaningfully, and appropriately. • Are varied, thematically coherent, but purposeful. • Give students many opportunities to personalize and own the language.
Communicative Activities ("The Purple Pages")	• Help students practice **grammar and communication in tandem.** • **Are engaging!** • Encourage students to **use their new language** both inside and outside the classroom. • Provide an opportunity to **practice reading, writing, listening, and speaking skills,** helping students realize the communicative value of the grammar they are learning.

Student Book Supplements

Audiocassettes	• **Provide listening activities for** each unit so students can practice listening to **grammar structures in context.**
Workbooks	• **Provide additional exercises** for each grammar point presented in the student text. • Offer question types found on the **TOEFL**® Test
Teacher's Editions	• **Facilitate teaching** by providing in one place notes and examples, answer keys to the Student Book and Workbook, page references to all of the components, the tapescript for the audiocassette activities, and tests with answer keys for each unit. • **Minimize teacher preparation time** by providing step-by-step teaching suggestions for every focus box and activity in the Student Book.

The *Grammar Dimensions, Platinum Edition* Student Books and the additional components help teachers teach and students learn to use English grammar structures in communication accurately, meaningfully, and appropriately.

Acknowledgments

Series Director Acknowledgments

This edition would not have come about if it had not been for the enthusiastic response of teachers and students using the previous editions. I am very grateful for the reception *Grammar Dimensions* has been given.

I am also grateful for all the authors' efforts. To be a teacher, and at the same time a writer, is a difficult balance to achieve . . . so is being an innovative creator of materials, and yet, a team player. They have met these challenges exceedingly well in my opinion. Then, too, the Heinle & Heinle team has been impressive. I am grateful for the leadership exercised by Erik Gundersen, formerly of Heinle & Heinle. I also appreciate all the support from Charlotte Sturdy, Eric Bredenberg, Mike Burggren, Mary Beth Hennebury, and Marianne Bartow. Deserving special mention are Amy Lawler and Nancy Jordan, who never lost the vision while they attended to the detail with good humor and professionalism.

I have also benefited from the counsel of Marianne Celce-Murcia, consultant for the first edition this project, and my friend. Finally, I wish to thank my family members, Elliott, Brent, and Gavin, for not once asking the (negative yes–no) question that must have occurred to them countless times: "Haven't you finished yet?"

Author Acknowledgments

This book is dedicated to the two Joels, Melanie, and Michele, who stood steadfastly by, tolerating all the moods and missed moments, as we reeled through this revision process. Their stamina was a great source of strength. Most importantly, this book also stands as an affirmation of the power of friendship.

We are deeply grateful to Diane Larsen-Freeman for her patient guidance and supportive ear.

We wish to extend our sincere thanks to The PRD Group, whose agreeable nature and "can do" spirit were instrumental and indispensable in the final stages of this revision.

We also wish to thank both our ESL students at the City University of New York, and our Methods students at Queens College and The New School for Social Research, for their insights.

Finally, our fondest thoughts and highest praise go to Amy Lawler for her talent, skill, humanity, and positive approach in bringing this project to fruition.

UNIT 1

THE VERB BE

Affirmative Statements, Subject Pronouns

UNIT GOALS:

- To use correct forms of the verb *be* in affirmative statements
- To use subject pronouns
- To use correct forms of contractions with subjects and the verb *be*
- To introduce and greet people formally and informally in English

▶ OPENING TASK
Introductions

STEP 1 Match the introductions to the pictures.

A.

B.

C.

D.

E.

F.

1. "Hello. My name is Monique. I'm French. I'm from Paris."

2. "I'm Chen. I'm Chinese. I'm from Beijing."

3. "We're the Mendoza family. This is my wife Maria. I'm Carlos. Our daughters' names are Rosita and Raquel."

4. "Hi. I'm Genya. I'm Russian. I'm from Moscow."

5. "I'm Fernando and this is Isabel. We are married. We are Colombian. We're from Bogota."

6. "Hi. My name is Oumar and this is my brother Alioune. We're from Senegal. Senegal is in West Africa."

STEP 2   Look at Monique's information card. Then complete the information card about yourself. Introduce yourself to the class.

Information Card

Name: Monique Delande
Country: France
Nationality: French
Age: 28 years old
Married/Divorced/Single: Single

Information Card

Name: _____
Country: _____
Nationality: _____
Age: _____
Married/Divorced/Single: _____

My name is _____ .
I am from _____ .
I'm _____ .
I'm _____ years old.
I'm _____ .

▶ *Be:* Affirmative Statements

SUBJECT	VERB *Be*		
Monique She Paris The city of Paris	is	single. from Paris. in France. beautiful.	singular (one)
Fernando and Isabel They The people in Colombia	are	Colombian. married. friendly.	plural (more than one)

EXERCISE 1

Fill in the blanks with the verb *be* or a name.

1. Genya _____is_____ from Russia.

2. Fernando and Isabel _____ married.

3. _____ is from the People's Republic of China.

4. Monique _____ twenty-eight years old.

5. Rosita and Raquel _____ sisters.

6. _____ are from Senegal.

7. Genya _____ divorced.

8. The Mendozas _____ Mexican.

9. _____ is from France.

10. Moscow _____ in Russia.

EXERCISE 2

Use the world map to complete each sentence. The first one has been done for you.

Continents/Regions

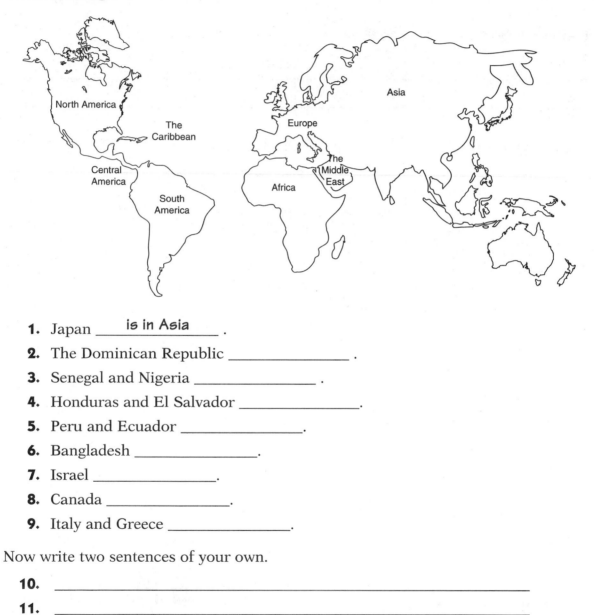

1. Japan _____is in Asia_____ .
2. The Dominican Republic _____ .
3. Senegal and Nigeria _____ .
4. Honduras and El Salvador _____.
5. Peru and Ecuador _____.
6. Bangladesh _____.
7. Israel _____.
8. Canada _____.
9. Italy and Greece _____.

Now write two sentences of your own.

10. _____
11. _____

▶ Subject Pronouns with Be

SUBJECT PRONOUN	VERB *Be*	
I	am	single.
You	are	married.
He She It	is	Brazilian.
We You They	are	from Korea.

Note: Use subject pronouns only after you know the subject.

Chen is Chinese. He is from Beijing.

EXERCISE 3

Read the dialogues. Fill in the blanks with a subject pronoun. The first one has been done for you.

1.

A. We are from Wellington.

B. Oh, *you* are from New Zealand! How interesting!

2.

B. I know_____ is from Helsinki.

A. That's Erik. He's Finnish.

EXERCISE 4

The subject pronouns in the sentences below are not correct. Circle the incorrect pronouns and write the correct sentences in the blanks.

1. Miyuki and Seung are from Asia. (You) are Asian. _They are Asian._
2. John is thirty years old. She is from Cyprus. _____
3. You and Hamid are Algerian. They are from Algiers. _____
4. Port-au-Prince is in Haiti. She is the capital city. _____
5. Clemente and I are from Rome. They are Italian. _____
6. Pedro and Miguel are from Puebla. You are Mexican. _____
7. Ayelet and Amir are from Tel Aviv. We are Israeli. _____

EXERCISE 5

Information Gap. Here is a list of students in an English-as-a-Second-Language (ESL) class. Work with a partner. You look at List A on the next page and make a statement about student number 1 on your list. Your partner looks at List B on page A-14 and makes a second statement with a subject pronoun about student number 1.

▶ **EXAMPLE:** **You say:** Mario is from Peru.

         Your partner says: He is Peruvian.

List A

Men	Country	Nationality
1. Mario	Peru	
2. Mohammed		Moroccan
3. Hideki and Yoshi	Japan	
4. Leonardo		Dominican
5. Oumar	Senegal	
Women		
6. Lilik		Indonesian
7. Krystyna	Poland	
8. Liisa and Katja		Finnish
9. Belen	Spain	
10. Margarita and Dalia		Brazilian

EXERCISE 6

Make summary statements about the students in the ESL class in Exercise 5.
Use the continents/regions and countries below.

▶ **EXAMPLE:** Africa

Two students are from Africa. One is from Morocco and one is from Senegal.

1. Africa

_____

2. Asia

_____

3. Europe

_____

4. South America

_____

5. Dominican Republic

_____

6. Finland

_____

▶ Contraction with *Be*

SUBJECT PRONOUN + *Be*		Be CONTRACTIONS	
I am		I'm	
You are		You're	
He is		He's	
She is	American.	She's	from the United States.
It is		It's	
We are		We're	
You are		You're	
		They're	

EXERCISE 7

Think about the people and places in this unit. Match the people and places on the left with the information on the right. Make two statements aloud. Use the name in the first statement and the subject pronoun and *Be* contraction in the second statement.

▶ **EXAMPLE:** **1.** Genya is Russian.   **2.** She's divorced.

1. Genya	a. Colombia/the capital
2. Japan	b. sisters/Mexican
3. Chen	c. Russian/divorced
4. Fernando and Isabel	d. an island/in the Caribbean
5. Monique	e. Chinese/twenty-five years old
6. Moscow	f. brothers/from Senegal
7. Bogotá	g. Russia/the capital
8. Rosita and Raquel	h. French/from Paris
9. Haiti	i. Colombian/married
10. Oumar and Alioune	j. an island/in the Pacific Ocean

EXERCISE 8

Go back to the Opening Task on page 1. Underline all the singular subjects and the verb *be*. Circle all the plural subjects and the verb *be*.

▶ **EXAMPLE:** <u>My name is</u> Monique.

⟨We're⟩ the Mendoza family.

EXERCISE 9

Choose information from Columns A and B that matches each famous person or group of people. Then make two statements.

▶ **EXAMPLE:** Madonna is American. She's a pop singer.

Famous People	A Nationality	B Occupation
1. Madonna	Tibetan	Opera singers
2. Arnold Schwarzenegger	South African	An actress
3. The Rolling Stones	Canadian	A baseball player
4. Nelson Mandela	Dominican	An actor
5. The Dalai Lama	French	A writer
6. Luciano Pavarotti & Cecilia Bartoli	Italian	A country music singer
7. Gabriel Garcia Marquez	British	A pop singer ✔
8. Catherine Deneuve	Colombian	A political leader
9. Sammy Sosa	American ✔	A religious leader
10. Shania Twain	Austrian	Rock singers

▶ **Introductions and Greetings**

USE

Introductions

EXAMPLES	EXPLANATIONS
(a) Hello. My name's Gustavo. I'm from the Philippines.	
(b) Hi! I'm Jennifer Brown. I'm from Florida. Please call me Jenny.	Introducing yourself
(c) Susan: Hello, John. This is Mario Ortiz. He's from the Philippines. John: Hi, Mario. Nice to meet you. Mario: Nice to meet you too, John.	Introducing another person
(d) Jeff: Hi, my name is Jeff Jones. I'm from California. What is your name? Alicia: Alicia Torres. Jeff: Where are you from, Alicia? Alicia: I'm from Chile. Jeff: Oh, really? Nice to meet you.	Meeting someone for the first time

EXAMPLES	EXPLANATIONS
(e) Ms. Chen: Good morning, Mr. Brown. Mr. Brown: Good morning, Ms. Chen. How are you today? Ms. Chen: I'm fine, thank you. How are you?	Greetings can be formal or informal (very friendly). Formal
(f) Bill: Hello, Lautaro. How's everything? Lautaro: Fine thanks, Bill. And how are you?	
(g) Jake: Hi, Yoshi. How are you doing? Yoshi: O.K., Jake. How about you? Jake: Not bad.	Informal
(h) Hello, Ms. Smith. **(i)** NOT: Hello, Ms. Susan Smith. Hello, Ms. Susan.	Use a title (*Mr., Mrs., Ms., Dr., Professor*) with a family name (last name), not with the full name, not with the first name.

EXERCISE 10

Introduce the person next to you to the class.

▶ **EXAMPLE:** This is Yoshi. He's from Japan.

EXERCISE 11

Fill in the blanks in the conversation.

▶ **EXAMPLE:** Susan: I'm Susan Wilson from New York.

Jim: __Nice to meet you__ Susan. __My name is__ Jim. __I'm__ from California.

1. **Fred:** Hello. I'm Fred.

   Phillippe: _____ , Fred. _____ Phillippe.

2. Lilik: Hi! I'm Lilik. _____ ?

Demos: My name's Demos.

Lilik: _____ ?

Demos: Greece. _____ ?

Lilik: I'm from Indonesia.

3. Michael: Hi, Gregg. _____ Jane.

Gregg: Hello, Jane. _____ ?

Jane: Fine, thanks. _____ ?

Gregg: Great!

Use Your English

ACTIVITY 1: WRITING

STEP 1 Make a list of all the students in your class. Make a list of the countries they come from and their nationalities.

Names	Countries	Nationalities
_____	_____	_____
_____	_____	_____
_____	_____	_____
_____	_____	_____
_____		

STEP 2 Write summary statements about the students in your class with the information from Step 1.

▶ **EXAMPLES:** Two students are Colombian.

Six students are from Asia.

ACTIVITY 2: WRITING/LISTENING

On a piece of paper write three sentences about yourself. Do not write your name on the paper. Give the paper to your teacher. Your teacher reads each paper and the class guesses who the person is.

▶ **EXAMPLE:** I am twenty-two years old. I'm from North Africa. I'm Algerian.

ACTIVITY 3: WRITING/SPEAKING

Work with a partner. Go back to your information card in the Opening Task on page 1. Exchange your information card with your partner. Introduce your partner to the class.

▶ **EXAMPLE:** This is Maria Gomez. She is from Mexico City. She is twenty-five years old. She is married.

ACTIVITY 4: SPEAKING

Role-play with a partner.

1. You are a student. Greet your professor in school.

2. Greet your classmate.

3. Greet your boss at work.

4. Introduce your partner to another student.

ACTIVITY 5: LISTENING

Listen and decide. Three different people greet Mr. Maxwell Forbes, a bank manager, at a job interview. In two of the conversations, the greetings are wrong. Who gets the job? Circle the person who gets the job.

1. Mr. Blake   2. Ms. Robbins   3. Kevin Dobbs

UNIT 2

THE VERB BE

Yes/No Questions, Be + Adjective, Negative Statements

UNIT GOALS:

- To ask *yes/no* questions with the verb *be* and give short answers
- To use the verb *be* with adjectives
- To make negative statements and contractions with *be*

▶ OPENING TASK
Asking Personal Questions

STEP 1 Here are some advertisements from the newspaper. Match each advertisement to the correct advertisers on the next page.

Are you single? Are you lonely? Are you ready to meet someone?
Call1-800-555-LOVE

A.

Is English hard for you? It isn't at our school. It's easy and fun!
Enroll now! Call ENG-LISH

B.

Are you sad? Are you nervous? Are you worried? You are not alone. I can help.
Call 554-HELP

C.

D.

Are you overweight? Are you out of shape? Are you tired? Call now! FIT-NESS

E.

Are you unemployed? Are you hardworking? We have a job for you. Call 500-JOBS

F.

Are you hungry? Are you busy? Our food is delicious and it isn't expensive. Call TAKE-OUT

(1) Dr. Friend, Psychologist _____

(2) ACME Employment Agency _____

(3) New Body Health Club _____

(4) Rose's Kitchen _____

(5) The Cool School of English _____

(6) The Lonely Hearts Dating Service _____

STEP 2 This is an advertisement for a cleaning company. Write the advertisement and give the company a name.

_____

_____

_____

_____

_____

FOCUS **1**

▶ *Be:* **Yes/No Questions
and Short Answers**

YES/NO QUESTIONS	SHORT ANSWERS			
		Affirmative		Negative Contractions
(a) Am I hardworking?		you are.		you aren't. you're not.
(b) Are you nervous?		I am.		I'm not.
(c) Is he/she lonely?		he/she is.		he/she isn't. he's/she's not.
(d) Is English difficult?	Yes,	it is.	No,	it isn't. it's not.
(e) Are we out of shape?		you are.		you aren't. you're not.
(f) Are you single?		we are.		we aren't. we're not.
(g) Are verbs difficult?		they are.		they aren't. they're not.

EXERCISE 1

Ask your partner *yes/no* questions from the Opening Task on pages 14 and 15.
Use short answers and contractions.

▶ **EXAMPLE:** **You:** Are you single?

   Your Partner: Yes, I am. **OR** No, I'm not.

16 | UNIT 2

EXERCISE 2

Read the conversations. Fill in the blanks with *yes/no* questions or short answers.

1. **A:** Hello, this is the New Body Health Club.

   B: Hello, _____ you open on Sundays?

   A: Yes, _____ _____. We're open from seven in the morning until ten at night.

2. **Mitch:** Hello, my name is Mitch Brown. _____ you Karen Jones?

   Karen: Yes, _____ _____.

   Mitch: I got your telephone number from the Lonely Hearts Dating Service. How are you, Karen?

   Karen: Fine, thanks. And you?

   Mitch: Not bad, thanks. _____ _____ free tonight?

   Karen: No, I'm sorry, _____ _____. How about tomorrow?

   Mitch: Great!

3. **A:** Hello, is this Dr. Friend's office?

   B: Yes, _____ _____.

   A: _____ Dr. Friend busy? I need to speak to him.

   B: Just a minute, please.

4. **Secretary:** Cool School of English. May I help you?

   Hui Chen: Yes, I'd like some information about your classes, please.

   Secretary: What would you like to know?

   Hui Chen: _____ the classes big?

   Secretary: No, _____ _____. We have only ten students in a class.

   Hui Chen: _____ the teachers good?

   Secretary: Yes, _____ _____. All the teachers are excellent.

   Hui Chen: _____ the tuition expensive?

   Secretary: No, _____ _____. It's only $800 for ten weeks.

   Hui Chen: O.K. Thank you very much.

   Secretary: You're welcome. Goodbye.

▶ *B*e + Adjective

EXAMPLES	EXPLANATIONS
(a) Dr. Friend is **busy**. **(b)** The health club is **open**. **(c)** Verbs are **difficult**.	An adjective describes a person, place, or thing. Adjectives can come after the verb *be*.
(d) They are **excellent**. **(e)** NOT: They are excellents.	Do not put "s" on the adjective when the subject is plural (more than one).
(f) The classes are **very good**.	*Very* makes the adjective stronger. *Very* can come before most adjectives.

EXERCISE 3

Go back to the Opening Task on pages 14 and 15 and circle all the adjectives.

▶ **EXAMPLE:** Are you (single)? Are you (lonely)?

EXERCISE 4

Information Gap. Work with a partner. You have two pictures: A and B. Your partner has one picture on page A-15. Ask your partner a question about his/her picture using the adjective in parentheses. Which picture does your partner have: A or B? You circle the correct picture.

▶ **EXAMPLE:** You look at pictures A and B.   You look at the adjective.

Picture A   Picture B   **(young)**

You say: Is he young?
Your partner says: No, he isn't. He's old.
You circle picture A.

	Picture A	Picture B	Adjective

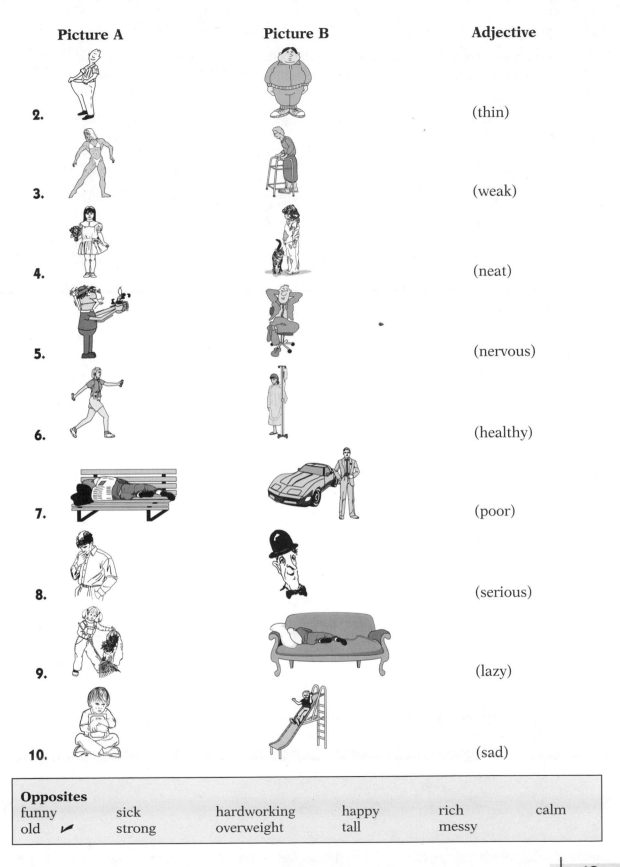

2. (thin)

3. (weak)

4. (neat)

5. (nervous)

6. (healthy)

7. (poor)

8. (serious)

9. (lazy)

10. (sad)

Opposites

funny	sick	hardworking	happy	rich	calm
old ✔	strong	overweight	tall	messy	

EXERCISE 5

Mark Heller is single and lonely. He wants a girlfriend. He puts this advertisement in the newspaper. Fill in the blanks with *am* or *are*. Use contractions where possible.

1) <u>I'm/I am</u> 28 years old. (2) _____ 6′2″ tall. (3) _____

single. (4) _____ handsome and athletic. (5) _____ romantic.

(6) _____ (negative) shy. (7) _____ you under 30?

(8) _____ you tall? (9) _____ you outgoing? (10) _____

ready for a serious relationship? Then call me: (718) 555-7954.

EXERCISE 6

Information Gap. Two women answer Mark's advertisement. Work with a partner. You have information about Cindy in Chart A and your partner has information about Shelly in Chart B on page A-16. Ask each other *yes/no* questions to find the information that you do not have in your chart. Then put a check in the correct place.

▶ **EXAMPLE:** **You:** Is Shelly tall?
 Your Partner: Yes, she is.
 Your Partner: Is Cindy tall?
 You: No, she isn't.

Chart A

	CINDY 24 years old	**SHELLY** 30 years old
1. Height		
tall		
average height		
short	✔	
2. Weight		
thin	✔	
average weight		
heavy		

3. Personality		
shy		
friendly	✔	
quiet		
talkative	✔	
neat		
messy	✔	
funny	✔	
serious		
nervous	✔	
calm		

EXERCISE 7
Ask a partner questions with the adjectives below.

talkative	funny	neat	lazy	messy
energetic	calm	strong	serious	shy

▶ **EXAMPLE:** **You:** Are you talkative?

Your Partner: Yes, I am. **OR** No, I'm not.

EXERCISE 8
What do you **like** about your partner? Write five statements.

▶ **EXAMPLE:** _____My partner is funny. He's energetic_.

_____

_____

_____

_____

_____

Be: Negative Statements and Contractions

NEGATIVE STATEMENT	CONTRACTION OF [SUBJECT + *BE*] + NOT	CONTRACTION OF [*BE* + *NOT*]
I am not shy.	I'm not shy.	*
You are not old.	You're not old.	You aren't old.
He She } is not ready. It	He's She's } not ready. It's	He She } isn't ready. It
We You } are not nervous. They	We're You're } not nervous. They're	We You } aren't nervous. They

Note: The contraction of [subject + *be*] followed by *not* (*he's not*) makes a negative statement stronger than a negative contraction of [*be* + not] (*he isn't*).

EXERCISE 9

Read the statements below each ID (identification) card. If the information is correct, say "That's right." If the information is not correct, make a negative statement with the *be* contraction + *not* and a correct affirmative statement.

▶ **EXAMPLE:** 1. His last name is Yu-ho.
His last name's not Yu-ho.
It's Oh.

Last Name:	Oh
First Name:	Yu-ho
Country:	Taiwan
Nationality:	Taiwanese
Age:	23
Marital Status:	single

Last Name:	Ryperman
First Name:	Aline
Country:	Holland
Nationality:	Dutch
Age:	32
Marital Status:	married

1. His last name is Yu-ho.
2. He is Korean.
3. He's twenty-five.
4. He's single.

5. Her first name is Alice.
6. She's from Germany.
7. She is Dutch.
8. She's fifty-two.

Last Name:	Mafegna		Last Name:	Shram
First Name:	Abiy		First Name:	Jehad
Country:	Ethiopia		Country:	Lebanon
Nationality:	Ethiopian		Nationality:	Lebanese
Age:	30		Age:	27
Marital Status:	single		Marital Status:	single

9. His first name is Mafegna.

10. He's Indian.

11. He's thirty.

12. He's married.

13. Jehad is Jordanian.

14. He is twenty-nine.

15. He's single.

EXERCISE 10

Complete each dialogue with an affirmative or a negative statement and an adjective from the list below.

Adjectives:
delicious   smart   ugly   beautiful   selfish   boring

1.
Ann: I'm short. I (a) _____ fat.

I (b) _____ ugly.

Marilyn: No, you (c) _____.

You (d) _____ , Ann!

2.
Woman: This dinner is terrible! I'm sorry.

Guest: No, it (a) _____.

It's (b) _____ !

3.
Mike: Sam, I (a) _____ nervous about this test. I (b)

_____ stupid, Sam!

Sam: No, you (c) _____,

Mike. You (d) _____ ! Your average is 98!

4.

Sally: You know Jill, I'm in love with Jack. He (a) _____ exciting and generous.

Jill: Exciting and generous??? No, he

(b) _____ . He

(c) _____ and

(d) _____ .

5.

Salesperson: That dress is perfect on you.

Customer: Perfect? Oh no, it

(a) _____ . It

(b) _____ .

Use Your English

Work with a partner. Make true statements with the subjects and adjectives below. Use the affirmative or negative form of the verb *be*. The pair with the most correct sentences wins.

▶ **EXAMPLE:** The United States is big.

SUBJECT	BE	ADJECTIVE	
My country		happy	difficult
I		single	rich
My classmates		tall	poor
The President		young	lonely
The United States		old	strong
My friends		beautiful	small
My father		smart	easy
English		big	powerful
My sister/brother		important	intelligent
		healthy	friendly

ACTIVITY 2: SPEAKING/WRITING

STEP 1   Check all the adjectives that describe you.

Adjective	Column A: You	Column B: Your Partner
shy		
quiet		
talkative		
romantic		
practical		
athletic		
lazy		
healthy		
funny		
friendly		
serious		
messy		
neat		

STEP 2   Ask your partner *yes/no* questions with the adjectives in the box. Check the adjectives in Column B.

▶   **EXAMPLE:**   **You ask:** Are you shy?
                   Your partner answers: Yes, I am. **OR** No, I'm not.

STEP 3   Write three ways you and your partner are similar and three ways you are different.

▶   **EXAMPLE:**   Similar
                   1. We are both athletic.

                   2. We are both healthy.
                   _____
                   _____
                   _____

                   Different
                   1. My partner is romantic. I'm practical.
                   2. He's serious. I'm funny.
                   _____
                   _____
                   _____

ACTIVITY 3: WRITING

Write your own personal advertisement for the newspaper or write one for a friend who is single.

▶ **EXAMPLE:**   My name is _____

I'm _____ (nationality).

I'm _____ years old.

I'm _____ (adjective).

I'm _____ (adjective).

And I'm _____ (adjective).

Are you _____ (adjective)?

Are you _____ (adjective)?

PLEASE CALL ME!

ACTIVITY 4: SPEAKING

Look at your answers to Exercise 6. Who is the best woman for Mark? Discuss your reasons.

ACTIVITY 5: LISTENING/ SPEAKING

STEP **1**   Consuela is at the Cool School of English to register for classes. Listen to the conversation and look at the questions below. Check Yes or No.

	Yes	No
1. Is Consuela a new student?		
2. Is Consuela an intermediate-level student?		
3. Is Consuela interested in morning classes?		

STEP **2**   With a partner, ask and answer the questions. If the answer is no, make a true statement.

STEP **3**   Role-play the conversation.

UNIT 3

THE VERB *BE*

Wh-Question Words, *It* with Time and Weather, and Prepositions of Location

UNIT GOALS:

- To ask *Wh*-questions with the verb *be*
- To use *it* to talk about the weather and the time
- To use prepositions of location

▶ **OPENING TASK**

Test Your World Knowledge

The Pyramids of Egypt

The Himalayas

The Kremlin

Pope John Paul II

STEP 1   Match the questions with the answers.

Questions

1. Who is the head of the Catholic Church?
2. Where is the Kremlin?
3. What's the Amazon?
4. How is the weather in Argentina in June?
5. Where are the Himalayas?
6. When is Thanksgiving in the United States?
7. It's 9 A.M.* in California. What time is it in Boston?
8. How old are the Pyramids in Egypt?
9. Where is Central America?
10. Why is July 4th special in the United States?
11. What are the names of the seven continents?
12. Where is Prague?

*A.M.: in the morning

Answers

a. It's a river.
b. the Pope
c. It's 12:00 noon.
d. about 4,700 years old
e. It's between Mexico and South America.
f. It's cold.
g. North America, South America, Africa, Asia, Australia, Europe, and Antarctica
h. because it is Independence Day
i. the last Thursday in November
j. It's in the Czech Republic, on the Vultava River.
k. in Moscow
l. in India, Nepal, and Tibet

STEP 2   Make up two questions of your own. Ask your classmates the questions.

Wh-Question Words with *Be*

Some *wh*-question words are: *what, where, who, when, how, what time, how old,* and *why.* Use *Wh*-question words to ask for specific information.

QUESTION WORD	BE	SUBJECT	ANSWER	MEANING
What	is 's	the Amazon?	a river	THING
Where	are	the Himalayas?	in India, Nepal, and Tibet	PLACE
Who	is 's	the head of the Catholic Church?	the Pope	PEOPLE
How	is 's	the weather in Argentina in June?	It's cold.	CONDITIONS
When	is 's	Thanksgiving in the United States?	the last Thursday in November	TIME
What time	is	it in New York?	It's 12:00.	TIME ON A CLOCK
How old	are	the Pyramids in Egypt?	about 4,700 years old	AGE
Why	is 's	July 4th special in the United States?	because it is Independence Day	REASON

EXERCISE 1

Fill in the blanks with one of these *wh*-question words: *what, where, how, who, when, how old, what time,* and *why.*

Questions   **Answers**

1. __How old_____ is the Great   about 2,200 years old
   Wall of China?

2. _____ are the
authors of *Grammar
Dimensions, Book I?*

Victoria Badalamenti and
Carolyn Henner Stanchina

3. _____ is Morocco?   in Africa

4. _____ is the
weather in the summer in
Washington, D.C.?

It's hot.

5. _____ is the
capital of Belgium?

Brussels

6. _____ is the first
day of summer?

June 21st

7. It's 10 A.M.* in Boston.
_____ is it in
Barcelona?

It's 4:00 P.M.*

8. _____ is
Independence Day in France?

July 14th

9. _____ are you in
this class?

to learn English

10. _____ are the Nile
and the Mississippi?

rivers

*A.M. = morning   *P.M. = afternoon, evening, night

EXERCISE 2

Match the question in Column A to the answer in Column B. Write the
letter in the blank on the left.

	Column A	Column B
_d_	**1.** What's your name?	**a.** October 17th.
_____	**2.** Where are you from?	**b.** I'm Turkish.
_____	**3.** What is the capital of	**c.** To study English.
	your country?	
_____	**4.** What's your nationality?	**d.** Mehmet.
_____	**5.** How old are you?	**e.** It's Ankara.
_____	**6.** When's your birthday?	**f.** I'm twenty-five.
_____	**7.** Why are you here?	**g.** Fine, thanks.
_____	**8.** How are you today?	**h.** Istanbul.

Now choose two of these questions. Memorize them. Go around the room and ask five other people your questions. They ask you their questions.

EXERCISE 3

Starting a Conversation at a Bus Stop: Write *wh*-questions in the blanks.

Carlos: Excuse me, (1) _____ please?

Maria: It's 10:15.

Carlos: Thank you. (2)_____?

Maria: Maria (3) _____?

Carlos: My name is Carlos.

Maria: (4) _____?

Carlos: I'm from Mexico.

Maria: (5) _____ your hometown?

Carlos: Mexico City.

Maria: (6) _____ in Mexico at this time of year?

Carlos: It's warm and sunny in Mexico now.

Maria: (7) _____?

Carlos: I'm here to study English. (8) _____ my English?

Maria: Your English is not bad.

Carlos: Thank you.

Maria: Here's the bus.

Carlos: O.K. Bye!

Maria: Bye! Good Luck!

EXERCISE 4

Write five questions about students in the class with the question word *who*. Then ask your partner the questions.

▶ **EXAMPLES:** Who's from Asia?

Who is twenty-five years old?

Who's tall?

▶ # How to Ask Questions about English

> When you need to ask about a word in English, you say:
>
> **(a)** **What** is the meaning of *crowded?*
> **(b)** **What** is the spelling of *crowded?*
> **(c)** **What** is the pronunciation of *c-r-o-w-d-e-d?*

EXERCISE 5

Read the paragraph below about Vancouver. Underline the words you don't know or can't pronounce. Ask your teacher or classmates questions.

▶ **EXAMPLE:** What is the meaning of <u>crowded</u>?

Vancouver is a city in Canada. It's on the Pacific coast. The city is magnificent. It is clean and open. It isn't <u>crowded</u>. Almost three-quarters of the population are of British ancestry. Other ethnic groups are the Chinese, French, Japanese, and East Indians. As a result, the food in Vancouver is varied and delicious. It is a wonderful place for a vacation.

FOCUS **3**

▶ # Using *It* to Talk about the Weather

QUESTIONS	ANSWERS		
How's the weather in Montreal?	**It's** sunny **It's** hot	in the	summer.
	It's cold **It's** snowy		winter.
	It's cloudy **It's** rainy		spring.
	It's windy **It's** cool		fall.
What's the temperature today?	**It's** 77 degrees Fahrenheit/25 degrees Celsius.		

EXERCISE 6

Information Gap. Work with a partner. You look at Map A and your partner looks at Map B (on page A-17). You have some information about the weather in the different cities on Map A. Your partner has different information on Map B. Ask each other questions to find out the missing information. Take turns asking questions.

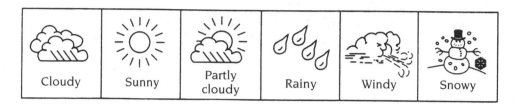

| Cloudy | Sunny | Partly cloudy | Rainy | Windy | Snowy |

MAP A

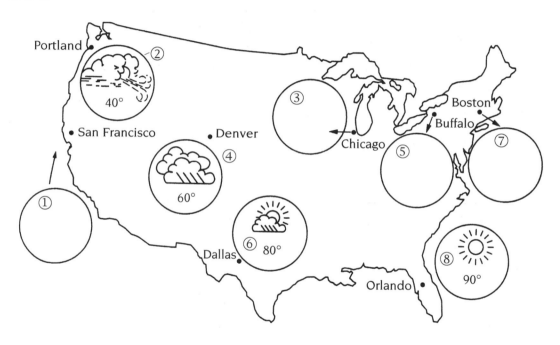

▶ **EXAMPLE:** **You:** ① How's the weather in San Francisco today?

Your Partner: It's sunny.

You: What's the temperature?

Your Partner: It's 65 degrees.

▶ **U**sing *It* to Talk about Time

WHAT TIME IS IT?

3:00	**It's** three o'clock. **It's** three.	

3:05	**It's** five after three.

3:15	**It's** three-fifteen. **It's** a quarter past three. **It's** a quarter after three.

3:30	**It's** three-thirty. **It's** half past three.

3:45	**It's** three forty-five. **It's** a quarter to four.

3:50	**It's** three-fifty. **It's** ten to four.

12:00	**It's** twelve o'clock. **It's** noon. **It's** midnight.

EXERCISE 7

Information Gap. Work with a partner. You look at the times on Chart B on page A-17. Say the time in different ways. Your partner draws the time on the clocks below.

▶ **EXAMPLE:** **You:** 1.   (6:30)   It's six thirty.   It's half past six.

Your partner:

Chart A

1.   2.   3.   4.

5.   6.   7.   8.

EXERCISE 8

Look at the map of the time zones in the United States. Ask and answer the questions.

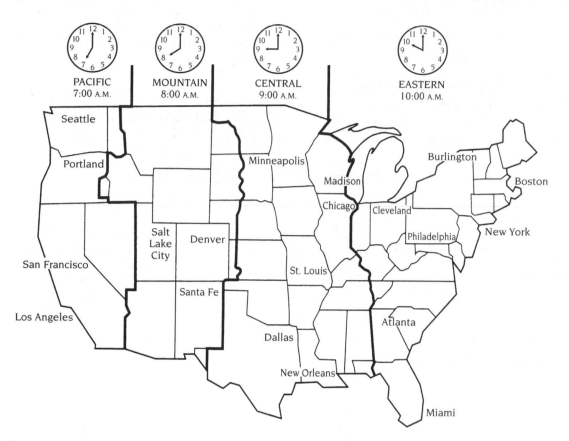

1. It's 7:00 A.M. in San Francisco. What time is it in Philadelphia? _____.

2. It's 10:45 P.M. in Miami. What time is it in Salt Lake City?_____.

3. It's 6:50 P.M. in Minneapolis. What time is it in New Orleans? _____.

4. It's 10:30 P.M. in Santa Fe. What time is it in Chicago? _____.

5. It's 2:15 A.M. in Los Angeles. What time is it in Boston? _____.

6. It's 9:10 A.M. in Dallas. What time is it in Portland? _____.

7. It's 10:20 A.M. in Atlanta. What time is it in Denver? _____.

8. It's 10:05 A.M. in Seattle. What time is it in Cleveland? _____.

Now make five questions of your own for your partner to answer.

▶ **P**repositions of Location

Prepositions of location tell where something is.

COMMON PREPOSITIONS OF LOCATION		
The ball is **in** the box.	The ball is **on** the box.	The ball is **above** the box.
The ball is **next to** the box.	The ball is **in back of** the box.	The ball is **under** the box.
The ball is **near** the box. It isn't next to the box.	The ball is **behind** the box.	The ball is **opposite** the box.
The ball is **between** the two boxes.	The ball is **in front of** the box.	

Prague
Vultava River
Czech
Republic

SUBJECT +	*Be* +	PREPOSITIONAL PHRASE (PREPOSITION + NOUN)
Prague	is	**in** the Czech Republic.
It	's	**on** the Vultava River.
The hotel	is	**near** the Vultava River.

EXERCISE 9

Sally and her family are in Prague, in the Czech Republic. Read the postcard and circle the prepositions of location. Who wrote this postcard?

Hi everybody. Here we are in Prague, the capital city of the Czech Republic. It is a beautiful city in Central Europe. I am between Ken and Jirka, our Czech friend. In this photo, we are at a cafe next to the Charles Bridge. Michele is trying to hide; she's camera shy! And right across from the cafe is a souvenir shop. Prague is very popular during the summer. Many tourists come here to visit. The couple next to us is from Italy. They love Prague too!

EXERCISE 10

Information Gap. You cannot find items 1–6 in Picture A. Your partner cannot find items 7–12 in Picture B on page A-18. Ask each other questions with *where*.

▶ **EXAMPLE:**   **Student A asks:** 1. Where are my slippers?
                 Student B says: They're under the sofa.

PICTURE A

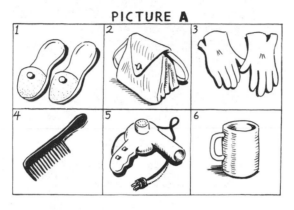

EXERCISE 11

This is a map of your neighborhood. The names of the places are missing. Read the sentences and fill in the names of the places on the map. The first one has been done for you.

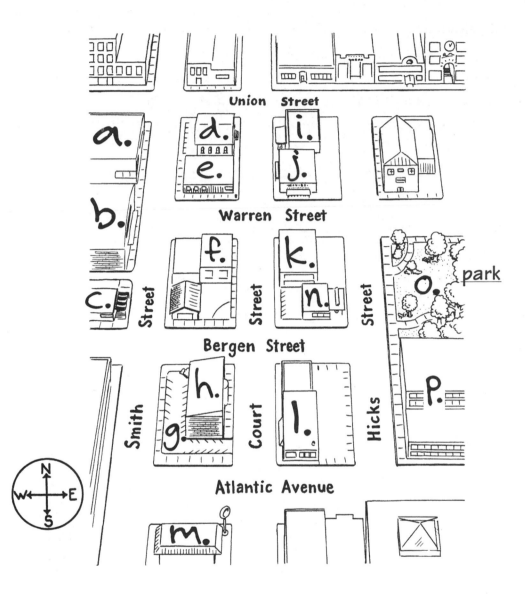

1. The park is on the corner of Hicks and Warren Street.
2. The hospital is next to the park.
3. The bank is on the southwest corner of Court Street and Union.

4. The drugstore is next to the bank.

5. The candy store is across the street from the drugstore on Court Street.

6. The video store is near the candy store.

7. The movie theater is on the west side of Court Street between Bergen and Atlantic.

8. The parking lot is behind the movie theater.

9. The bakery is across the street from the movie theater.

10. The gas station is on the corner of Hicks and Bergen.

11. The hardware store is on the southeast corner of Court Street and Warren.

12. The bookstore is across from the hardware store.

13. The newsstand is on the corner of Bergen and Smith Streets.

14. The pet store is on the southwest corner of Union Street and Smith Street.

15. The supermarket is between the pet store and the newsstand on Smith Street.

16. The diner is on Atlantic Avenue.

Use Your English

ACTIVITY 1: SPEAKING

TEST YOUR KNOWLEDGE GAME

Get into two teams.

STEP 1 Team 1 chooses a category and an amount of money. Team 2 asks a question with *what* or *where*. If Team 1 answers correctly, they get the money.

STEP 2 Team 2 chooses a category and an amount of money. Team 1 asks a question with *what* or *where*. If Team 2 answers correctly, they get the money. The team with the most money at the end wins.

▶ **EXAMPLES:** Step 1.

Team 1: Monuments for $30.

Team 2: Where is the Colosseum?

Team 1: It's in Rome, Italy.

Categories					
Amount $$$	**Monuments**	**Capitals**	**Countries**	**Continents**	**Rivers, Mts, Deserts**
Question	**Where is/ are**	**What's the capital of**	**Where's**	**Where's**	**Where is/are**
$10	The Eiffel Tower	Afghanistan	Managua	Canada	The Sahara Desert
$20	The Great Wall	Greece	Nagasaki	Chile	The Rocky Mts.
$30	The Colosseum	Israel	Budapest	India	The Amazon River
$40	The Pyramids	Peru	Capetown	Egypt	Mount Everest
$50	The Taj Mahal	Turkey	Zurich	Portugal	The Nile River

ACTIVITY 2: SPEAKING/WRITING

STEP 1 Ask a classmate about his or her hometown. Ask questions with *is/are* . . . or *wh*-question words.

▶ **EXAMPLE:** **You:** Where are you from?   **Your Partner:** Acapulco.
Where's Acapulco?   It's in Mexico.
How is the weather?   It's hot in the summer and mild in the winter.

Are the people friendly?   Yes, they are.

The words in the box will help you:

Weather	People	Other
hot warm mild cold sunny dry humid rainy cloudy	happy friendly hard-working cold religious outgoing quiet rich poor	expensive cheap small big crowded delicious safe dangerous clean

STEP 2 Write about your partner's hometown.

▶ **EXAMPLE:** My classmate is from Mexico City. Mexico City is the capital of Mexico. Mexico City is big. It is crowded. It is hot in the summer. People are friendly. The food is delicious.

ACTIVITY 3: LISTENING

Listen to the telephone conversation between a student and a secretary at a college. Fill in the following places on the campus map:

- Parking Lot B
- Administration Building
- library
- bookstore

- English as a Second Language Department
- auditorium
- cafeteria

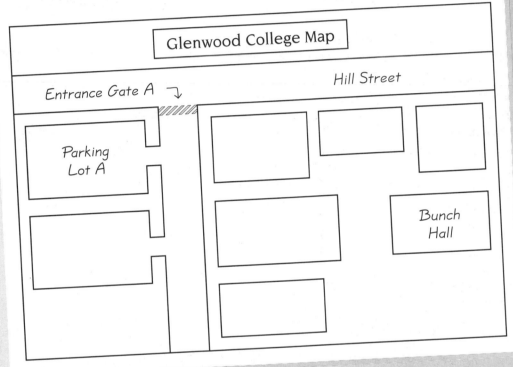

ACTIVITY 4: SPEAKING/WRITING

Draw a map of your hometown or the place where you live now. Describe your map to your partner. Then write down the description, using prepositions.

▶ **EXAMPLES:** This is my house. It's on Main Street. The drugstore is on the corner of Main and 1st Avenue. The supermarket is opposite the drugstore.

NOUNS

Count and Noncount Nouns, *Be* + Adjective + Noun

UNIT GOALS:

- To understand the difference between count and noncount nouns
- To use *a/an* with singular count nouns
- To know how to spell and pronounce regular plural nouns
- To know how to form the irregular plurals of nouns
- To ask questions with *how much* . . .
- To make statements with *be* + *adjective* + *noun*

▶ **OPENING TASK**
Categories

STEP 1   Write each word in the box in one of the three circles below.

milk	dresses	cash
dollars	bread	a shoe
a shirt	cents	an egg

Category

1. Food

3. Money

2. Clothing

STEP 2   Now the same words from above are in different categories. Write a name for each category. Note: The new categories are types of nouns.

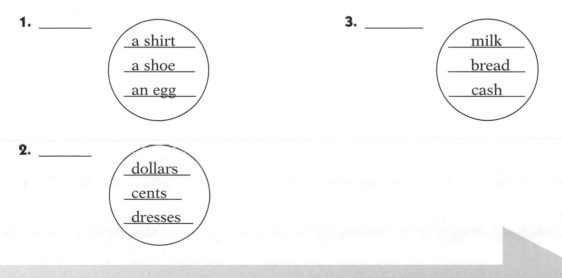

1. _____
- a shirt
- a shoe
- an egg

3. _____
- milk
- bread
- cash

2. _____
- dollars
- cents
- dresses

▶ Count Nouns and Noncount Nouns

Money

Coins

We can see things as whole or as separate things we can count. We use noncount nouns like *money* when we see a thing as whole. We use count nouns like *coins* when we refer to things we can count.

EXAMPLES		EXPLANATIONS
Count Nouns		**Things we can count**
SINGULAR	PLURAL	Count nouns take *a/an* in the singular. They take *-s* or *-es* in the plural.
an egg	eggs	
a dress	dresses	
Noncount Nouns		**Things we don't count**
money		Noncount nouns have one form. They are not singular, not plural.
cash		
clothing		

EXERCISE 1

Look at the list of words from the Opening Task. Check count or noncount.

	COUNT NOUN	NONCOUNT NOUN
food		
milk		
egg		
bread		
clothing		
dresses		
shirt		

	COUNT NOUN	NONCOUNT NOUN
shoe		
money		
dollars		
cents		
cash		

FORM

▶ *A*/*An* with Singular Count Nouns

A	AN
a house **a** movie **a** uniform*	**an** orange **an** egg **an** hour*
Use *a* before a word beginning with a consonant or a consonant sound. *uniform* begins with a vowel but has the consonant sound of "y" as in *you*.	Use *an* before a word beginning with a vowel (a, e, i, o, u) or a vowel sound. *hour* begins with a consonant but the "h" is silent.

EXERCISE 2

List the words below under the correct categories. Then, read your lists to your partner with *a* or *an*.

earring	bed	watch	necklace
dormitory	table	apple	house
orange ✔	apartment	ring	desk
armchair	banana	pear	hotel

Fruit	**Furniture**	**Jewelry**	**Housing**
an orange	_____	_____	_____
_____	_____	_____	_____
_____	_____	_____	_____
_____	_____	_____	_____

EXERCISE 3

For each picture write a sentence to show the person's occupation. Use *a/an*.

▶ **EXAMPLES:**

_____He's a waiter._____   _____She's an athlete._____

1. actor

_____

2. secretary

_____

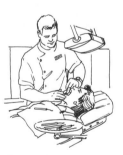

3. dentist

_____

4. cashier

_____

5. engineer

_____

6. doctor

_____

7. nurse

_____

8. hairdresser

_____

9. flight attendant

_____

10. accountant

_____

EXERCISE 4

Test your knowledge. Work with a partner. You read the question on the left. Your partner finds the answer on the right and reads it using _a/an_.

▶ **EXAMPLE:** **You:** What's Poland?

Your Partner: (m) It's a country.

1. What's Poland?	**a.** It's _____ continent.
2. What is Thanksgiving?	**b.** It's _____ car.
3. What is the Atlantic?	**c.** It's _____ hour.
4. What is Puerto Rico?	**d.** It's _____ clock.
5. What's the Sahara?	**e.** It's _____ river.
6. What is Africa?	**f.** It's _____ island.
7. What's New York?	**g.** It's _____ holiday in the United States and Canada.
8. What's the Concorde?	**h.** It's _____ museum.
9. What's Big Ben?	**i.** It's _____ university.
10. What is the Louvre?	**j.** It's _____ ocean.
11. What is Harvard?	**k.** It's _____ city.
12. What's sixty minutes?	**l.** It's _____ airplane.
13. What's a Mercedes?	**m.** It's _____ country.
14. What's the Amazon?	**n.** It's _____ desert.

Spelling of Regular Plural Count Nouns

SINGULAR	PLURAL	EXPLANATIONS
(a) a car a book	two cars three books	To make the plural form of most count nouns, add -*s*.
(b) a boy a radio	four boys two radios	Nouns that end in: vowel + *y* vowel + *o* Plural form: add -*s*.
(c) a class a sandwich a dish a box	two classes two sandwiches two dishes three boxes	Nouns that end in: *ss* *ch* *sh* *x* Plural form: add -*es*.
(d) a potato a tomato	six potatoes four tomatoes	Nouns that end in: consonant + *o* Plural form: add -*es*.
(e) a baby a city	babies cities	Nouns that end in: consonant + *y* Plural form: change *y* to *i*, add -*es*.
(f) a thief a life	two thieves three lives	Nouns that end in: *f* or *fe* Plural form: change *f* to *v*, add -*es*. Exceptions: *chief—chiefs* *chef—chefs*

EXERCISE 5

Write the plural form of the words below.

1. party _____parties_____
2. shoe _____
3. fox _____
4. dictionary _____
5. week _____
6. glass _____

7. wife _____
8. watch _____
9. leaf _____
10. lady _____
11. month _____
12. key _____

EXERCISE 6

Complete the sentences with the plural of one of the nouns in the box.

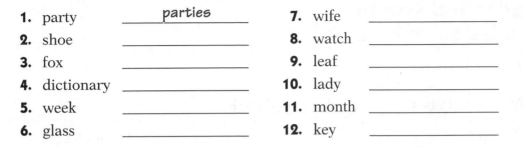

desert	city	story	holiday ✔	university	state
river	mountain	country	continent	company	ocean

1. Thanksgiving and Christmas are _____holidays_____.
2. The Atlantic and the Pacific are _____.
3. Africa and Asia are _____.
4. Princeton and Yale are _____.
5. IBM and Sony are _____.
6. "Cinderella" and "Beauty and the Beast" are _____.
7. The Alps are _____.
8. Colombia and Venezuela are _____ in South America.
9. Colorado and Vermont are _____ in the United States.
10. Vienna and Oslo are two _____ in Europe.
11. The Sahara and the Gobi are _____.
12. The Amazon and the Nile are _____.

▶ **R**egular Plural Nouns: Pronunciation of Final *-s,* and *-es*

EXAMPLES	EXPLANATIONS
(a) books, students, groups months, desks, cats	**/S/** Final *-s* is pronounced /s/ after voiceless sounds.*
(b) beds, rooms, lives years, days, dogs	**/Z/** Final *-s* is pronounced /z/ after voiced sounds.**
(c) classes, faces exercises, sizes dishes, wishes sandwiches, watches colleges, pages class-es	**/IZ/** Final *-es* is pronounced /iz/ after "s" sounds "z" sounds "sh" sounds "ch" sounds "ge/dge" sounds This adds an extra syllable to the noun.
	*Voiceless sounds: /p/t/k/f/th. **Voiced sounds: /b/d/g/v/m/n/l/r/ and vowels.

EXERCISE 7

Make the words below plural. Then, write each word in the correct pronunciation group on the next page. Read each group aloud.

✔ book	radio	dress	house	ticket	rule
thing	horse	head	list	bus	cup
car	train	boat	church	peach	hat

/S/	/Z/	/IZ/
books	_cars_	_horses_
radios	_things_	_dresses_
train	_lists_	_houses_
_____	_beads_	_church_
boots	_____	_buses_
lists	_____	_____

EXERCISE 8

Look at the list of common measurements. Make the measurement on the right plural. Then, read the statements aloud using the verb *equals*.

▶ **EXAMPLE:** 98.6 degrees Fahrenheit = 37 degree_s___ Celsius.

  98.6 degrees Fahrenheit equals 37 degrees Celsius.

1. one foot = 12 inch ____   **6.** one year = 365 day ____

2. one pound = 16 ounce ____   **7.** one quart = 2 pint ____

3. one minute = 60 second ____   **8.** one gallon = 4 quart ____

4. one hour = 60 minute ____   **9.** one inch = 2½ centimeter ____

5. one day = 24 hour ____   **10.** one kilo = 2.2 pound ____

EXERCISE 9

Rhymes. Make the nouns in italics plural. Then, read the rhymes aloud.

1. On Education

*Word*____, *sentence*____, *exercise*____, *rule*____,
*Dictionary*____, *textbook*____, *page*____, *school*____,
*Classroom*____, *teacher*____, *student*____, —all *jewel*____
Of education, these are the *tool*____.

2. On Age

*Day*____, *week*____, *month*____, *year*____.
Getting old? Please, no *tear*____!!!

3. On Imports

The *shoe*____ are Brazilian,
The *glove*____ are Italian,
The *chef*____ are from France;
from South America—the salsa dance.
The *toy*____ are Chinese,
The *camera*____ are Japanese:
Tell me, what's American, please?

▶ **Irregular Plural Nouns**

EXAMPLES	EXPLANATIONS
(a) child children man men woman women foot feet tooth teeth mouse mice person people	Some nouns change spelling in the plural.
(b) a deer two deer a sheep three sheep a fish four fish	Some nouns do not change in the plural.
(c) scissors pajamas eyeglasses shorts clothes pants	Some nouns are always plural. They have no singular form.

EXERCISE 10

STEP 1 Work in pairs. Match each noun to the correct part of the picture by asking questions. Use *a/an* when necessary.

STEP 2 Then label the picture.

▶ **EXAMPLES:** What's number 1?   An eyebrow.

What's number 2?   Toes.

eyebrow	sunglasses	teeth	lips	nose	ear
hand	fingers	arm	tee shirt	shorts	feet
toes	sandal	freckles	baseball cap	eye	hair

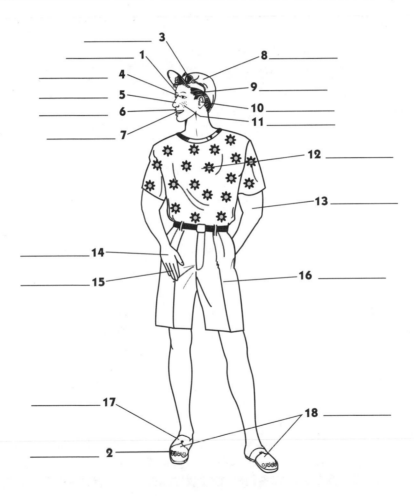

▶ **Count and Noncount Nouns**

COUNT NOUNS	NONCOUNT NOUNS
Can take *a/an* or *one* in the singular. **(a)** It's a job. **(b)** I'm on vacation for one week.	Cannot take *a/an* or *one* in the singular. **(c)** It's work.
Can take *-s* or *-es* in the plural. **(d)** They are earrings. **(e)** They're watches.	Cannot take *-s* or *-es*. **(f)** It's jewelry.
Can take a singular or plural verb. **(g)** It is a table. **(h)** They are chairs.	Always take a singular verb. **(i)** Furniture is expensive.
To ask about prices with count nouns, use: **(j)** How much is a television set in Taiwan? (singular) **(k)** How much are newspapers in Russia? (plural)	To ask about prices with noncount nouns, use: **(l)** How much is gas in Italy?

Some Common Noncount Nouns

advice	electricity	help	mail	salt
bacon	fish	homework	milk	sugar
bread	food	information	money	tea
cheese	fruit	jewelry	music	traffic
clothing	furniture	love	news	transportation
coffee	garbage	luck	pollution	water
crime	hair	luggage	rice	work

EXERCISE 11

Donald is an international student arriving in Wisconsin with his wife. Read his conversations. Check count or noncount for each underlined noun.

	COUNT	NONCOUNT

1. Donald is at the airport with his wife.
   Donald: It's cold here in Wisconsin.
   - a. I need warm <u>clothing</u>.
   - b. Where's my <u>coat</u>?

   Wife: c. It's in the black <u>suitcase</u>.
   Donald: d. Where is the <u>luggage</u>?
   Wife: It's still on the plane!

   a. _____ _____
   b. _____ _____
   c. _____ _____
   d. _____ _____

2. Donald is at the University of Wisconsin.
   Secretary: a. Donald, here are three <u>letters</u> for you.
   Donald: b. Thank you. <u>Mail</u> from home is very important to me.

   a. _____ _____
   b. _____ _____

3. Donald is with an American student.
   Donald: a. How's the <u>food</u> in the cafeteria?
   Student: b. The <u>vegetables</u> are good.
   - c. The <u>fruit</u> is fresh.
   - d. The <u>meat</u> is terrible.

   a. _____ _____
   b. _____ _____
   c. _____ _____
   d. _____ _____

EXERCISE 12

Work with a partner. Use the words below to ask questions about the country your partner comes from.

▶ **EXAMPLE:** hamburgers/popular/in . . .?

Are hamburgers popular in Russia?

Yes, they are.

OR No, they aren't.

1. pizza/popular/in . . .?
2. fruit/cheap/in . . .?
3. cars/big/in . . .?
4. electricity/cheap/in . . .?
5. American music/popular/in . . .?
6. rent/expensive/in . . .?
7. families/big/in . . .?
8. taxes/high/in . . .?
9. public transportation/good/in . . .?
10. American movies/popular/in . . .?

Now ask five questions about the price of the following items in your partner's country using: *How much is/are?*

hamburgers	public transportation	rent
gas	movies	a local telephone call
fruit	a daily newspaper	a CD (compact disc)

▶ *Be* + Adjective + Noun

EXAMPLES	EXPLANATIONS
(a) Princeton and Yale are **private** universities.	An adjective can come before the noun.
(b) They are **excellent** colleges.	Do not put -*s* on the adjective when the noun is plural.
(c) It's **a** large university. **(d)** English is **a** universal language.	Use *a* before an adjective with a consonant or a consonant sound.
(e) He's **an** "A" student. **(f)** She's **an** honor student.	Use *an* before an adjective with a vowel sound.
(g) Psychology is a **very** interesting subject.	Put *very* before most adjectives to make the adjectives stronger.

EXERCISE 13

Tour the United States. Choose an adjective from the box. Make sentences using *be* + *adjective* + *noun*. You can also use *very*. Remember: you can use an adjective more than once.

beautiful	exciting	spectacular	famous
small	crowded	expensive	tall
huge	popular	long	important

▶ **EXAMPLE:** Disneyworld <u>is a very popular</u> place in Florida.

1. The Twin Towers _____ buildings in New York City.
2. The Golden Gate _____ bridge in San Francisco.
3. The Keys _____ islands off the coast of Florida.
4. The Mississippi _____ river flowing from Minnesota to the Gulf of Mexico.
5. Bryce and Zion _____ national parks in Utah.
6. Niagara Falls _____ waterfall between the U.S. and Canada.
7. The Lincoln Memorial _____ monument in Washington.
8. Alaska and Hawaii _____ vacation spots in the U.S.

Use Your English

CATEGORIZING GAME.

STEP 1 Get into two teams. Write the words in the box in the correct categories below.

STEP 2 Then, next to each word, write C for count nouns and NC for noncount nouns.

STEP 3 Each correct answer is one point. The team with the most points wins. Find the winning team.

shirts	ears	coffee	shoes	feet	tea
toothpaste	underwear	lemonade	soap	coat	rice
cheese	shampoo	bread	jacket	eyes	head
hair	toothbrush	juice	beans	milk	pizza
soda	hairbrush	hamburger	socks	towels	arm

Things to Wear

shirts C
_____

_____

_____

_____

_____

Things to Eat

_____

_____

_____

_____

_____

Things to Drink

_____

_____

_____

_____

_____

Things in the Bathroom

_____

_____

_____

_____

Parts of the Body

_____

_____

_____

_____

ACTIVITY 2: SPEAKING

Plan a party for the class. Get into groups. Each group plans what they are going to bring to the party under the following categories.

Food   **Drinks**   **Entertainment**

Compare your plans with the other groups'. Which group has the best plan?

ACTIVITY 3: SPEAKING

Tell your classmates what you have for:

Breakfast	Lunch	Dinners	Snack
coffee			
cereal			
orange juice			

ACTIVITY 4: LISTENING / SPEAKING

STEP 1 Listen to what kind of pizza the woman orders.

STEP 2 Check (✔) what the woman wants on the pizza. Then mark C for count nouns and NC for noncount nouns.

- ❑ cheese _____
- ❑ tomatoes _____
- ❑ olives _____
- ❑ peppers _____
- ❑ pepperoni _____
- ❑ mushrooms _____
- ❑ anchovies _____
- ❑ onions _____

STEP 3 Ask a classmate about his or her favorite pizza.

STEP 4 Role play. Telephone the pizza store with your order.

ACTIVITY 5: SPEAKING

Work in groups. Bring in a picture of friends or family. Talk about your friends or family members to your group.

▶ **EXAMPLE:** I have two brothers. Juan is an engineer. Carlos is a student.

ACTIVITY 6: SPEAKING

Work with a partner. Bring in a clothing catalogue. You have $200 and you need to buy some clothes for a party. Here are some things you might look for:

Checklist:

Shoes _____

Pants _____

Shirt _____

Blouse _$27_

Skirt _____

Tie _____

socks/stockings _____

jacket _____

belt _____

dress _____

hat _____

vest _____

▶ **EXAMPLE:** You (looking in the catalogue): "I want to buy the blouse on page 52."

Your Partner: "How much is it?"

You: "It's $27.00."

Your Partner: (Write down $27 next to the blouse on the checklist. Make sure your total isn't over $200.)

THE VERB *HAVE*

Affirmative and Negative Statements, Questions and Short Answers, *Some/Any*

UNIT GOALS:

- To make affirmative statements with the verb *have*
- To make negative statements with *do*
- To ask *yes/no* questions with *do* and give short answers
- To use *some/any*
- To ask for something politely
- To use the verb *have* to describe people

▶ OPENING TASK
Modern and Traditional Lifestyles

Look at the photographs of two Inuit women in North Canada, and at the chart on the next page. Check (✔) and say the things you think Mary has. Check and say the things you think Nilaulaq and her husband have.

Mary

Nilaulaq

	Mary	Nilaulaq (Nila) and her husband, Napachee
1. a house		
2. an Inuit name		
3. Inuit clothing		
4. dogs		
5. furniture		
6. electricity		
7. fresh fish		
8. a bed		
9. a tent		
10. canned food		

In the photographs, who has a traditional lifestyle? Who has a modern lifestyle? Say why.

1. _____ a traditional lifestyle.

2. _____ a modern lifestyle.

FOCUS 1

▶ *Have* and *Has:*
Affirmative Statements

The verb *to have* means to own or possess.

SUBJECT	VERB	
I You	have	a telephone.
He She It Mary	has	
We You They (Nila & Napachee)	have	children.

EXERCISE 1

Fill in the blanks about Nilaulaq and Mary with *have* or *has*. Read the sentences aloud.

A. Nilaulaq _____has_____ an Inuit name. She ____has____ a husband. He ____has____ an Inuit name too. They ____have____ two children. They ____have____ two dogs. Nilaulaq is proud. She says, "I ____have____ a beautiful family."

B. Mary ____has____ wallpaper in her house. Mary ____has____ a clock. She ____has____ photographs and a map. She ____has____ furniture. She ____has____ canned food on the shelf.

C. Modern Inuit people live in towns. The towns ____has____ stores. Modern Inuit people _____ money. They _____ jobs.

▶ *Have:* **Negative Statements and Contractions**

EXAMPLES	DO/DOES	BASE FORM OF VERB	
I You We They Nilaulaq and her husband	do not (don't)	have	a telephone.
He She It Nilaulaq	does not (doesn't)		

EXERCISE 2

What are some differences between traditional and modern families? Make the words below into sentences with *has/have* or *doesn't have/don't have.*

Traditional families are big.

1. They/many children.
2. They also/grandmothers and grandfathers living with them.
3. In a traditional family, only the father/a job.
4. The mother/a job.
5. The children/a babysitter.

Modern families are different.

6. Sometimes they/only two people.
7. Sometimes the parents/one or two children.
8. Sometimes, they/children.

Now make four sentences of your own about modern families.

9. _____
10. _____
11. _____
12. _____

▶ *H*ave: Yes/No questions and Short Answers

DO/DOES	SUBJECT	HAVE	
Do	I you we they Nilaulaq and Napachee	**have**	children?
Does	he she it Mary		

AFFIRMATIVE SHORT ANSWERS		
Yes,	I you we they	**do.**
	he she it	**does.**

NEGATIVE SHORT ANSWERS		
No,	I you we they	**do not.** **(don't)**
	he she it	**does not.** **(doesn't)**

EXERCISE 3
Find Someone Who
Ask your classmates if they have the things on the left. Write the names of the students who say "yes."

▶ **EXAMPLE:** Do you have a cordless telephone?
  Yes, I do. **OR** No, I don't.

Things   **Students' Names**

  1. a cordless telephone   _____

  2. pets   _____

  3. a car   _____

  4. children   _____

5. relatives in this country   _____

6. a job   _____

7. English-speaking friends   _____

8. a bicycle   _____

9. a driver's license   _____

10. a video cassette recorder (VCR)   _____

EXERCISE 4

Work with a partner. Take turns asking and answering questions. Make questions about the Inuit people in the Opening Task. Use short answers.

▶ **EXAMPLE:**   **You:** Does Mary have a house?

          Your Partner: Yes, she does.

1. Nila/children   **4.** Nila/wallpaper in her house   **7.** Nila/a television set

2. Mary/bed   **5.** Nila/furniture   **8.** Mary/canned food

3. Napachee/boat   **6.** Mary/an Inuit name

EXERCISE 5

Work with a partner. Write questions using the words on the next page. Try to answer the questions by looking at the pictures below. Then, read the text and check your answers to the questions.

Horse and carriage in Lancaster, Pennsylvania

Daniel

An Amish family

John Lapp

Questions

▶ **EXAMPLE:** An Amish man/car?

          You: Does an Amish man have a car?

          Your Partner: No, he doesn't.

1. Amish people/a simple life?   _____?
           _____.

2. Amish women/jewelry?   _____?
           _____.

3. An Amish home/electricity?   _____?
           _____.

4. An Amish farmer/horses?   _____?
           _____.

5. An Amish home/telephone?   _____?
           _____.

6. Amish people/their own language?   _____?
           _____.

7. An Amish child/computer?   _____?
           _____.

8. Amish people/colorful clothing?   _____?
           _____.

9. An Amish home/television?   _____?
           _____.

10. Amish children/special teachers?   _____?
           _____.

11. Amish children/school after eighth grade?   _____?
           _____.

12. Amish people/a modern lifestyle?   _____?
           _____.

The Amish are a special group of Americans. There are about 85,000 Amish people in the United States. They have their own language. They also have a simple way of life.

The Amish are farmers, but they don't have machines on their farms. They have horses. They do not have electricity or telephones in their homes.

The Amish are called "the plain people." They wear dark clothing. The men all have beards and wear hats. The women wear long dresses and hats.

Amish children have one-room schoolhouses. They have Amish teachers. They have no school after the eighth grade. The Amish have a very traditional lifestyle.

▶ *Some/Any*

EXAMPLES			EXPLANATIONS
STATEMENT	**(a)**	The children have **some** books.	Use *some* in statements (with plural count nouns and noncount nouns).
	(b)	They have **some** money.	
NEGATIVE	**(c)**	They don't have **any** books.	Use *any* in negative statements (with plural count nouns and noncount nouns).
	(d)	She doesn't have **any** money.	
QUESTION	**(e)**	Do they have **any** books?	Use *any* in questions (with plural count nouns and noncount nouns.)
	(f)	Does she have **any** money?	

EXERCISE 6

Complete the rhyme with *some* or *any*.

I don't have (1) _____ time today.

I have (2) _____ problems to solve.

I have (3) _____ bills to pay.

Do you have (4) _____ time to play?

I have (5) _____ places to go.

I have (6) _____ people to see.

Do you have (7) _____ advice for me?

Yes, I do: "Slow down!"

EXERCISE 7

Read the sentence. Say if it is true or not true. If it's not true, change it to make a true sentence.

▶ **EXAMPLES:**   John Lapp has some electrical machines on his farm.
False. He doesn't have any electrical machines on his farm.
The Amish people have a close community.
True.

1. Daniel has some colorful T-shirts.
2. John Lapp's wife has some expensive jewelry.
3. The Amish people have different ideas about education.
4. The Amish have very big telephone bills.
5. Amish schools have some non-Amish teachers.
6. Amish people have strong religious beliefs.
7. The Amish people have some very different habits.
8. The Amish people have some problems with modern lifestyles.
9. The Amish people have some beautiful farmland in the state of Pennsylvania.
10. Amish children have some experience in the outside world.

▶ # Asking for Something Politely

Use *Do you have . . .* ? to ask for something politely.

EXAMPLES	EXPLANATIONS

Say:
   (a) Do you have an eraser?
Answer
   (b) Yes, I do. **OR** Sure.
	• to ask for something politely.

Say:
   (c) Excuse me, do you have the time?
Answer
   (d) No, I don't. **OR** Sorry, I don't.
	• to stop a person and ask for something.

EXERCISE 8

Work in pairs. You need to borrow five items from your partner. Keep asking questions until you get the five items. The words in the box may help you.

▷ **EXAMPLE:** Do you have an eraser?   Do you have any gum?

   Yes, I do.   **OR**   Sorry, no I don't.

Eraser	Gum	Notebook
Pen	Whiteout	Piece of paper
Pencil	Stapler	English-English dictionary
Calculator	Ruler	Electronic dictionary
Stamp	Quarter (25 cents)	Change
Tissue	Pencil sharpener	Aspirin

▶ **U**sing *Have* **to Describe People**

He **has** short hair.
He **has** a mustache.

HAIR COLOR	HAIR LENGTH	HAIR TYPE	OTHER	EYE COLOR
dark	long	straight	a mustache	black
light	short	wavy	a beard	brown
black	medium-length	curly	bangs	blue
brown			freckles	green
red				gray
blond				hazel
gray				
white				

EXERCISE 9

You need to seat these guests at the dinner table on p. 75. Match each description to the correct photograph. Write the number of the photograph on the correct name card at the table.

Photographs:

1.

2.

3.

4.　　　　　　　　　**5.**　　　　　　　　　**6.**

Descriptions:

a.　Rodrigo has a mustache and short, dark, curly hair. He wears glasses. He has an oval face and bushy eyebrows. He's at the head of the table on the left side.

b.　Opposite Rodrigo is Chita. Chita is exotic. She has big, round, happy eyes. She has a diamond in her nose. Her hair is dark and she has two shoulder-length braids.

c.　Theresa is to the left of Rodrigo. She has short, dark hair and bangs. She has dark round eyes.

d.　Next to Theresa is Gonzalo. Gonzalo has a kind face. He has a beard and mustache. His hair and beard are dark, but a little grey. He has bright, round eyes.

e.　Across from Theresa is Karl. Karl is almost bald. He has a white mustache and beard. He has wrinkles in his forehead. He has a long, narrow face.

f.　Across from Gonzalo and next to Karl is Dominique. Dominique is a very cute woman. She has short hair. It's light brown. She has thin eyebrows and high cheek bones. She has a nice smile.

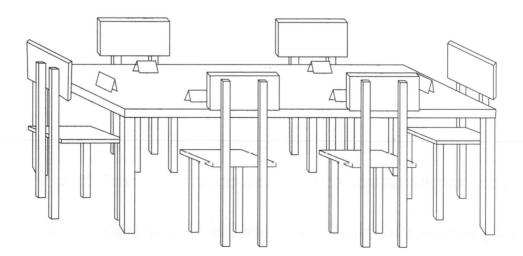

EXERCISE 10

Look at the photographs of Mary and Nilaulaq and of the Amish on pages 64, 65, and 69. Fill in the blanks with *be* or *have* and the correct nouns.

1. John Lapp is Amish.

   a. He _____is_____ married.

   b. He _____ long _____.

   c. He _____ a long _____.

2. a. Nilaulaq _____ an Inuit name.

   b. She _____ long black _____.

   c. She _____ a nice smile.

3. a. Daniel _____ a young Amish boy.

   b. He _____ long blond hair.

   c. He _____ bangs.

4. a. Mary _____ a modern Inuit woman.

   b. Mary _____ a round face.

   c. She _____ dark hair.

EXERCISE 11

Correct the mistakes in the sentences.

1. He ~~have~~ has a car.

2. She have not a house.

3. He no have a TV set.

4. He doesn't is rich.

5. She doesn't has children.

6. Does he has a sister?

7. Does she is an Inuit?

8. Excuse me, have you change?

Use Your English

ACTIVITY 1: WRITING/SPEAKING

WHO IS HE OR SHE?
Write a description of one of your classmates. Do not write the person's name. Read your description to the class. Your classmates guess who it is.

▶ **EXAMPLE:** This student is tall. He has short black hair. He has brown eyes. He has a mustache. Who is he?

ACTIVITY 2: WRITING/SPEAKING

Think of a person or people you know with traditional lifestyles. Write about these people. Write about what they look like. Tell how their lives are different. Tell what they have and what they don't have. Then make an oral presentation to the class.

ACTIVITY 3: RESEARCH

Go to the library and take out a book about the Inuit, the Amish, or another culture you want to learn about. Write down five new things you have learned about what they have and don't have. Report to the class.

ACTIVITY 4: SPEAKING

Work in groups. These are aspects of United States culture. Do you have them in your country today? What is your opinion of these things? Discuss this with your group.

▶ **EXAMPLE:** In my country today, we have fast-food restaurants. I like them because the food is good and not expensive.

  or

  I don't like them because the food is not good and we have no time to talk.

- fast-food restaurants
- take-out restaurants
- 24-hour supermarkets
- cell phones
- social security
- daycare centers
- nursing homes
- health insurance

ACTIVITY 5: LISTENING/ 🎞️ SPEAKING

STEP 1 Listen to this news report. Then fill in the blanks with information from the news report.

In Zorlik—*Not Any*

_____

_____

_____

On the American airplanes—*Some*

_____

_____

_____

STEP 2 With a partner, ask and answer questions about the information above. Use *some* and *any*.

ACTIVITY 6: SPEAKING

STEP 1 **The Dream List** Look at the Dream List and choose five items you want in your life, or think of some others. Write the items in the chart.

A beautiful house	A car	A computer
15 minutes of fame	Some freedom	An interesting job
Some help in English	A spouse	Some money
Some good friends	A good education	Some free time
Some excitement in my life	Some good luck	Some advice for a problem

My Dream List	Classmate #1	Classmate #2	Classmate #3
1.			
2.			
3.			
4.			
5.			

STEP 2 Find three other students who want the same items.

▶ **EXAMPLE:** You: What do you want?

Classmate #1: I want some free time. I also want some good friends.

UNIT 6

THIS/THAT/THESE/THOSE AND POSSESSIVES

UNIT GOALS:

- To use *this, that, these, those* correctly
- To ask what things are
- To use possessive nouns, adjectives, and pronouns
- To ask questions with *whose*

▶ **OPENING TASK**

Wally the Waiter

Wally the waiter is new at his job.

STEP 1 Ask your partner questions to name all the foods on Wally's tray.

STEP 2 Read the conversation.

Wally: Uh, excuse me, whose steak is this?

Charles: It's not ours. Maybe it's theirs at the next table.

Wally: Oh, I'm sorry. Is this your soup?

Charles: Yes, it is.

Wally: Then this bread is yours too . . . and what about these french fries?

Jim: No, they aren't ours. The french fries are theirs, too.

Wally: This salad?

Jim: Yes, that's mine.

Wally: And the pizza?

Charles: That's his pizza.

Wally: Is the hamburger for this table?

Charles: No, it isn't. But those strawberries are.

Wally: I'm very sorry. Today is my first day on this job. I'm a little confused.

Jim: No problem. But those are our sodas too, please.

Wally: Sure, thanks again for your patience!

STEP 3 Try to help Wally remember whose foods these are. Where are the vegetarians—Table 1 or Table 2?

Foods	Charles	Jim	Table 2
a. sodas	❏	❏	❏
b. hamburger	❏	❏	❏
c. french fries	❏	❏	❏
d. strawberries	❏	❏	❏
e. salad	❏	❏	❏
f. steak	❏	❏	❏
g. soup	❏	❏	❏
h. pizza	❏	❏	❏
i. bread	❏	❏	❏

▶ *This, These, That, Those*

NEAR SPEAKER	FAR FROM SPEAKER
Singular	
(a) **This** is a hamburger. **(b)** **This** hamburger is good.	**(c)** **That** is a steak. **(d)** **That** steak is delicious.
Plural	
(e) **These** are baked potatoes. **(f)** **These** baked potatoes are hot.	**(g)** **Those** are french fries. **(h)** **Those** french fries are salty.
Noncount	
(i) **This** is Italian bread. **(j)** **This** Italian bread is cheap.	**(k)** **That** is French bread. **(l)** **That** French bread is expensive.

EXERCISE 1

Go back to the Opening Task on page 81. Find at least five sentences with *this, these, that,* and *those*. Write them below.

1. _____

2. _____

3. _____

4. _____

5. _____

EXERCISE 2

Are the things in the pictures on the next page singular, plural, or noncount? Are the things near or far from the speaker? Fill in the blanks with *this/that/ these/those* and the correct form of the verb *be*.

1. That _____ is _____
a sweater.

2. _____ _____
high-heeled shoes.

3. _____ _____
a belt.

4. _____ _____
shorts.

5. _____ _____
a dress.

6. _____
sunglasses.

7. _____
jewelry.

8. _____
a skirt.

9. _____
blouses.

10. _____
women's clothing.

▶ **Asking What Things Are**

QUESTIONS	ANSWERS
(a) What's **this**? **that**	**Singular** **It's a** sandwich. **It's an** egg.
(b) What are **these**? **those**	**Plural** **They are** french fries. **They're** cookies.
(c) What's **this** dish? **that** dish?	**Noncount** **It's** soup.

EXERCISE 3

Work with a partner. Go back to Exercise 2. Partner A asks questions about the items of clothing. Use *What's this/that? What are these/those?* Partner B responds.

▶ **EXAMPLES:**   **Partner A:** What's that?   **Partner B:** It's a sweater.

Partner A: What are these?   **Partner B:** They're high-heeled
                                                                        shoes.

EXERCISE 4

This is Maria's first American party. She doesn't know about American food.
She asks her American friend, Chris, about the food on the table.

Ask questions with *what*. Then fill in the subject, verb, and *a/an* where
necessary. Then match each sentence to the picture.

Letter in the Picture

1. <u>What's this? It's a</u> _____ hamburger.   <u> d </u>
2. _____ hot dog.   _____
3. _____ french fries.   _____
4. _____ ketchup.   _____
5. _____ pizza.   _____
6. _____ sandwich.   _____
7. _____ doughnuts.   _____
8. _____ cookies.   _____
9. _____ muffin.   _____
10. _____ ice cream cone.   _____

▶ **Possessive Nouns**

EXAMPLES	EXPLANATIONS
(a) The boy has a dog. The **boy's dog** is small. **(b)** Carol has a magazine. **Carol's magazine** is on the table.	Add an apostrophe (') and **-s** to a singular noun.
(c) The boss has an office. The **boss's office** is big. The **boss' office** is neat. **(d)** Charles has a sister. **Charles's** sister is twenty-six. **Charles'** sister is successful.	Add an apostrophe (') and **-s** or just an apostrophe (') to singular nouns and names that end in **-s**.
(e) The waiters have trays. The **waiters' trays** are heavy.	Add only an apostrophe (') at the end of a plural noun.
(f) The **children's school** is near here. **(g)** **Women's clothing** is cheap here.	Add apostrophe (') **-s** to irregular plural nouns.
(h) Paul and **Mary's dog** is friendly. **(i)** My mother-in-**law's cookies** are delicious.	For two or more subjects or a subject with hyphens (-), add '**-s** at the end of last noun.

EXERCISE 5

A *hobby* is an activity we do in our free time. Look at the pictures. Match each person to a hobby. Complete the statement using possessive nouns.

▶ **EXAMPLE:**

BERNIE

a. <u>Bernie's hobby is photography.</u>
b. <u>The man's hobby is photography.</u>

HOBBIES			
photography	playing the piano	hiking	reading
gardening	dancing	astronomy	collecting stamps
traveling	surfing the Internet		

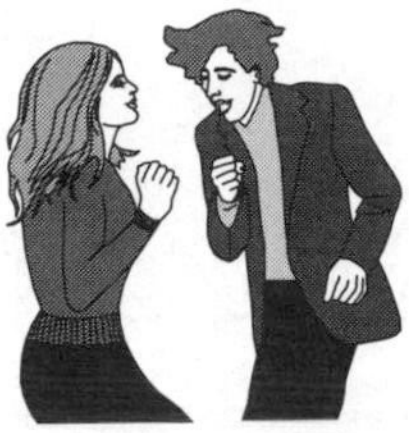

1. KARLA & JULIO

a. ____________________

b. ____________________

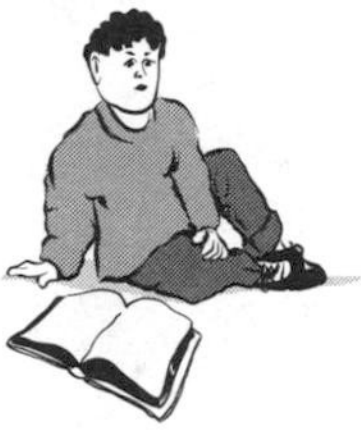

2. CHRIS

a. ____________________

b. ____________________

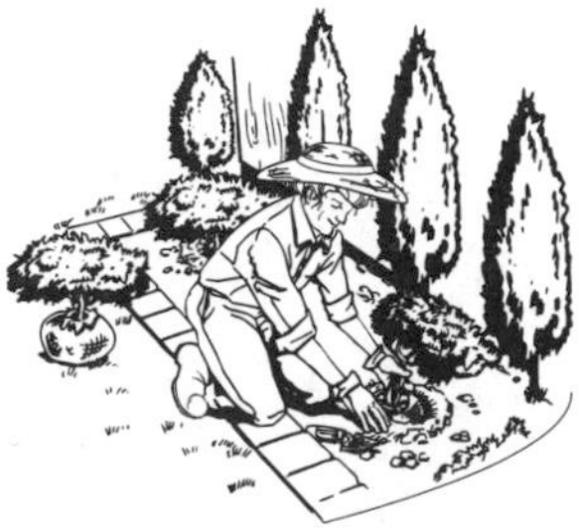

3. CAROL

a. ____________________

b. ____________________

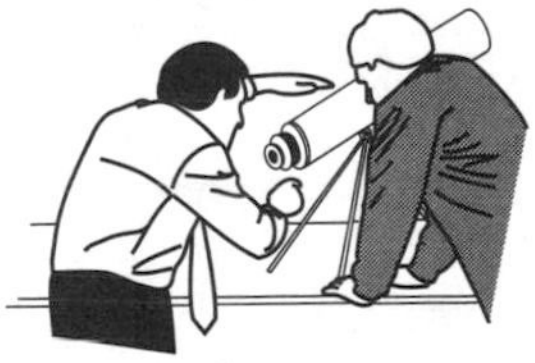

4. JOEL & EUGENE

a. ____________________

b. ____________________

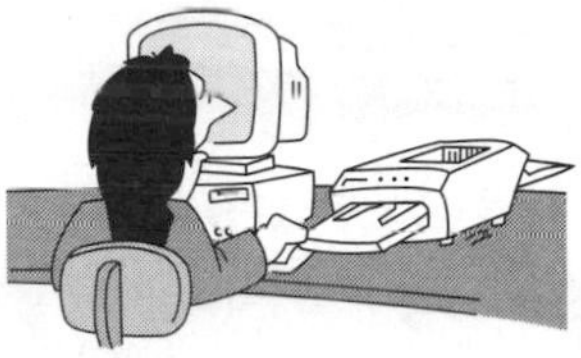

5. ALEXIS

a. ____________________

b. ____________________

6.

DONALD

a. _____

b. _____

7.

JUDY, ELLEN & GINA

a. _____

b. _____

8.

ALICE

a. _____

b. _____

9.

SONIA & TOMMY

a. _____

b. _____

EXERCISE 6

This is Charles' family tree. Read the sentences. Write each person's relationship to Charles under the name in the box.

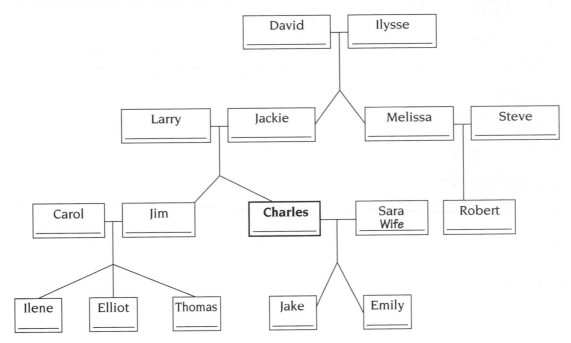

1. Sara is Charles' wife.
2. Emily is Sara and Charles' daughter.
3. Jake is Sara and Charles' son.
4. Jim is Charles' brother.
5. Carol is Charles' sister-in-law.
6. Elliot and Thomas are Charles' nephews.
7. Ilene is Charles' niece.
8. Melissa is Charles' aunt.
9. Steve is Charles' uncle.
10. Robert is Charles' cousin.
11. Jackie is Charles' mother.
12. Larry is Charles' father.
13. David is Charles' grandfather.
14. Ilysse is Charles' grandmother.

EXERCISE 7

Write the correct possessive nouns in the blanks. Say each sentence aloud.

▶ **EXAMPLE:** Sara is __Charles'__ wife.

1. Charles is _____ brother.
2. David is _____ father.
3. Emily is _____ sister.
4. Jim is _____ husband.
5. Melissa is _____ daughter.
6. Elliot is _____ cousin.
7. Charles is _____ uncle.
8. Jake is _____ nephew.
9. Carol is _____ sister-in-law.
10. Ilysse is _____ mother-in-law.

EXERCISE 8

Look carefully at the apostrophes in the sentences below. How many people are there in each sentence? How many dogs? Check *one* or *more than one* for each sentence.

	How many people?		How many dogs?	
	One	More than one	One	More than one
1. My daughter's dog is big.	✔	_____	✔	_____
2. My daughters' dogs big.	_____	_____	_____	_____
3. My son's dog is big.	_____	_____	_____	_____
4. My sons' dogs are big.	_____	_____	_____	_____
5. My sons' dog is big.	_____	_____	_____	_____
6. My son's dogs are big.	_____	_____	_____	_____
7. My children's dog is big.	_____	_____	_____	_____
8. My children's dogs are big.	_____	_____	_____	_____

▶ **P**ossessive Adjectives, Pronouns

POSSESSIVE ADJECTIVES		POSSESSIVE PRONOUNS	
My	car is new.	The car is	**mine**.
Your	house is beautiful.	The house is	**yours**.
His	dog is old.	The dog is	**his**.
Its	fur is white.	(**Its** cannot be a possessive pronoun.)	
Her	jewelry is expensive.	The jewelry is	**hers**.
Our	children are cute.	The children are	**ours**.
Their	television is big.	The television is	**theirs**.

NOTES: Do not confuse a possessive adjective (*its*) with the contraction of *it + is* (*it's*). **Example:** I have a Siamese cat. **It's** a pure breed. Its eyes are deep blue.

Use possessive adjectives with parts of the body.

My hair is black.   **Your** eyes are blue.

EXERCISE 9

Fill in each blank with a possessive adjective or possessive pronoun.

1.

Man: Excuse me, miss. Is this _____ scarf?

Woman: No, it's not _____. I have _____ scarf, thanks.

Man: Oh, I'm sorry. By the way, what's _____ name?

Woman: Anna. What's _____?

2.

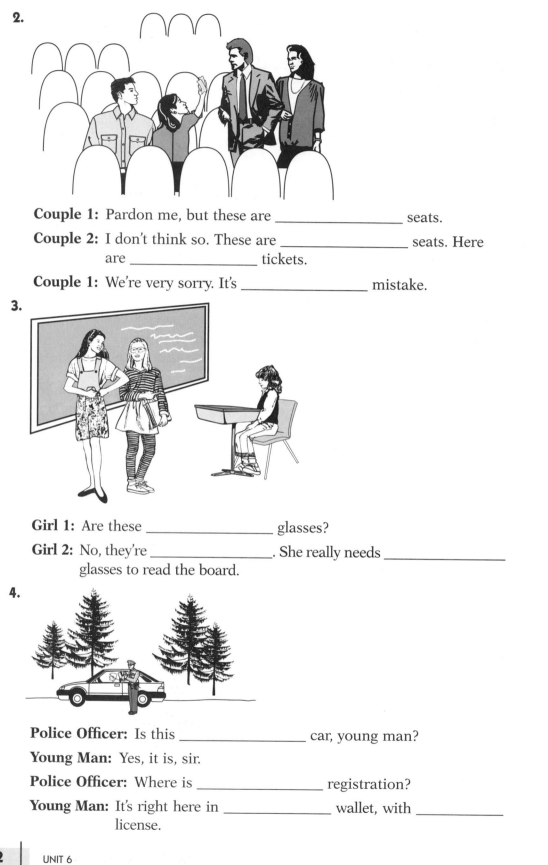

Couple 1: Pardon me, but these are _____ seats.

Couple 2: I don't think so. These are _____ seats. Here are _____ tickets.

Couple 1: We're very sorry. It's _____ mistake.

3.

Girl 1: Are these _____ glasses?

Girl 2: No, they're _____. She really needs _____ glasses to read the board.

4.

Police Officer: Is this _____ car, young man?

Young Man: Yes, it is, sir.

Police Officer: Where is _____ registration?

Young Man: It's right here in _____ wallet, with _____ license.

5.

Boy #1: Who's _____ new friend?

Boy #2: That's Zack. He's a real computer wiz. He has _____ own website. Zack's parents have _____ own computer company. Maybe computers are in _____ genes!

EXERCISE 10

Fill in each blank with a possessive word (a possessive adjective or a possessive pronoun). Then look at the two dogs. Whose dog is A? Whose dog is B?

Many people have pets. (1) _____Their_____ pets are very important to them. Charles' family loves pets. (2) _____ children have a dog. Emily says the dog is (3) _____ ; Jake says the dog is (4) _____ . (5) _____ dog is small. (6) _____ legs are short, (7) _____ ears are long. It's very cute.

Charles' parents have a dog too. They introduce their dog: "This is (8) _____ dog. (9) _____ name is Buck. He's strong. (10) _____ nose is flat. (11) _____ fur is short. We love Buck. He's part of (12) _____ family."

A. This is _____ dog.   **B.** This is _____ dog.

Questions with *Whose*

Use *whose* to ask who owns or possesses something.

WHOSE	NOUN	VERB		ANSWERS
Whose	dog	is	this?	It's Carol's dog. It's her dog. It's hers. Carol's.
Whose	glasses	are	these?	They're Jim's glasses. They're his glasses. They're his. Jim's.

EXAMPLES	EXPLANATIONS
(a) **Who's** she? My sister. (b) **Whose** car is that? Mine.	Do not confuse *who's* and *whose*. *Who's* and *whose* have the same pronunciation. *Who's* = *who is*. *Whose* asks about who owns something.

EXERCISE 11

Ask questions with *whose* to find out who owns each object. Answer in two ways as in the example.

▶ **EXAMPLE:** Whose hammer is this?

It's Jackie's hammer. It's hers.

A. John is a hairdresser. **B.** Jackie is a carpenter **C.** Jim is a secretary **D.** Pierre and Daniel are cooks

1. spoon

2. pencil sharpener

3. shampoo

4. screwdriver

5. computer

6. comb

7. hammer

8. hairbrush

9. sauce pan

10. scissors

11. envelope

12. can opener

13. ladder

14. nails

15. frying pan

16. paperclip

EXERCISE 12

Correct the mistakes in the following sentences.

1. This is Jim magazine.
2. Charles is married. Sara is her wife.
3. That computer is her's.
4. Is Jim the brother of Charles?
5. Who's son-in-law is Charles?
6. Charles and Sara have two children. Jake and Emily are theirs children.
7. What's that name's man?
8. The Larry's dog is small.
9. Whose hungry?
10. This dogs are cute.
11. A: Is this the dog's food?
    B: Yes, that's its.
12. The teacher has chalk on the face.

Use Your English

ACTIVITY 1: WRITING

STEP 1 Draw your family tree.

STEP 2 Ask a classmate about his or her family tree. Draw your classmate's family tree. Then write five sentences about your classmate's family.

ACTIVITY 2: SPEAKING

The teacher asks each student to put a personal object into a bag. One student picks an object and asks, "Whose is this?" The class guesses who the owner is. If the class is not correct, the owner says, "It's mine."

ACTIVITY 3: SPEAKING/WRITING

STEP 1 Bring something to class from your country or another country you know that is special (something you eat, something you wear, something people use, etc.). Tell the class about the special thing. Tell why it is special.

► **EXAMPLES:** This is a special dress. It's for a wedding.
These are ankle bracelets from India.
They're made of silver.

STEP 2 Choose one of the objects from the class presentations. Write about it.

ACTIVITY 4: SPEAKING

Bring in a menu from an American restaurant. Ask questions about the foods on the menu. Role-play a dialogue between a confused waiter (like Wally) and two customers in a restaurant.

ACTIVITY 5: LISTENING

STEP 1 Listen to the conversation. What are the people talking about?

STEP 2 Listen again. In the chart, write *this/that/these* or *those* next to each thing. Then check (✔) if each thing is *near* or *far from* the speaker.

This/that/these/those?		*Near*	*Far from*
1. these	chairs	✔	
2.	table		
3.	lamp		
4.	pictures		
5.	statue		
6.	sofa		

UNIT 7

THERE IS/THERE ARE, A/AN VERSUS THE

UNIT GOALS:

- To understand the meaning of *there* + *be*
- To know when to use *there* + *be* to focus on new information
- To make affirmative and negative statements, and *yes/no* questions with *there* + *be*
- To choose between *a/an* and *the*

▶ OPENING TASK
Whose Apartment is This?

Read the statements on the next page. Then circle the type of person you think lives in this apartment. Give reasons for your choices.

1.	The person	is a man.	is a woman.
2.	The person	has a baby.	doesn't have a baby.
3.	The person	has a pet.	doesn't have a pet.
4.	The person	is athletic.	is not athletic.
5.	The person	drinks coffee.	doesn't drink coffee.
6.	The person	is well-educated.	is not well-educated.
7.	The person	likes music.	doesn't like music.
8.	The person	is on a diet.	is not on a diet.

I think this person is a man/woman because … List your reasons.

▶ *There + Be*

EXAMPLES	EXPLANATIONS
(a) **There are** a lot of things in the apartment.	Use *there + be:* • to show something or somebody exists.
(b) **There is** a cat under the bed.	• to show something or somebody's location.
(c) **There is** a mouse in the house. There's a mouse in the house. NOT: A mouse is in the house.	• when you talk about something or somebody for the first time.
(d) **There are** two men in the picture below. **They are** not happy.	Do not confuse *there are* and *they are*.

EXERCISE 1

Circle (a) or (b) for the correct sentence.

▶ **EXAMPLE:**   (a)   Two men are in this picture.

(b)   There are two men in this picture.

1. An angry restaurant customer says,
   (a) "Waiter, a fly is in my soup."
   (b) "Waiter, there's a fly in my soup."

2. The waiter answers,
   (a) "Sorry, sir. There's more soup in the kitchen."
   (b) "Sorry, sir. More soup is in the kitchen."

3. The customer gets the bill. He says,
   (a) "Waiter, a mistake is on the bill."
   (b) "Waiter, there's a mistake on the bill."

▶ *There Is/There Are*

The form of the *be* verb depends on the noun phrase that follows it.

THERE + BE	NOUN PHRASE		EXPLANATIONS
(a) **There is**	an angry man	at the table.	singular count noun
(b) **There are**	two people	in the restaurant.	plural count noun
(c) **There is**	soup	in his dish.	noncount noun
(d) **There is**	a dining room, kitchen, and restroom	in this restaurant.	When there is more than one noun, *be* agrees with the first noun.

Contraction: *There is = There's.*

EXERCISE 2

Go back to the Opening Task on page 98. Write sentences about the picture with *there is/are* and the words below.

▶ **EXAMPLE:** one bed in the apartment

There's one bed in the apartment.

1. a tennis racquet in the closet
2. high-heeled shoes in the closet
3. women's clothing in the closet
4. sneakers in the closet
5. a coat in the closet
6. CDs on the shelf
7. a CD player on the shelf
8. books on the shelf
9. women's jewelry in the box on the table
10. coffee in the coffee pot
11. a big cake on the counter
12. an exercise bicycle in the apartment
13. an expensive rug on the floor
14. two pillows on the bed

EXERCISE 3

STEP 1 Get into groups. Choose one student to read the following sentences. Listen to the description and draw the picture.

1. There's a table in the center of the room.
2. There are two chairs at the table—one at each end.
3. There's a tablecloth on the table.
4. There's a plate on each end of the table. On one plate, there's a steak and potatoes.
5. The other plate is empty. There's only a napkin.
6. Next to the empty plate, there's an empty glass.
7. Next to the plate with food, there's a half-full glass.
8. There's a bottle of water on the right side of the table. The bottle is half full.
9. There is a vase in the center of the table.
10. There are eight flowers on the floor next to the table.

STEP 2 Compare your drawings. Whose is correct? Who is a good artist?

STEP 3 Choose the best title for your picture.
   A. A Wonderful Dinner
   B. Disappointed Again!
   C. Always Eat Your Vegetables

▶ *There Isn't/There Aren't/ There's No/There Are No*

THERE	BE + NOT		TYPE OF NOUN
There	isn't	a vase on the table.	singular count noun
There	aren't	any children in this restaurant.	plural count noun
There	isn't	any water on the table.	noncount noun

THERE	BE	NO	
There	is	no	vase on the table.
There	are	no	children in the restaurant.
There	's	no	water on the table.

EXERCISE 4

Go back to the Opening Task on page 98. Make sentences with *there is/are, there isn't/there aren't,* or *there's no/there are no* with the words below.

▶ **EXAMPLE:**   There isn't an armchair in the apartment.

        OR There's no armchair in the apartment.

1. television set   **4.** computer   **7.** books   **10.** plants

2. rug   **5.** window   **8.** toys   **11.** coffee pot

3. men's clothing   **6.** desk   **9.** exercise bicycle   **12.** ties

EXERCISE 5

Use the information in the chart below about the city Utopia. Write sentences with *there is/are, there isn't/there aren't,* or *there's no/there are no.*

EXAMPLE: In Utopia, there aren't any guns.

In Utopia, there are no guns.

THE CITY OF UTOPIA

	Yes	No		Yes	No
1. guns		✔	6. universities	✔	
2. public transportation	✔		7. noise		✔
3. crime		✔	8. jobs	✔	
4. museums	✔		9. parks	✔	
5. traffic problems		✔	10. poor people		✔

EXERCISE 6

Read the politician's speech about the city of Utopia. Fill in the blanks with *there is/are, there isn't/there aren't,* or *there's no/there are no.*

Good evening, Ladies and Gentlemen. I am the Mayor of Utopia. I am here tonight to talk about our wonderful city.

Today, (1) ____there are____ 50,000 people in our city. We are all happy. (2) _____ problems in our city.

(3) _____ jobs for all our people. (4) _____ good schools for the children. (5) _____ nice houses for all our families. The houses are comfortable. They aren't expensive.

(6) _____ homeless people on our streets. Our streets are safe. (7) _____ crime here. (8) _____ drugs. Our streets are clean. (9) _____ garbage on the streets. (10) _____ pollution.

(11) _____ many museums, theaters, and parks in our city. (12) _____ entertainment for everyone. (13) _____ good and cheap public transportation for everyone.

(14) _____ many reasons why Utopia is a great city! (15) _____ a good quality of life here in Utopia. And don't forget: (16) _____ an election this year. I want to be your Mayor for four more years. Are you happy in Utopia? Then (17) _____ only one thing to do: VOTE FOR ME, your Mayor Lucas Lime, on November sixth!

FOCUS **4**

▶ *Yes/No* **Questions with**
There Is/There Are

YES/NO QUESTIONS	SHORT ANSWERS	TYPE OF NOUN
(a) **Is there** a computer in the room?	Yes, there is. No, there isn't.	singular count noun
(b) **Are there** any books on the shelves?	Yes, there are. No, there aren't.	plural count noun
(c) **Is there** any jewelry in the box?	Yes, there is. No there isn't.	noncount noun

EXERCISE 7
Complete the questions for each picture.

1. <u>Are there</u> any messages for me?

3. _____ any food in here, Mom?

2. _____ a doctor in the house?

4. Excuse me, _____ a post office near here?

5. _____ any tickets available for the 10:00 show?

6. _____ any room for me?

7. _____ any more instructions in the box?

8. _____ any mail for me?

9. _____ any small sizes?

10. _____ a seat for me?

EXERCISE 8

Test your knowledge. Ask your partner *yes/no* questions with *Is there/Are there* and the words below.

▶ **EXAMPLE:** eggs in an eggplant?

Are there any eggs in an eggplant?

No, there aren't.

1. rain in a desert
2. two billion people in China
3. fifty-two states in the United States
4. earthquakes in Japan
5. billions of stars in the sky
6. life on the moon
7. trees at the North Pole
8. cure for the common cold

FOCUS **5**

▶ **Choosing *A/An* or *The***

A/An and *the* are articles. *A/An* are indefinite articles (see Unit 4). *The* is the definite article.

A/AN	THE
Use only with singular count nouns. **(a)** Susan has **a** bicycle.	Use with all nouns. **(b)** **The** bicycle is new. *(singular)* **(c)** **The** books are on the shelf. *(plural)* **(d)** **The** jewelry is in the box. *(noncount)*
Use to talk about a person or thing for the first time. **(e)** Susan has **a** necklace.	Use the second time you talk about a person or thing. **(f)** Susan has a necklace. **The** necklace is beautiful.
Use to classify people, animals, and things. **(g)** She is **an** investment banker.	Use when both speakers know which noun they are talking about. **(h)** When's **the** party? It's at 8:00.
	Use when the noun is the only one. **(i)** **The** sun is hot.

EXERCISE 9

Look at the pictures. Fill in the blanks with *a/an* or *the*.

1. **Nurse:** It's _____ girl!

   Congratulations, Mr. Spade.

2. **Passenger:** Boy, it's hot. Do you have _____ air conditioner in this car?

   Driver: Yes, but _____ air conditioner doesn't work. Sorry about that!

3. **Husband:** What's in _____ box?

   Wife: I have _____ surprise for you.

   Husband: What's _____ surprise?

   Wife: Open it!

4. **Man:** Do you have _____ room for tonight?

   Clerk: Sorry, sir. _____ motel is full tonight.

5. **Jeff:** Do you have _____ key or do I?

   Matt: I think _____ key's in the car.

6. **Receptionist:** Take your feet off _____ table, please young man!

7. **Woman:** Who is it?

   Mailman: It's _____ mailman, Mrs. Wallace. Here's your mail.

   Woman: Thanks, Mr. Brown. Have a good day!

EXERCISE 10

Read the paragraph. Fill in *a/an* or *the*.

Susan owns (1) _____ neighborhood restaurant.

(2) _____ restaurant is very small. It has

(3) _____ cook, (4) _____ cashier, and

(5) _____ waiter. Susan is (6) _____ boss. Susan has

(7) _____ excellent cook in (8) _____ kitchen: her

mother! Susan has (9) _____ sister. Her sister is

(10) _____ cashier in (11) _____ restaurant. Her sis-

ter's husband is (12) _____ waiter. Susan's sister is

(13) _____ good cashier, but her brother-in-law is not

(14) _____ very good waiter. He doesn't have

(15) _____ good memory and is always confused. This is

(16) _____ big problem for Susan.

EXERCISE 11

Correct the mistakes in the following sentences.

1. It's a picture on a wall.
2. There are a bathroom, a kitchen, and a living room in my house.
3. There have three bedrooms and two bathrooms in the apartment.
4. Is a good restaurant in my neighborhood.
5. There aren't milk in the refrigerator.
6. In my picture, have one woman and two men.
7. Are homeless people in your city?
8. Is there a jewelry in Susan's apartment?
9. Susan owns a restaurant.
   Really? Where is a restaurant?
10. Are there any museums in your town?
    Yes, they are.
11. Excuse me, is there the men's room in this restaurant?
12. Do you have any children?
    Yes, I have the daughter.
13. Are there pollution in your city?
14. There no are women in the restaurant.
15. There are no any poor people in Utopia.

Use Your English

ACTIVITY 1 : WRITING/SPEAKING

Work with a partner. Look at the two pictures. Find eight differences and write sentences with *there is/isn't* or *there are/aren't*. Compare your sentences with those of another pair of students.

▶ **EXAMPLE:** In picture A, there is a dog. In picture B, there's a cat.

Picture A

Picture B

ACTIVITY 2: SPEAKING

Find out about your partner's neighborhood.

STEP 1 Ask questions with *Is there . . .? Are there . . .?* Check **Yes** or **No** in the chart.

▶ **EXAMPLE:** A: Is there a hospital in your neighborhood?

B: Yes, there is. **OR** No, there isn't.

	Yes	No
supermarkets		
movie theaters		
bookstore		
hospital		
bank		
fast-food restaurants		
gas station		
post office		
public library		
schools		
crime		
coffee shop		
trees		
public transportation		

STEP 2 Tell the class or group about your classmate's neighborhood.

ACTIVITY 3: SPEAKING/WRITING

STEP 1 Use the categories below to find out about your classmates. Fill in the blanks with numbers of students.

Total number of classmates _____

Sex: Male _____ Female _____

Physical Characteristics: Dark eyes _____ Blue/Green eyes _____

Women with short hair _____ Women with long hair _____

Nationalities: _____

Personalities: Shy _____ Outgoing _____

Marital Status: Married _____ Single _____

Add your own categories.

STEP 2 Write sentences about your classmates.

▶ **EXAMPLE:** There are ten Mexicans, two Chinese, three Koreans, one Vietnamese, and one Brazilian in my class.

ACTIVITY 4: WRITING

Think of a place that's important to you. Write a short description of this place.

▶ **EXAMPLE:** There's an island off the coast of Sicily called Filicudi. There aren't many houses on the island.

ACTIVITY 5: WRITING

Write a letter to the mayor of your city. Write about the problems in your city or neighborhood.

▶ **EXAMPLE:** Dear Mr. Mayor,

I live in _____. There are many problems in my

neighborhood.

ACTIVITY 6: LISTENING

STEP 1 Listen to Tom's description of his neighborhood and write in the places on the map.

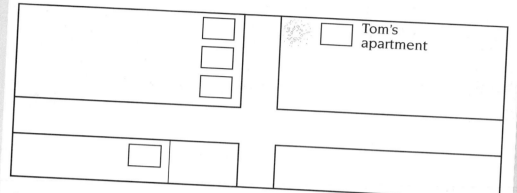

Tom's apartment

STEP 2 Work with a partner. Ask about these places in Tom's neighborhood:

1. police station
2. supermarket
3. banks
4. gas station

5. laundromat
6. mini-market
7. library
8. schools

▶ **EXAMPLE:** Is there a police station?
No, there isn't.

UNIT 8

SIMPLE PRESENT TENSE

Affirmative and Negative Statements, Time Expressions: In/On/At, Like/Need/Want

UNIT GOALS:

- To make affirmative and negative statements using the simple present tense
- To know how to spell and pronounce the third person singular form of verbs in the simple present tense
- To use frequency and time expressions
- To use the simple present tense to:
  -talk about habits and routines
  -talk about things that are always true
  -talk about what you like, want, or need

▶ **OPENING TASK**
Looking at Healthy and Unhealthy Habits

Fran Tic and Rhee Lakst are university students. Fran attends a large university in California and Rhee goes to a small New England school in Massachusetts.

STEP 1 Look at a typical day in their lives. Whose life is healthier? Whose lifestyle is more stressful? Why? Discuss this with a partner.

A Typical Day in the Life of:		
	Fran Tic	**Rhee Lakst**
6:30 A.M.	Wake up and skip breakfast	
7:30 A.M.	Rush to subway station	Wake up and eat breakfast
8:30 A.M.	Go to class	
9:30 A.M.		Walk to school
10:30 A.M.		Go to class
12:30 P.M.	Eat a fast lunch, study in the library	Eat lunch with friends in the cafeteria
1:30 P.M.		Go to work
2:30 P.M.	Rush to work	
4:30 P.M.	Work out in the gym	Go home and take a nap
5:30 P.M.	Meet with her study group	
6:30 P.M.		Buy dinner at a take-out restaurant
7:30 P.M.	Go grocery shopping	Study
8:30 P.M.	Cook dinner at home	Watch TV
10:30 P.M.	Go out with friends	Have milk and cookies and go to bed
12:30 A.M.	Go to bed	

STEP 2 Write statements to complete the chart about the healthy and unhealthy/stressful things Fran and Rhee do.

	Healthy Things They Do	**Unhealthy/Stressful Things They Do**
Fran	Fran goes to the gym.	Fran skips breakfast.
Rhee		
Fran and Rhee		

▶ # Simple Present Tense:
Affirmative Statements

SUBJECT	VERB
I You* We They	work.
He She It	work**s**.
*Both singular and plural.	

EXERCISE 1

Compare Fran and Rhee's lifestyles. Circle the correct form of the verb in each statement.

1. Fran (lead/leads) a busy life in a big city.
2. Rhee (live/lives) a quiet life in a small city.
3. Fran and Rhee both (like/likes) their colleges.
4. Fran (fill/fills) her schedule with many activities.
5. Rhee (need/needs) time to rest during the day.
6. Fran and Rhee (worry/worries) about their grades.
7. They both (work/works) part-time.
8. Fran (sleep/sleeps) about 6 hours a night.
9. Fran (drink/drinks) coffee every night to stay awake.
10. Fran (skip/skips) meals.
11. Rhee (get/gets) a good night's sleep.
12. Rhee (eat/eats) regular meals.
13. Fran and Rhee (study/studies) hard.
14. Fran (exercise/exercises) every day.
15. Rhee (walk/walks) to school.
16. Fran (make/makes) time for her friends.
17. Rhee (spend/spends) a lot of time alone.
18. Fran and Rhee (enjoy/enjoys) their independence.

EXERCISE 2

Go back to the chart in Step 2 of the Opening Task. Correct the statements you wrote.

FOCUS **2**

USE

▶ **Talking about Habits and Routines**

EXAMPLES	EXPLANATION
(a) Fran and Rhee **listen** to music together. **(b)** Fran **goes** to the gym every afternoon.	Use the simple present tense to talk about habits or things that happen again and again.

EXERCISE 3

Match the occupations with what the people do. Use the correct verb forms and make statements aloud.

▶ **EXAMPLE:** A doctor takes care of sick people.

1. A doctor
2. Construction workers
3. A mechanic
4. Air traffic controllers
5. A receptionist
6. Taxi drivers
7. Police officers
8. A fire fighter

a. repair cars
b. protect people
c. answer the telephone
d. take care of sick people
e. build houses
f. direct airplanes
g. work in emergencies
h. take passengers to different places

Which of these jobs are the most stressful? Explain why.

FORM

▶ **T**hird Person Singular:
Spelling and Pronunciation

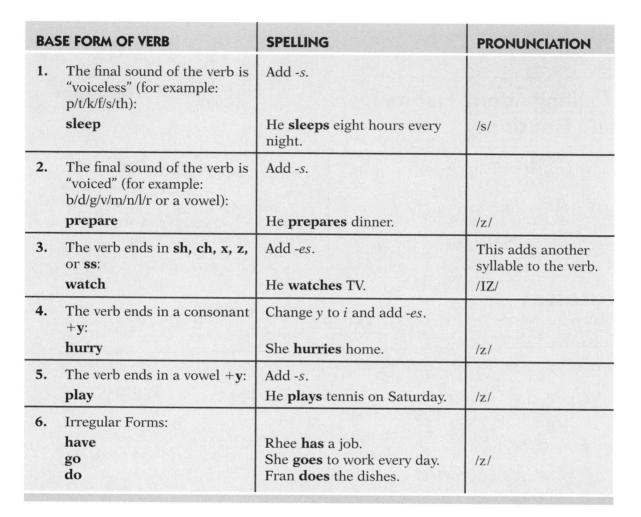

BASE FORM OF VERB	SPELLING	PRONUNCIATION
1. The final sound of the verb is "voiceless" (for example: p/t/k/f/s/th):	Add -*s*.	
sleep	He **sleeps** eight hours every night.	/s/
2. The final sound of the verb is "voiced" (for example: b/d/g/v/m/n/l/r or a vowel):	Add -*s*.	
prepare	He **prepares** dinner.	/z/
3. The verb ends in **sh, ch, x, z,** or **ss**:	Add -*es*.	This adds another syllable to the verb.
watch	He **watches** TV.	/IZ/
4. The verb ends in a consonant +**y**:	Change *y* to *i* and add -*es*.	
hurry	She **hurries** home.	/z/
5. The verb ends in a vowel +**y**:	Add -*s*.	
play	He **plays** tennis on Saturday.	/z/
6. Irregular Forms: **have** **go** **do**	Rhee **has** a job. She **goes** to work every day. Fran **does** the dishes.	/z/

EXERCISE 4

The pictures of Lazy Louie and his wife Hannah are not in the correct order. Number the pictures in the correct order. Then write the number of the picture next to the sentences below.

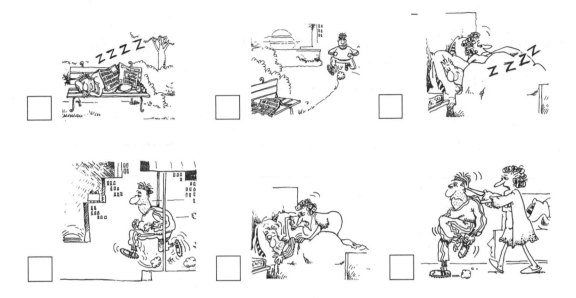

_____ **A.** Poor lazy Louie leaves the house and goes jogging.

_____ **B.** He lies down on the bench and says, "Finally, I am free!" Then he goes to sleep.

_____ **C.** Lazy Louie hates exercise. He wants to sleep, but he gets up. He puts on his clothes and sneakers with his eyes closed. Hannah pushes him out of the house.

_____ **D.** Lazy Louie loves to sleep. He dreams about sleeping! But he snores all the time and his wife gets no sleep. Hannah is tired and needs to do something.

_____ **E.** He runs to the park and finds his favorite bench.

_____ **F.** Hannah finds a way to get Louie out of bed. She wakes him at 6:45 every morning. He continues to sleep. She shakes him. She shouts in his ear, "Time to get up! You need your exercise, dear!"

EXERCISE 5

Here is a list of third-person singular verbs from the story about Lazy Louie. Check (✔) the sound you hear at the end of the verb. Then read the verbs aloud.

Verb	/s/	/z/	/iz/
1. loves		✔	
2. dreams			
3. snores			
4. gets			
5. needs			
6. finds			
7. wakes			
8. continues			
9. shakes			
10. shouts			
11. hates			
12. wants			
13. puts			
14. pushes			
15. leaves			
16. goes			
17. runs			
18. lies			
19. says			

EXERCISE 6

Sit in a circle. The first person in the circle starts to tell the story of Louie and Hannah and the next continues, and so on all around the circle. The pictures in Exercise 4 and the verb list in Exercise 5 will help you.

FOCUS 4

▶ **Frequency and Time Expressions**

EXAMPLES	EXPLANATIONS
every morning/afternoon/evening/night every day/week/year every summer/winter/spring/fall all the time once a week twice a month three times a year	*Frequency expressions* tell how often we do something.

in + the morning   more general
          the afternoon
          the evening
in + June
          1969
          the summer
on + Wednesday(s)
          March 17
          the weekend
at + 7:30
          night
          noon   more specific
	Time expressions tell when we do something.

EXERCISE 7

Lifestyles of Urban Kids. Fill in the blanks with a frequency or time expression.

Michele and Nadia live in a big city. They get up (1) _____
6:00 (2) _____ day of the week, but not (3) _____
weekends. (4) _____ Saturdays, they get up (5) _____
8:00. They go to dancing school (6) _____ Saturday morning
for 3 hours. (7) _____ the afternoon, they go to swimming
lessons. (8) _____ 5:30, they take art lessons at the local college.
(9) _____ Saturday nights, they go out with friends.
(10) _____ , on Sunday morning, they sleep late. They have breakfast (11) _____ 12:00 noon! They do homework
(12) _____ the afternoon. They talk on the phone and read their
e-mails (13) _____ the evening. These big city kids are busy
(14) _____ .

▶ **Frequency and Time Expressions**

EXAMPLES	EXPLANATIONS
(a) They cook dinner **every night.** **(b)** She gets up at 7:00 **every morning.**	Frequency and time expressions usually come at the end of a sentence.
(c) They cook dinner **every night at 7:00.** **(d)** They cook dinner **at seven every night.**	When there is both a frequency and a time expression in one sentence, the frequency expression can come before or after the time expression.
(e) **Once a week,** they go out to eat. **(f)** **On weekends,** they stay in.	Frequency and time expressions can sometimes come at the beginning of a sentence. Use a comma (,) after the expressions at the beginning of a sentence.
(g) I work **on Saturdays.** **(h)** I work **Saturdays.** **(i)** I work **on July 4th.** **(j)** I work **July 4th.**	With days and dates, *on* is not necessary.

EXERCISE 8

Make true statements about yourself using the time and frequency expressions below and the simple present tense.

▶ **EXAMPLE:**   once a week

   You say: I go to the library once a week.

1. once a week
2. every weekend
3. twice a week
4. on my birthday
5. once a year
6. at 7:30 in the morning
7. on Friday nights
8. in September
9. in the summer
10. all the time
11. on December 31
12. at 6:00

EXERCISE 9

Look at Wendy's weekly schedule. Then fill in the blanks in the exercise with the simple present tense or a frequency or time expression.

	Monday	Tuesday	Wednesday	Thursday	Friday
7:00	wake up				
7:30	eat breakfast at home				go out for breakfast
9:30	teach French	go jogging	teach French	do aerobics	teach French
12:00	eat lunch at school	eat lunch at home	eat lunch at school	eat lunch at home	attend meetings
3:00	play tennis	prepare lessons	play tennis	go food shopping	clean apartment
6:00	meet a friend for dinner	go to cooking class	go to the movies	take dancing lessons	go out with friends
8:00	do the laundry	use the Internet	read the newspaper	prepare lessons	
10:30	go to bed early				
12:00					go to bed

1. Wendy _goes food shopping_ on Thursday afternoon.
2. Wendy cleans her apartment _on Friday afternoon_ .
3. Wendy _____ every day at 7:00.
4. She eats breakfast at home _____ .
5. Once a week, on Friday mornings, she _____ .
6. She _____ three times a week.
7. She does aerobics _____ .
8. She eats lunch at school _____ .
9. She attends meetings _____ .
10. She eats lunch at home _____ .
11. She goes to cooking class _____ .

12. She reads _____ .

13. On Friday evening, she _____ .

14. She goes to bed early _____ .

15. She _____ at midnight on Friday.

16. She does the laundry _____ .

17. She _____ at 8:00 on Thursday night.

Now make three more statements about Wendy's schedule.

18. _____ .

19. _____ .

20. _____ .

FOCUS **6**

▶ **Simple Present:
Negative Statements**

SUBJECT	DO/DOES NOT	BASE FORM OF VERB
I You* We They Jim and Peter	do not don't	work.
He She It Mary	does not doesn't	

*Both singular and plural.

EXERCISE 10

Do you have a healthy life? Check (✔)Yes or No.

		Yes	No
1.	I smoke.	_____	_____
2.	I exercise every day.	_____	_____
3.	I drink three or more cans of soda every day.	_____	_____
4.	I eat fruit and vegetables.	_____	_____
5.	I eat fast food every day.	_____	_____
6.	I live a quiet life.	_____	_____
7.	I go to bed late.	_____	_____
8.	I skip meals.	_____	_____
9.	I feel tired every day.	_____	_____
10.	I eat red meat every day.	_____	_____
11.	I cook fresh food at home.	_____	_____
12.	I find time to relax.	_____	_____
13.	I overeat.	_____	_____
14.	I worry all the time.	_____	_____

Now look at your partner's **Yes** and **No** checks. Tell the class why your partner has a healthy or unhealthy life.

▶ **EXAMPLE:** My partner has a very healthy life. He doesn't smoke. He exercises every day.

EXERCISE 11

For each verb below, make a true negative statement about Fran or Rhee.

▶ **EXAMPLE:**   skip meals

Rhee doesn't skip meals.

1. go to bed late
2. get a good night's sleep
3. have a healthy diet
4. take naps
5. have milk and cookies every night
6. take time to relax
7. cook
8. skip breakfast
9. eat breakfast
10. go to the gym

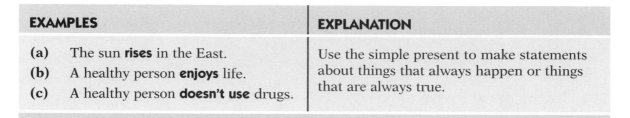

Talking about Things that Are Always True

EXAMPLES	EXPLANATION
(a) The sun **rises** in the East. **(b)** A healthy person **enjoys** life. **(c)** A healthy person **doesn't use** drugs.	Use the simple present to make statements about things that always happen or things that are always true.

EXERCISE 12

Use the simple present affirmative or negative to complete the definitions of the new words below.

1. Workaholics (love) _____*love*_____ to work all the time.
2. Vegetarians (eat) _____ meat.
3. Couch potatoes (sit) _____ in front of the TV all the time.
4. An alcoholic (drink) _____ a lot of wine, beer, or liquor every day.
5. A pacifist (like) _____ war.
6. An insomniac (sleep) _____ at night.
7. A stressed person (worry) _____ a lot.
8. A health-conscious person (care) _____ about his or her health.
9. Environmentalists (like) _____ pollution.

EXERCISE 13

Fill in the blanks. Use the simple present affirmative or negative of the verbs in parentheses.

Today, many Americans are under stress. They (move) (1) _____*move*_____ at a fast pace. They (work) (2) _____ all the time. They often (work) (3) _____ overtime. People (have) (4) _____ time for themselves or their families. An average worker (have) (5) _____ too much work and (have) (6) _____ enough time to finish it. As a result, many Americans (take) (7) _____ vacations.

Why are Americans so busy all the time? One reason is modern technology. Modern technology (keep) (8) _____ us busy and (give) (9) _____ us stress. Technology (let) (10) _____ us relax. We (wear) (11) _____ beepers. We (use) (12) _____ fax machines to send messages fast. We (take) (13) _____ time to rest. Even on Sundays, many stores (stay) (14) _____ open and people (go shopping) (15) _____ . Today, stress is one of the top reasons why Americans (get) (16) _____ sick.

▶ *Like, Want, Need*

EXAMPLES	EXPLANATIONS
I $\left\{\begin{array}{l}\textbf{like} \\ \textbf{want} \\ \textbf{need}\end{array}\right\}$ coffee.	Subject + Verb + Noun
I $\left\{\begin{array}{l}\textbf{like} \\ \textbf{want} \\ \textbf{need}\end{array}\right\}$ to drink coffee.	Subject + Verb + Infinitive
(a) I love animals. I **want** a cat. **(b)** I love Joel. I **want** to marry him.	*Want* expresses desire.
(c) I have a headache. I **need** some medicine. **(d)** You don't look well. You **need** to see a doctor.	*Need* expresses something that is necessary.

EXERCISE 14

What do these people need? Write one sentence with *need* + noun and another sentence with want + infinitive. Use the nouns and verbs in the box.

▶ **EXAMPLE:**

He needs some flour.

He wants to bake some cookies.

Nouns	Verbs
cup of coffee	write down a message
hammer	hang a picture
a quarter	fix a broken cup
peace and quiet	paint a room
pen	wake up
glue	get some sleep
a can of paint	make a telephone call

1.

_____

_____

2.

_____

_____

3.

_____

_____

4.

_____

_____

5.

_____

_____

6.

_____

_____

7.

_____

_____

EXERCISE 15
Correct the mistakes in the following sentences.

1. She is smile every day.
2. He every day takes a walk.
3. He finish his dinner every night.
4. He don't cook dinner on Sundays.
5. We are study in the library on Saturdays.
6. She don't work on Tuesdays.
5. English classes begin at September.
8. She need a pen to write.
9. He want to make a sandwich.
10. Wendy plays tennis on 3:00.

Use Your English

ACTIVITY 1: SPEAKING

Who is a person you admire? Tell your partner about this person. Then answer questions your partner may have.

▶ **EXAMPLE:** I admire my mother. She loves our family. She enjoys her work. She cooks great food. She doesn't get angry.

Tell your partner about a person you are worried about. Then answer the questions your partner may have.

▶ **EXAMPLE:** I am worried about my friend. He doesn't eat healthy food. He doesn't exercise. He doesn't sleep. He sits in front of the TV all the time.

ACTIVITY 2: WRITING/SPEAKING

What do you and your partner have in common? Write two affirmative statements and two negative statements with *like* for each of the categories below. Share your sentences with your partner and find out what you both have in common. Report your results to the class.

Music	Books	Food
I like to listen to classical music. I also like rock. I don't like rap. I don't like to listen to opera.		

Movies	Sports	Cars

ACTIVITY 3: WRITING/SPEAKING

STEP 1   Fill out your own daily schedule using only the base form of the verb.

My schedule: <u>(Name)</u> _____

	Mon.	Tues.	Wed.	Thurs.	Fri.	Sat.	Sun.
Morning		6:00 go jogging					
Afternoon				3:00 go to the library			
Evening					8:00 go bowling		

STEP 2   Exchange your schedule with a partner. Write several sentences about your partner's habits and routines. Report to the class.

▶ **EXAMPLE:**   My partner wakes up at 10:00 on Sundays.

My schedule: <u>(Name)</u> _____

	Mon.	Tues.	Wed.	Thurs.	Fri.	Sat.	Sun.
Morning							10:00 wake up
Afternoon							
Evening							

ACTIVITY 4: WRITING/SPEAKING

Write ten statements about the habits of people in the country you come from. Share your information with your classmates. Compare the habits of people in different countries.

▶ **EXAMPLES:**   1. In Korea, women don't change their names when they get married.
                                        people eat rice every day.
                                        men go into the army.
                     2. In China, people like to exercise in the morning.
                                        people go to work by bicycle.
                     3. In Italy,   people eat pasta.

ACTIVITY 5: SPEAKING

What is a typical day for you?
Look at the activities below and say how much time you spend on each activity.

sleep _____

study in school _____

watch TV _____

commute _____

other _____

eat _____

exercise _____

do homework _____

cook _____

work _____

clean my room _____

talk on the phone _____

get dressed _____

Get into a group and talk about each activity. What is the average time the group spends on each activity? Each group should report to the class.

▶ **EXAMPLE:** In our group, everyone sleeps eight hours a night.

ACTIVITY 6: LISTENING

Listen to the two people talk about their jobs. Complete the chart.
S = Sunday
M = Monday
T = Tuesday
W = Wednesday
T = Thursday
F = Friday
S = Saturday

Job	Start	Circle workdays	Work on Sundays?
1.		S M T W T F S	
2.		S M T W T F S	

Which job do you like? 1 or 2? Why?

UNIT 9

SIMPLE PRESENT TENSE

Yes/No **Questions, Adverbs of Frequency,** *Wh***-Questions**

UNIT GOALS:

- To ask *yes/no* and *Wh*-questions in the simple present tense
- To understand the meaning and correct position of adverbs of frequency
- To ask questions with *who* and *whom*
- To ask for information about English

▶ OPENING TASK
What Do Good Language Learners Do?

You are all "language learners" in this class. But are you **good** language learners? What is a good language learner? What does a good language learner do?

STEP 1   Read the text below. Do you think you are a good language learner?

Good language learners think about how to learn. They try to use the new language every day. They read, write, and listen to the new language. They find people to speak to. When they don't understand, they don't get nervous. They try to guess the meanings of new words and expressions. They always ask questions about the language. They find ways to remember new words. They try to use new words and expressions in sentences. They listen to correct pronunciation. They repeat words out loud. They sometimes talk to themselves in the new language. They also think about grammar. They try to understand how the new language works.

Good language learners know that learning a new language is not easy. They don't feel bad when they make mistakes. They try to understand their problems in the new language. They review every day.

STEP 2   With a partner, make up five comprehension questions about this text. For example: Do good language learners think about how to learn? Does a good language learner practice the new language? Then ask another pair of students the questions.

▶ Simple Present: *Yes/No* Questions

DO/DOES	SUBJECT	BASE FORM OF VERB	SHORT ANSWERS	
			Affirmative	**Negative**
Do	I you we they	work?	Yes, you I we do. they	No, you I we do not. they don't.
Does	he she it		Yes, he she does. it	No, he she does not. it doesn't.

EXERCISE 1

Are your classmates good language learners?

Ask one classmate *yes/no* questions with the words below. Then ask another classmate the questions.

▶ **EXAMPLE:** **You:** Do you speak English outside of class?

Classmate: Yes, I do./No, I don't.

	Classmate 1		Classmate 2	
	Yes	No	Yes	No
1. speak English outside of class				
2. practice pronunciation				
3. ask people to correct your English				
4. ask people questions about English				
5. watch TV in English				
6. guess the meaning of new words				
7. make lists of new words				
8. read something in English every day				
9. write something in English every day				
10. think about grammar				

Discuss your answers with the class. Decide who is a good language learner.

EXERCISE 2

Information Gap

Nahal and Sang-Woo are two different types of language learners. Work with a partner to find out how they are different. Student A looks at the chart below. Student B looks at the chart on page A-19. Ask and answer questions to complete your chart.

▶ **EXAMPLE:** **Student A:** Does Nahal want to meet English-speaking people?

   Student B: Yes, she does.

   Student B: Does Sang-Woo want to meet English-speaking people?

   Student A: No, he doesn't.

Student A:

	Nahal		Sang-Woo	
	Yes	No	Yes	No
1. like to learn English	✔			
2. want to meet English-speaking people				✔
3. feel nervous when speaking English		✔		
4. like to work in groups			✔	
5. need grammar rules to learn English	✔			
6. learn by speaking and listening to English				✔
7. learn by reading and writing English		✔		
8. learn slowly, step by step			✔	
9. try new ways of learning	✔			

EXERCISE 3

What kind of language learner are you?
Look at Exercise 2 and write statements about yourself.

▶ **EXAMPLE:** I like to learn English. I want to meet English-speaking people. I don't feel nervous when speaking English.

EXERCISE 4

What are some of your personal habits? Ask a partner *yes/no* questions with the words below. Check *yes* or *no*. Then your partner asks you.

▶ **EXAMPLE:** **You:** Do you wake up early?

Your Partner: Yes, I do./No, I don't.

	Your Partner's Answers	
	Yes	**No**
1. wake up early	_____	_____
2. watch TV a lot	_____	_____
3. listen to loud music	_____	_____
4. cook	_____	_____
5. have parties on weekends	_____	_____
6. make friends easily	_____	_____
7. go to bed late	_____	_____
8. talk on the telephone a lot	_____	_____
9. study hard	_____	_____
10. clean your apartment every week	_____	_____

EXERCISE 5

Read about students in the United States.

(1) In the United States, a child usually starts kindergarten at age five. (2) In public schools, boys and girls study together. (3) Children go to school five days a week. (4) They don't go to school on Saturdays. (5) They go to school from 8:30 a.m. to 3:00 p.m. (6) They don't wear uniforms. (7) In public schools, children do not study religion.

(8) In high school, some students take difficult exams to enter college. (9) A private college costs a lot of money. (10) The government doesn't pay for private colleges. (11) Many parents pay for their children's education. (12) Many students work after school to help pay for college.

Write twelve *yes/no* questions from the sentences marked 1–12 in the reading. Interview a classmate about his or her country with the questions you wrote. Compare students in the United States to students in your home countries.

QUESTIONS

1. Does a child usually start kindergarten at age five in your country _____ ?

2. Do boys and girls usually study together _____ ?

3. _____ ?

4. _____ ?

5. _____ ?

6. _____ ?

7. _____ ?

8. _____ ?

9. _____ ?

10. _____ ?

11. _____ ?

11. _____ ?

12. _____ ?

Now write five sentences about school in your partner's home country.

1. In Korea, a child usually starts kindergarten at age four or five. _____

2. _____

3. _____

4. _____

5. _____

▶ **Adverbs of Frequency**

Adverbs of frequency tell how often something happens.

QUESTION: HOW OFTEN DOES NAHAL WATCH TELEVISION?			
Nahal	**always** **almost always** **usually** **often/frequently** **sometimes** **seldom/rarely** **never**	watches television.	100% 0%

EXERCISE 6

Read the questions and answers. Circle the correct adverbs of frequency.

▶ **EXAMPLE:** **Q:** Does Belinda read English/American newspapers?

   A: She (often/seldom) reads an English or American newspaper. She buys one every morning.

1. Q: Does Hamid ever use his hands when he speaks English?
   A: He (never/always) uses his hands. His hands help him explain things.

2. Q: Does Belinda ever guess the meanings of words?
   A: She (never/always) guesses the meanings of new words. She uses her dictionary all the time.

3. Q: Does Hamid ever think in English?
   A: He (never/usually) thinks in his own language first. Then he translates his words into English.

4. Q: Does Belinda ever sing in English?
   A: She (often/seldom) sings in English. She doesn't like to sing.

5. Q: Does Hamid ever write letters in English?
   A: He has an American friend in Boston. He misses him. He (rarely/sometimes) writes letters to him in English.

6. Q: Does Belinda ever make telephone calls in English?
   A: She lives with her aunt. Her aunt speaks English. Her aunt makes the phone calls. Belinda (never/always) makes phone calls in English.

7. Q: Does Belinda ever talk to herself in English?
   A: She likes English. She (usually/rarely) talks to herself in English.

8. Q: Does Hamid ever think about how English works?
   A: He thinks grammar is very interesting. He (never/always) tries to understand how English works.

EXERCISE 7

The chart below shows learning habits and adverbs of frequency. Check the box that is true for you.

Learning Habits	Adverbs of Frequency						
	Always	Almost always	Usually	Often/ Frequently	Sometimes	Seldom/ Rarely	Never
1. use a dictionary							
2. make telephone calls in English							
3. speak to native speakers							
4. discuss learning problems with classmates							
5. practice English pronunciation							
6. record my voice on tape							
7. read books or newspapers in English							
8. ask questions about English							
9. think in English							
10. dream in English							

▶ **Position of Adverbs of Frequency**

EXAMPLES	EXPLANATIONS
(a) They **always** come to class. **(b)** He **sometimes** asks questions in class. **(c)** He **never** asks questions.	Adverbs of frequency usually come between the subject and the verb.
(d) **Sometimes** I ask questions in class. **(e)** That's not true. He asks questions **often**.	Some adverbs of frequency can come at the beginning or at the end of a sentence for emphasis.
(f) They **are always** in class. **(g)** I **am never** late to class.	Adverbs of frequency come after the verb *be*.

EXERCISE 8

Go back to the chart in Exercise 7. Exchange books with a partner. Write statements about your partner's learning habits using adverbs of frequency.

▶ **EXAMPLES:** He always uses a dictionary.

She rarely speaks to native speakers.

EXERCISE 9

Make true statements about your home country by adding an adverb of frequency.

Name of country: _____

In schools in my home country:

1. The students are of the same nationality.
    The students are usually of the same nationality.
    _____

2. The teachers are women.

    _____

3. Teachers hit students.

    _____

4. Teachers are young.

_____

5. Teachers give homework.

_____

6. Teachers are relaxed and friendly.

_____

7. Students work together to learn.

_____

8. The classrooms are noisy.

_____

9. Students take tests.

_____

10. Students cheat on tests.

_____

Now discuss what you think is true for the United States.

▶ Simple Present: *Wh*-Questions

Wh-QUESTION WORD	*DO/DOES*	SUBJECT	BASE FORM OF VERB	
(a) **What**	**do**	I	**do**	in class?
(b) **When**	**do**	you	**review**	new vocabulary?
(c) **What time**	**do**	we	**begin**	class?
(d) **Where**	**do**	they	**study**	English?
(e) **Why**	**does**	he	**need**	English?
(f) **How**	**does**	she	**get**	to school?
(g) **How often**	**does**	Maria	**talk to**	native speakers of English?
(h) **Who(m)**	**does**	George	**meet**	after school?

EXERCISE 10

Match each question to its answer. Write the letter on the line.

_f_ 1. Why does he need English?   a. on weekends

___ 2. When does the semester begin?   b. by car

___ 3. What do they do in class?   c. at the City University of New York

___ 4. What time does your class start?   d. They speak, read, write, and listen to English.

___ 5. Where does he study English?   e. at 8:30

___ 6. How often does he speak English?   f. because he wants to go to college in the United States

___ 7. When does she go out with her American friends?   g. on September 10th

___ 8. How does he go home?   h. every day

EXERCISE 11

Read the story of a student named Denise. Write *Wh*-questions with the words in parentheses. Then read the story again and take turns asking a partner the questions and answering them aloud.

Denise is a Haitian student in Washington, D.C. She speaks three languages—Creole, French, and English. She wants to be a bilingual teacher. Her English is very good, but she speaks with an accent. Sometimes people don't understand her when she speaks. She often meets her Haitian friends to talk about her problem. Denise feels embarrassed and seldom speaks English. She feels angry at Americans. She says Americans only speak English. They don't understand the problems people have when they learn a new language.

▶ **EXAMPLE:** (Denise/live) _Where does Denise live_____?

1. (Denise/come from) _____?

2. (Denise/want to be) _____?

3. (Denise/speak English) _____?

4. (Denise/feel when she speaks English) _____?

5. (Denise/feel this way) _____?

6. (Denise/feel angry) _____?

Now ask two questions of your own about the story.

7. _____?

8. _____?

▶ ***Wh*-Questions with *Who/Whom***

EXAMPLES	EXPLANATIONS

(a) **Q: Who** usually meets her friends?
   A: Denise.
(b) **Q: Who** speaks Creole?
   A: Denise and her Haitian friends.
	Who asks a question about the **subject** (Denise) of the sentence. Do not use *do/does.*

(c) **Q: Who(m)** does Denise meet? **A:** Denise meets her friends.	*Who(m)* asks a question about the **object** (her friends) of the sentence.
(d) **Whom** does Denise call on Sundays? **(e)** **Who** does Denise call on Sundays?	Formal written English Informal or spoken English
(f) **Q: What** goes up but never comes down? **A:** ¡ǝƃɐ ɹno⅄	*What* can also be the subject of a question. Do not use *do/does* in this case.

EXERCISE 12

Fill in the blanks with *who* or *whom.*

▶ **EXAMPLE:** ____Who____ speaks English?

   __Who(m)__ do you call every week?

1. _____ likes English?

2. _____ avoids English?

3. _____ bites his or her nails before a test?

4. _____ do you meet after class?

5. _____ do you usually visit on weekends?

6. _____ makes mistakes in English?

7. _____ do you call at night?

8. _____ understands the difference between *who* and *whom*?

9. _____ helps you with English?

EXERCISE 13
Read about immigrant families in the United States.

Many families immigrate to the United States. At the beginning, the parents often have problems. They don't speak English. They don't learn English fast. The children usually learn English before the parents, so they translate for their parents. The children always help their parents. Sometimes, the children pay the rent to the landlords. They often talk with doctors about their parents' health. The children take their parents to job interviews. They solve the family's problems. This is a big responsibility for the children, and they feel important. But their parents sometimes feel sad and helpless. Life is often difficult for new immigrant families.

Fill in the blanks with *who* (subject) or *whom* (object). Then answer the questions.

▶ **EXAMPLES:** Q: _____Who_____ learns English before the parents?

A: The children (learn English before the parents.)

Q: _____Whom_____ do the children help?

A: (The children help) their parents.

1. _____ translates for the parents?

2. _____ helps the parents?

3. _____ do the children pay the rent to?

4. _____ do the children often talk to about their parents' health?

5. _____ do the children take to job interviews?

6. _____ solves the family's problems?

7. _____ feels important?

8. _____ feels sad and helpless?

▶ # Getting Information about English

In a new language, you do not always know the words to say what you want. When you have a problem, ask for help.

EXAMPLES	EXPLANATIONS
You say:	**When you:**
(a) What does the word *decision* mean? **(b)** What does *strategy* mean?	• want to know the **meaning** of a word.
(c) How do you spell *remember?*	• want to know the **spelling** of a word.
(d) How do you pronounce *communicate?*	• want to know the **pronunciation** of a word.
(e) How do you say *a machine to clean floors?* **(f)** How do you say *the opposite of happy?*	• don't know the word for something, and you want to communicate your meaning and learn new words.

EXERCISE 14

Ask *Wh-*questions for the answers below.

▶ **EXAMPLE:** **Q:** How do you say *special shoes you wear in the house?*

   A: You say *slippers.*

1. **Q:** _____?

   A: You pronounce it læŋ-gwIdz.

2. **Q:** _____?

   A: The word *guess* means you don't know the answer, but you try to find the answer in your head.

3. **Q:** _____?

   A: You say *thin.*

4. **Q:** _____?

   A: You spell it: *c-o-m-m-u-n-i-c-a-t-e.*

5. Q: _____?

   A: *Strategy* means an action or actions you take to achieve a goal; for example. to learn English.

EXERCISE 15

Correct the mistakes in the following sentences.

1. Is he read books?
2. Do they good students?
3. What means *routines*?
4. I watch sometimes TV.
5. How often you listen to native speakers of English?
6. Does he studies in the library?
7. What does the class on Mondays?
8. How you say *not correct*?
9. I am never make mistakes.
10. Why you feel embarrassed to speak English?

Use Your English

ACTIVITY 1: WRITING/SPEAKING

Work with a partner.

STEP 1 Write at least ten questions you have about family life in your partner's country. Include people's roles, habits, and routines.

STEP 2 Ask each other questions about family life in your countries. Find five similarities and five differences in family life. Report to the class.

▶ **EXAMPLES:**

	Same	Different
Do women make important family decisions?	_____	_____
What decisions do women make?	_____	_____
Do men cook at home?	_____	_____
Who cooks?	_____	_____

ACTIVITY 2: WRITING/SPEAKING

Find the perfect roommate. You want to share an apartment with another student. Write ten questions to ask your classmates. Find a good "roommate" in your class.

▶ **EXAMPLES:**
- Do you smoke?
- What time do you get up?

ACTIVITY 3: WRITING/SPEAKING

What do you know about the countries your classmates come from? Write ten questions about customs, habits, etc. Find a classmate who comes from a different country and ask the questions. Then report to the class.

▶ **EXAMPLES:** What do people usually do on weekends?

How often do people go to the movies?

How do people usually celebrate their birthdays?

ACTIVITY 4: WRITING/SPEAKING

United States Knowledge Quiz

STEP 1 Get into two teams. Write ten *Wh*-questions in the simple present that test knowledge about the United States.

STEP 2 Team A asks Team B the first question. Team B can discuss the question before they answer. Then Team B asks Team A the second question and so on.

Score: Score 1 point for each grammatically correct question. Score 1 point for each correct answer. The team with the most points is the winner.

▶ **EXAMPLES:** Where does the President of the United States live?

When do Americans vote?

ACTIVITY 5: WRITING

Write about the educational system in your native country. Answer these questions:

- What do students usually do?
- What do teachers usually do?
- What are the differences between the school system in your country and in the United States?

ACTIVITY 6: LISTENING/ SPEAKING

STEP 1 Listen to the conversation between Pedro and Yuko. Who is the hard-working student?

STEP 2 Listen again. Make a list of the things Pedro and Yuko do on Sundays.

Pedro   Yuko

_____   _____

_____   _____

_____   _____

STEP 3 Role-play the conversation with a partner.

UNIT 10

IMPERATIVES AND PREPOSITIONS OF DIRECTION

UNIT GOALS:

- To make affirmative and negative imperatives
- To understand the many functions of imperatives
- To use prepositions of direction
- To give directions

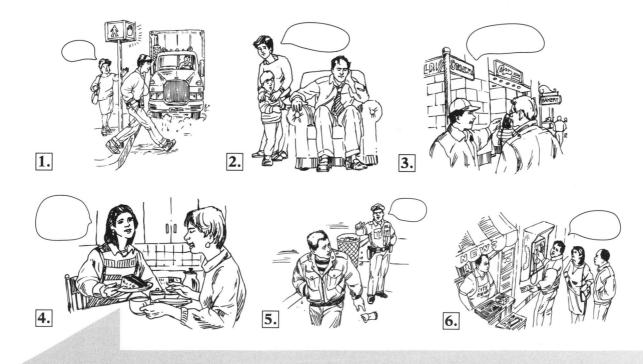

STEP 1   Match each statement to a picture.

**Picture
Number**

(a)   "Please give me change for a dollar, Sir."   _____

(b)   "Have a piece of cake with your coffee, Mary."   _____

(c)   "Don't ask your father now. He's very angry."   _____

(d)   "Don't throw your litter on the street.
      Pick it up!"   _____

(e)   "Go straight down Eighth Avenue and
      turn left at the bakery."   _____

(f)   "Watch out!"   _____

STEP 2   What is the mother saying? Write her words.

▶ Imperatives: Affirmative and Negative

Affirmative

BASE FORM OF VERB	
(a) Have	a piece of cake
(b) Give	me change for a dollar.

Negative

DO NOT/DON'T + BASE FORM OF VERB	
(c) Do not throw	your litter on the street.
(d) Don't ask	your father now.

Polite imperatives

> (e) **Please give** me change for a dollar.
> (f) **Please don't do** that again.
> (g) **Don't do** that again, **please.**

NOTE: Don't use a subject with imperatives:
> *Have a piece of cake.* **NOT:** ~~You~~ *have a piece of cake.*

EXERCISE 1
Go back to the Opening Task on pages 156–157. Underline all the affirmative imperative verbs and circle all the negative imperative verbs.

▶ **EXAMPLE:** "Please <u>give</u> me change for a dollar, Sir."

▶ **U**ses of Imperatives

Imperatives have different uses or functions. Look at the pictures and notice what the imperative does in each situation.

a.
b.
c.
d.
e.
f.

IMPERATIVE	USE
(a) "Don't worry. Relax."	Give advice or make a suggestion.
(b) "Be careful!"	Give a warning when there is danger.
(c) "Make a right at the corner."	Give directions or instructions.
(d) "Please give me some aspirin, Mom."	Make a polite request.
(e) "Have some coffee, dear."	Offer something politely.
(f) "Don't come home late again!"	Give an order.

EXERCISE 2

Look back at the Opening Task on pages 156–157. Write the number of the picture that matches each use.

Use	Picture Number
A. Give advice	2
B. Give an order	
C. Give a warning when there is danger	
D. Make a polite request	
E. Offer something politely	
F. Give directions	

EXERCISE 3

Fill in each blank with an affirmative or negative imperative.

use	keep	drink	be	drive
wear	obey	leave	look	use

To be a good driver, remember these rules:

1. _____ prepared to stop.

2. _____ at the road ahead.

3. _____ your rearview mirrors.

4. _____ the speed limit.

5. _____ space between your car and the car in front of you.

6. _____ your seat belt.

7. _____ if you are very tired or are on medication.

8. _____ and drive.

9. _____ your horn to warn others of danger.

10. _____ your car in good condition.

EXERCISE 4

Work with a partner. You read each sentence on the left. Your partner gives an appropriate response from the right.

1. I don't like my landlord.
2. I have a headache.
3. I am overweight.

4. I have the hiccups.
5. I have a toothache.
6. I don't have any friends here.
7. I feel tired every morning.

8. I miss my family.

9. I worry too much.
10. I can't speak English very well.

a. Go on a diet.
b. Go to the dentist.
c. Make friends with your classmates.
d. Move to a different apartment.
e. Call home.
f. Go to bed early.
g. Practice speaking to native speakers.
h. Hold your breath for two minutes.
i. Take it easy.
j. Take some aspirin.

FOCUS **3**

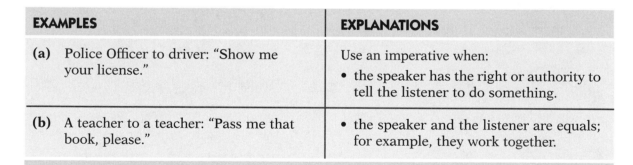

▶ **U**sing Imperatives Appropriately

EXAMPLES	EXPLANATIONS
(a) Police Officer to driver: "Show me your license."	Use an imperative when: • the speaker has the right or authority to tell the listener to do something.
(b) A teacher to a teacher: "Pass me that book, please."	• the speaker and the listener are equals; for example, they work together.

EXERCISE 5

Check (✔) Yes if the imperative is appropriate in each situation. Check (✔) No if the imperative is not appropriate.

Situation	Imperative	Yes	No
1. A student says to a teacher:	"Give me my paper."		
2. A student says to a classmate:	"Wait for me after class."		
3. A man stops you on the street. He says:	"Hey, mister. Tell me the time."		
4. A worker says to his boss:	"Don't bother me now. I'm busy."		
5. You get into a taxi and say:	"Take me to the airport, and please hurry!"		
6. A father says to his teenage son:	"Turn down that music! I can't take it anymore!"		

FOCUS **4**

MEANING

▶ **Prepositions of Direction:**
To, Away From, On (to), Off (of),
In (to), Out of

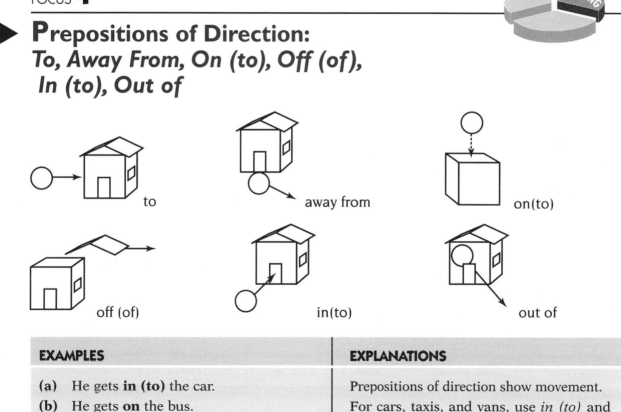

EXAMPLES	EXPLANATIONS
(a) He gets **in (to)** the car.	Prepositions of direction show movement.
(b) He gets **on** the bus.	For cars, taxis, and vans, use *in (to)* and *out of*.
(c) He gets **out of** the taxi.	
(d) He gets **off of** the train.	For buses, trains, and planes, use *on (to)* and *off (of)*.

EXERCISE 6

Here is a story about the hard life of a mouse. Fill in the blanks with a preposition of direction from Focus 4.

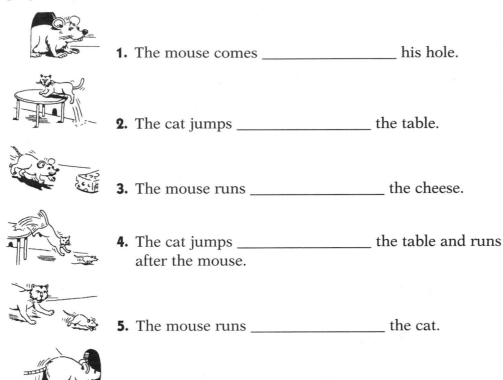

1. The mouse comes _____ his hole.

2. The cat jumps _____ the table.

3. The mouse runs _____ the cheese.

4. The cat jumps _____ the table and runs after the mouse.

5. The mouse runs _____ the cat.

6. The mouse runs _____ his hole.

▶ **P**repositions of Direction:
Up, Down, Across, Along, Around, Over, Through, Past

MEANING

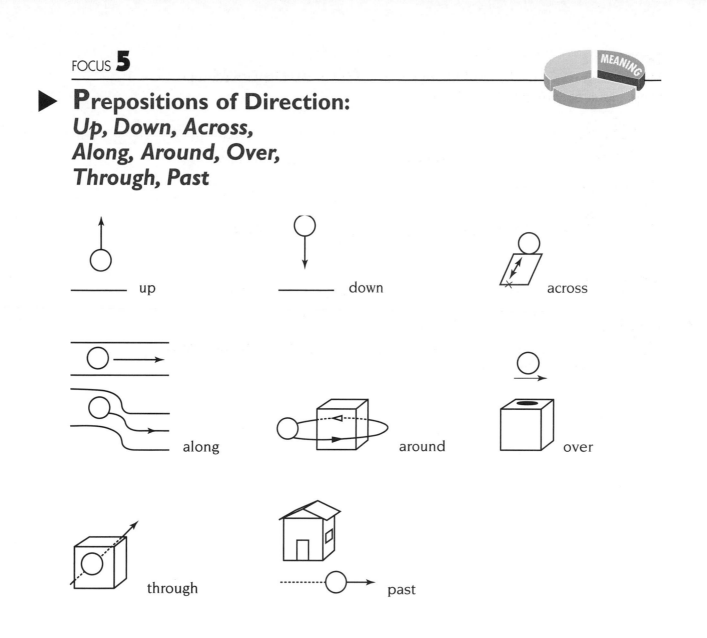

up

down

across

along

around

over

through

past

EXERCISE 7

Here is a story about the hard life of a cat. Fill in the blanks with a preposition of direction from Focus 5.

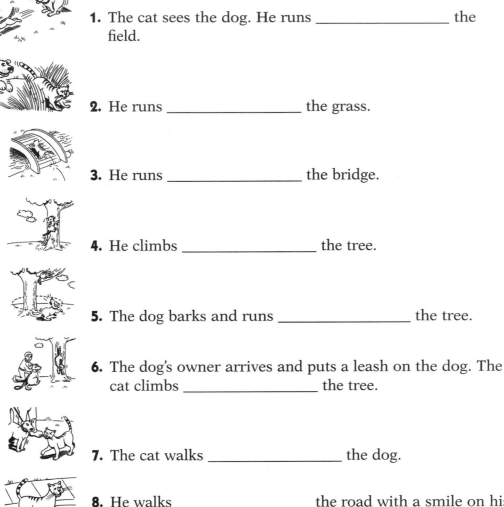

1. The cat sees the dog. He runs _____ the field.

2. He runs _____ the grass.

3. He runs _____ the bridge.

4. He climbs _____ the tree.

5. The dog barks and runs _____ the tree.

6. The dog's owner arrives and puts a leash on the dog. The cat climbs _____ the tree.

7. The cat walks _____ the dog.

8. He walks _____ the road with a smile on his face.

▶ Giving Directions

Look at the map and read the conversation below.

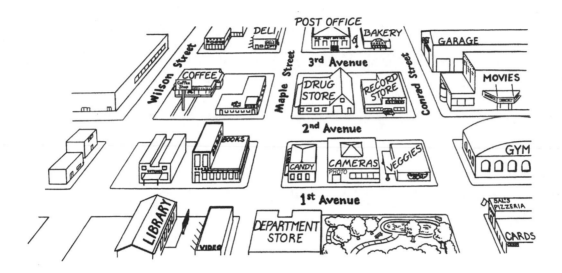

(Person A is at the bakery.)

A: Excuse me, how do I get to the department store?

B: Walk **down** Conrad Street until you get to First Avenue. Then turn **right** at the corner. Go **straight**. Walk one block. The department store is on the corner on the left.

EXERCISE 8

Look at the map in Focus 6. Follow the directions. Then answer the questions.

▶ **EXAMPLE:** You are at the record store on the corner of Second Avenue and Conrad Street. Walk down Conrad Street until you get to Third Avenue. Turn left at the corner. Walk one block. Cross Third Avenue. This place is on the right. Where are you? Answer: *At the Post Office.*

   1. You are at the bakery. Walk down Conrad Street and make a right on Second Avenue. Go straight and make a left on Maple Street. Walk across the street. Where are you? _____

   2. You come out of the coffee shop on Second Avenue. Walk down Second Avenue and go two blocks. Turn right on Conrad Street. Go straight until you get to First Avenue. Make a left. Walk into the building on your right. Where are you? _____

3. You are at the library on First Avenue. Walk up Wilson Street. Make a right on Third Avenue. Go straight for two blocks. Then make a left on Conrad Street. Go across the street from the bakery. Where are you? _____

Now write two sets of directions and questions of your own.

EXERCISE 9

Work with a partner. Take turns giving the commands. Your partner acts out the commands you give.

1.	Step off the bus.	Step onto the bus.
2.	Put your hand into your pocket.	Take your hand out of your pocket.
3.	Walk to the blackboard.	Walk away from the blackboard.
4.	Put a pencil into the desk drawer.	Put a pencil on the desk.
5.	Climb up a mountain.	Climb down a mountain.
6.	Walk on the grass.	Walk through tall grass.
7.	Walk away from your classmate.	Walk around your classmate.
8.	Walk past a group of people.	Walk through a group of people.
9.	Walk across the room.	Step over a book on the floor.

Use Your English

DO'S AND *DON'TS*

STEP 1 Make a list of *do's* and *don'ts* for someone who plans to travel to your country or the United States.

▶ **EXAMPLE:** Korea

	DO'S	DON'TS
Hand and body movements	Bow to say goodbye.	Don't touch or pat a man on the back—only if you are very good friends.
Eating		
Manners for a guest at a person's house		
Other		

STEP 2 Make an oral presentation of the *do's* and *don'ts* to your class.

ACTIVITY 2: WRITING/SPEAKING

PROBLEMS AND ADVICE

STEP 1 Write down three problems you have.

STEP 2 Work with a partner. Tell your partner your problems.

STEP 3 Your partner gives you advice.

▷ **EXAMPLE:** **You:** I can't sleep at night.

   Your Partner: Drink a cup of hot milk.

Problems	Advice
1.	
2.	
3.	

ACTIVITY 3: WRITING

Work in a group. Create an information booklet to give advice to new students in the United States. Choose from the ideas below.

- How to Learn English
- How to Find a Job
- How to Do Well in School
- How to Find an Apartment
- How to Meet People

ACTIVITY 4: WRITING/SPEAKING

DIRECTIONS GAME

STEP 1 Work in groups of two or three. Write directions for someone to go to different parts of the building you are in (restrooms, snack bar, etc.).

▷ **EXAMPLE:** Go out of the room. Turn left and go to the end of the corridor. Turn right. It's on the right.

STEP 2 Ask the rest of the class to find out where your directions lead.

ACTIVITY 5: RESEARCH

Look around your neighborhood or your home. Find imperatives in public notices and signs. Discuss the meaning of the notices.

ACTIVITY 6: LISTENING/ SPEAKING

REMEDIES

STEP 1 Listen to the three different remedies. Match the remedy to one of the titles below.

    Remedies

    (a) _____ How to cure a headache

    (b) _____ How to cure a cold

    (c) _____ How to treat a burn

STEP 2 Describe a remedy you know.

UNIT 11

QUANTIFIERS

UNIT GOALS:

- To understand the meaning of quantifiers
- To choose between *a few* and *few, a little* and *little*
- To use the correct form of quantifiers with count/noncount nouns
- To ask questions with *How many . . . , How much . . .*
- To understand the meaning of measure words

▶ **OPENING TASK**

Who Eats a Healthy Breakfast?

The chart on page 173 shows the number of **calories** and the amount of **fat** and **cholesterol** in the foods Billy, Juanita, and Brad eat for breakfast every day.

Calories are the amount of energy a food produces in the body. To lose weight, we need to reduce our calories.

There is **fat** in foods like butter, cheese, and meat. Too much fat is bad for your health.

There is **cholesterol** in foods like eggs, butter, and cheese. Too much cholesterol can give you heart disease.

Look at the chart and answer the questions.

	Calories	Fat (grams)	Cholesterol (milligrams)
Billy			
eggs (3)	140	9.8	399
sausages (2)	180	16.3	48
muffin	170	4.6	9
whole milk	165	8	30
Brad			
cereal	80	1.1	0
orange juice	80	0	0
nonfat milk	85	0	0
banana (1)	130	less than 1	0
Juanita			
pancakes (3)	410	9.2	21
vanilla milkshake	290	13	10
doughnuts (2)	240	20	18

1. Is there a lot of fat in Juanita's breakfast?
2. Who eats a breakfast with only a little fat?
3. Whose breakfast has a lot of calories?
4. Are there any calories in Brad's breakfast?
5. How much cholesterol is there in each breakfast?
6. Which foods don't have any cholesterol?
7. Which foods have little fat?
8. Which food has a lot of cholesterol?

STEP 2 Whose breakfast is healthy? Write three sentences to explain why.

_____ has a healthy breakfast.

1. _____ calories.

2. _____ fat.

3. _____ cholesterol.

▶ **R**eview of Count and
Noncount Nouns

EXAMPLES	EXPLANATIONS
(a) Billy eats a **muffin** and an **egg.** (b) Brad likes **pancakes.** (c) Billy eats three **eggs.** (d) There is a **fast-food restaurant** near here. (e) There are a lot of **calories** in a **milkshake.** (f) How many **eggs** does Billy eat?	**Count nouns:** • can have *a/an* in front of them. • can have plural forms. • can have a number in front of them. • can take singular or plural verbs. • can be in questions with *how many*.
(g) **Cereal** is healthy. (h) He eats **bread** and **butter.** (i) It has a little **cholesterol.** (j) Nonfat **milk** is good for you. (k) How much **cholesterol** does an egg have?	**Noncount nouns:** • can't have *a/an* in front of them. • can't have plural forms. • can't have a number in front of them. • can't take plural verbs. • can be in questions with *how much*.

EXERCISE 1

Go back to the Opening Task on page 173. Make a list of the count and noncount nouns.

Count Nouns	Noncount Nouns
eggs	milk

▶ Quantifiers

Quantifiers are words or phrases that show how many things or how much of something we have.

Positive Meaning

COUNT NOUNS			
	Quantifiers		
(a) There are	**many**	eggs	
(b) There are	**a lot of**	apples	in the
(c) There are	**some**	carrots	refrigerator.
(d) There are	**a few**	oranges	

NONCOUNT NOUNS			
	Quantifiers		
(e) There is	**a lot of**	milk*	
(f) There is	**some**	juice	in the refrigerator.
(g) There is	**a little**	cake	

NOT: There is much milk in the refrigerator. Do not use *much* in affirmative statements.

Negative Meaning

COUNT NOUNS			
	Quantifiers		
(h) There aren't	**many**	oranges	
(i) There aren't	**a lot of**	oranges	
(j) There are	**few**	tomatoes	in the refrigerator.
(k) There aren't	**any**	onions	
(l) There are	**no**	onions	

NONCOUNT NOUNS			
	Quantifiers		
(m) There isn't	**much**	cake*	
(n) There isn't	**a lot of**	cake	
(o) There is	**little**	coffee	in the refrigerator.
(p) There isn't	**any**	jam	
(q) There is	**no**	jam	

*Use *much* in negative statements.

EXERCISE 2

Match the picture to the statement. Write the letter next to each statement.

Community Bank	January 31
	Account #536
Debits: $325.00	
Credits: $325.00	
	Balance: $ ____.00

A.

Community Bank	January 31
	Account #741
Debits: $458.31	
Credits: $958.31	
	Balance: $ 500.00

B.

Community Bank	January 31
	Account #289
Debits: $312.80	
Credits: $412.80	
	Balance: $100.00

C.

Community Bank	January 31
	Account #125
Debits: $ 7,096.10	
Credits: $12,096.10	
	Balance: $ 5,000.00

D.

___d___ **1.** Carlos has a lot of money in the bank.

_____ **2.** François has a little money in the bank.

_____ **3.** Kim has no money in the bank.

_____ **4.** Lee has some money in the bank.

E.

F.

G.

_____ **5.** The Greens have a lot of plants in their home.

_____ **6.** The Smiths don't have any plants.

_____ **7.** The Taylors have a few plants.

H.

I.

J.

_____ **8.** Jody has no friends.

_____ **9.** Irene has a few friends.

_____ **10.** Helene has many friends.

K.   L.   M.

_____ **11.** Bill has a lot of hair.

_____ **12.** Jim doesn't have any hair.

_____ **13.** Albert has a little hair.

EXERCISE 3

Cross out the incorrect quantifier in each sentence.

▶ **EXAMPLE:** My new apartment has ~~many~~ furniture.
                                     some
                                     a lot of

1. Middletown has   a lot of   pollution.
                        a little
                        a few

2. The teacher gives us some   homework.
                         many
                         a little

3. Billy has   a little   girlfriends.
                        a few
                        many

4. Mario speaks   much   languages.
                        three
                        a few

5. Majid has   a lot of   money.
                        a little
                        many

EXERCISE 4

Test your knowledge about food. Check *True* or *False*. Then compare your answers to your partner's answers.

	True	False
1. There are no calories in water.	✔	
2. There's a lot of salt in fast food.		
3. There are no calories in soda.		
4. There's a lot of fat in cheese.		
5. There are few calories in a small baked potato.		
6. There's little cholesterol in fish.		
7. There are few vitamins in orange juice.		
8. There's some fat in low-fat yogurt.		
9. There isn't any sugar in fruit.		
10. There's a little caffeine in herbal tea.		

EXERCISE 5

Use the chart in the Opening Task on page 173 to complete the statements by adding quantifiers.

1. Doughnuts have _____*a lot of*_____ calories.

2. A banana doesn't have _____ calories.

3. There is _____ cholesterol in eggs.

4. There is _____ cholesterol in a muffin.

5. There is _____ fat in bananas.

6. Orange juice has _____ calories.

7. Sausages have _____ fat.

8. Eggs and pancakes have _____ fat.

9. There are _____ calories in cereal.

10. There is _____ cholesterol in orange juice.

11. There is _____ fat in cereal.

12. There is _____ fat in whole milk.

FOCUS **3**

▶ A *Few/Few, A Little/Little*

EXAMPLES	EXPLANATIONS
(a) She has **a few** books. = She has *some* books. **(b)** I have **a little** time. = I have *some* time.	*A few* and *a little* have a positive meaning for the speaker. The speaker means: *some,* or more than zero (a sufficient quantity).
(c) They have **few** books. = They don't have many books. **(d)** They have **little** time. = They don't have much time.	*Few* and *little* have a negative meaning for the speaker. The speaker means: *not much, not many,* almost zero (an insufficient quantity).

EXERCISE 6

Linda and Kathy are both Americans living in Europe for a year. Their experiences are very different. Fill in the blanks with *few/a few* or *little/a little.*

Linda is very lonely. She doesn't have a full-time job. She has

(1) _____few_____ friends and (2) _____ money. She works

part-time as a baby sitter. She doesn't like this kind of work. She has

(3) _____ patience for children. She speaks very

(4) _____ Spanish.

Kathy loves to live in different countries. She speaks (5) _____

languages. She goes to a language school in Spain and she has

(6) _____ very close friends. Kathy learns (7) _____

Spanish every day. She also works as a baby sitter and makes

(8) _____ extra money. Kathy works hard, but she always has

(9) _____ time to go out and have fun. She has (10) _____

problems in Spain.

▶ Questions with *How Many* and *How Much*

QUESTION			ANSWER	EXPLANATIONS
How many	**Count Noun**			
(a) **How many**	universities	are there?	A lot.	Use *How many* with **count nouns.**
(b) **How many**	brothers	do you have?	Two.	
(c) **How many**	oranges	do you eat every week?	A few.	
How much	**Noncount Noun**			
(d) **How much**	money	do you have in your account?	$200	Use *How much* with **noncount nouns.**
(e) **How much**	time	do you have?	Not much.	
(f) **How much**	gas	do you need?	Five gallons.	

EXERCISE 7

Go back to the Opening Task on page 173. Make questions with *how much* or *how many*. Then answer the questions.

1. ___How many___ pancakes does Juanita usually eat for breakfast?

2. ___How much___ juice does Brad drink?

3. _____ eggs does Billy have?

4. _____ cholesterol is there in three eggs?

5. _____ calories are there in a vanilla milkshake?

6. _____ cholesterol is there in a bowl of cereal?

7. _____ fat is there in two doughnuts?

8. _____ calories are there in three pancakes?

9. _____ sausages does Billy eat?

10. _____ money does Brad spend on breakfast?

EXERCISE 8

Fill in the blanks with *how much* or *how many* or a quantifier (*a lot, a little, some, any, much, many*). Then read the conversations aloud.

1. **Mom:** How was school today, dear?

   Child: O.K., Mom . . .

   Mom: (a) _____ homework do you have tonight?

   Child: I have (b) _____ homework—three compositions plus a spelling test tomorrow!

   Mom: Don't worry, I have (c) _____ time to help you tonight.

2. **Doctor:** Please remember to take this medicine, Mr. Josephson.

   Patient: (a) _____ medicine do I need to take every day?

   Doctor: These are pills. You need three red pills a day, one after every meal. And you need two blue pills a day, one in the morning and one before bed.

   Patient: Say that again, please . . . (b) _____ red pills? (c) _____ blue pills? And (d) _____ pills do I need to take in all?

   Doctor: Three red pills and two blue pills. Five pills a day in all. Take these for a week. Then call me.

   Patient: O.K. Thanks, Doctor.

EXERCISE 9

Ask your partner questions about a city he or she knows. First ask a *yes/no* question. Then ask a question with *how many* or *how much*.

1. skyscrapers   Are there any skyscrapers in your city?
                   How many skyscrapers are there?

2. crime   Is there any crime in your city?
                   How much crime is there?

3. noise
4. universities
5. pollution
6. trash on the streets

7. parks
8. poor people
9. traffic
10. museums
11. beaches

12. American fast-food restaurants
13. public transportation
14. shopping malls
15. hospitals

► **Measure Words**

Measure words change the way we see a thing. A measure word before a noncount noun tells us about the specific quantity.

► **EXAMPLES:** I have a lot of coffee.   (coffee = noncount noun)

I have four cans of coffee.   (specific quantity)

a **can** of tuna a **jar** of jam a **tube** of toothpaste	a **box** of cereal a **bottle** of beer a **bag** of sugar	Containers
a **slice** of pizza a **piece** of pie	a **glass** of milk a **cup** of coffee	Portions
a **cup** of flour a **pint** of ice cream a **teaspoon** of salt	a **quart** of milk a **pound** of sugar a **gallon** of water	Specific quantities
a **head** of lettuce a **sheet** of paper	a **loaf** of bread a **bar** of soap	Other
a **bag** of apples a **pound** of onions BUT: a **dozen** eggs NOT: a **dozen** of eggs	a **can** of beans a **box** of chocolates **five thousand** people NOT: five thousand of people	Measure words can also be used with count nouns.

EXERCISE 10

Here is Maggie at the checkout counter. Write down her shopping list on the next page. Use measure words in the list.

Shopping List

a pound of	coffee	_____	oil
_____	milk	_____	soda
_____	rice	_____	bread
_____	soup	_____	soap
_____	toothpaste	_____	lettuce
_____	candy	_____	toilet paper
_____	eggs	_____	beef
_____	butter	_____	peanut butter

EXERCISE 11

How much food do you have in your refrigerator? Use measure words to tell your classmates what you have.

▶ **EXAMPLE:** I have a quart of milk.

EXERCISE 12

Correct the mistakes in the following sentences.

1. **Jane:** Can I talk to you for a minute?

   Kevin: Sure, I have little time.

2. John has much friends.

3. How many money do you have?

4. My teacher gives us many homeworks.

5. Her hairs are black.

6. Elsie is in great shape. She runs few miles a day.

7. We don't sell no newspapers here.

8. There are much stores in this city.

9. I would like some informations please.

10. My best friend gives me many advices.

11. This school has little students.

12. We have few time to finish this book.

Use Your English

ACTIVITY 1: SPEAKING

FOOD HABIT SURVEY

Ask three students questions with *how much* and *how many* to complete the chart.

▶ **EXAMPLES:**   How much coffee do you drink a day?

   I drink three cups a day.

   How much sugar do you put in your coffee?

   Two teaspoons.

	Student 1	Student 2	Student 3
cups of coffee or tea/drink/a day			
teaspoons of sugar/put in coffee or tea			
meat/eat/a week			
fish/eat/a week			
soda/drink/a day			
money/spend on food/a week			
bread/eat/a day			
fruit/eat/a day			
salt/put on food			
glasses of water/drink/a day			
eggs/eat/a week			
meals/have/a day			
other			
other			

ACTIVITY 2: SPEAKING

Play a circle game with all the students in the class. Make a statement starting with "I want to buy . . ." One student says an item that begins with the letter A and uses a measure word. The second student repeats the statement and adds a second item that starts with the letter B. The third student does the same and adds on an item with the letter C, and so on.

▶ **EXAMPLE:**   **Student 1:** I want to buy a bag of <u>a</u>pples.

Student 2: I want to buy a bag of <u>a</u>pples and a loaf of <u>b</u>read.

Student 3: I want to buy a bag of <u>a</u>pples, a loaf of <u>b</u>read, and a head of <u>c</u>abbage.

ACTIVITY 3: WRITING/SPEAKING

Choose a recipe you like and write the ingredients without writing the quantity. The other students ask you questions with *how much* and *how many* to fill in the exact quantity. Make a book of the class' favorite recipes.

▶ **EXAMPLE:**   Recipe: *Italian Tomato Sauce*

Ingredients: tomatoes

onions

garlic

oil

salt and pepper

Questions: How many tomatoes do you use?

How many onions do you use?

How much garlic is there?

How much oil do you use?

How much salt do you add?

A C T I V I T Y   4 :   R E S E A R C H

Go to a supermarket. Look at three food labels. Write the nutrition facts on the chart below.

Nutrition Facts
Serving Size 1 Container

Amount Per Serving

Calories 170	Calories from Fat 15

% Daily Value*

Total Fat 2g	3%
Saturated Fat 1g	5%
Cholesterol 10mg	3%
Sodium 110mg	4%
Total Carbohydrate 31g	10%
Dietary Fiber 0g	0%
Sugars 28g	
Protein 7g	

| Vitamin A 2% | • | Vitamin C | 6% |
| Calcium 25% | • | Iron | 2% |

*Percent Daily Values are based on a 2,000 calorie diet.

VANILLA YOGURT

8 OZ (226g)

	Example	Label 1	Label 2	Label 3
Food	yogurt			
Calories per serving	170			
Fat	2g			
Cholesterol	10 mg			
Sodium	110 mg			
Sugars	28g			
Protein	7g			

Tell the class about the foods. Are they healthy or not?

ACTIVITY 5: WRITING

Your friend wants to come and live where you are living now. Write a letter to your friend explaining why this is or is not a good idea. Use the vocabulary in the box to help you.

▶ **EXAMPLE:** I live in a really wonderful neighborhood. There isn't much crime. There are a lot of trees and parks. There are many good restaurants.

crime	parks	trees
traffic	hospitals	flowers
noise	houses	grass
spacious apartments	bookstores	drugstores
good restaurants	movie theaters	job
clean streets	ethnic markets	good schools
people from my country	friendly neighbors	open spaces

ACTIVITY 6: LISTENING

Sara is calling a supermarket. She has a shopping order.

STEP 1 Listen to her order and check the things she wants.

STEP 2 Listen again. Write the amount she wants.

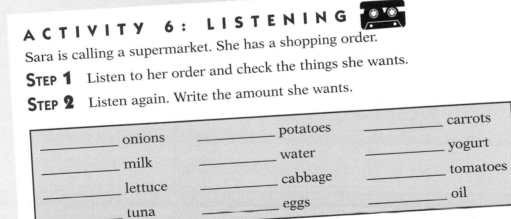

_____ onions	_____ potatoes	_____ carrots
_____ milk	_____ water	_____ yogurt
_____ lettuce	_____ cabbage	_____ tomatoes
_____ tuna	_____ eggs	_____ oil

U N I T 12

ADVERBS OF MANNER

UNIT GOALS:

- To understand the meaning of adverbs of manner
- To know the position of adverbs of manner in a sentence
- To know how to spell adverbs of manner
- To focus on either an action or a person

▶ OPENING TASK
Do You Want to Give Bill Rogers Life Insurance?

You work for a life insurance company. Look at Bill Rogers' record and read the sentences below. Check *True* or *False*.

Long Life Insurance Company
Health and Accident Record

Name:	Bill Rogers	Sex:	Male
Date of Birth:	9/20/48	Marital Status:	Single
Height:	5'7"	Weight:	225 pounds
Health Information:	Heart Problems		
	Smokes 2 packs a day		

Previous Offenses: Speeding: 5/19/92, 8/15/96
Not stopping at a red light: 7/14/89, 9/21/93, 12/31/94, 7/4/95

Drunk driving: 12/31/95
Crashing into a wall: 3/17/96

	True	False
1. Bill is a careful driver.		
2. He drives slowly.		
3. He drives carelessly.		
4. He is a big eater.		
5. He drives fast.		
6. He drinks excessively.		
7. He eats moderately.		
8. He is a heavy smoker.		
9. He takes his health seriously.		
10. He lives dangerously.		

STEP 2 Work with a group. Are you going to give Bill Rogers life insurance? Explain why or why not.

▶ **A**dverbs of Manner

EXAMPLES	EXPLANATIONS
(a) He is a **careful** driver.	*Careful* is an adjective. It describes the noun *driver*. The adjective goes before the noun.
(b) He drives **carefully**.	*Carefully* is an adverb of manner. It describes the verb *drive*. The adverb answers the question "how?" The adverb goes after the verb.
(c) He drives his car **carefully**. NOT: He drives carefully his car.	When there is an object after the verb, the adverb goes after the object (*his car*).

EXERCISE 1
Go back to the Opening Task on page 189. Underline all the adjectives and circle all the adverbs of manner.

▶ **EXAMPLE:**   Bill is a <u>careful</u> driver.

   He drives ⟨slowly.⟩

▶ **S**pelling of Adverbs of Manner

ADJECTIVE	ADVERB	RULE
slow beautiful	slowly beautifully	Add *-ly*.
heavy	heavily	Adjectives that end in *-y*: change *y* to *i* and add *-ly*.
fantastic	fantastically	Adjectives that end with *-ic*: add *-ally*.
terrible	terribly	Adjectives that end with *-le*: drop the *-e*, and add *-y*.

EXAMPLES		EXPLANATIONS
(a) She's a **fast** driver. **(b)** She drives **fast**. **(c)** We have an **early** dinner. **(d)** We have dinner **early**. **(e)** We eat a **late** lunch. **(f)** We eat lunch **late**. **(g)** We are **hard** workers. **(h)** We work **hard**.		Some adverbs have the same form as adjectives.
(i) Joel's a **good** cook. **(j)** He cooks **well**.		Some adverbs are irregular.
(k) He works **hard**. **(l)** He **hardly** works.		Do not confuse *hard* with *hardly*. In example (l), *hardly* is an adverb of frequency. It means "he doesn't work very much."
(m) She is lovely. **(n)** Marco is lonely. **(o)** That dress is ugly. **(p)** Maria is friendly. **(q)** The party is lively.		Some words that end in *-ly* are not adverbs. They are adjectives.

EXERCISE 2

Find three sentences that describe each occupation. Write the letters next to the occupation.

Occupations

1. I am a teacher.   _____*c*_____

                                    _____

2. I am a lawyer.   _____

                                    _____

3. I am an artist.   _____

                                    _____

4. I am the Secretary General   _____ <br> of the United Nations.   _____

a. I respond to medical emergencies very quickly.

b. I defend my clients successfully.

c. I prepare lessons carefully.

d. I draw beautifully.

e. I take care of international problems urgently.

f. I give medical treatment to people carefully.

g. I paint well.

h. I speak three languages fluently.

i. I stay at the office very late.

j. I drive very fast.

5. I am an emergency medical _____   **k.** I talk to my students politely

technician in an ambulance. _____   **l.** I use colors creatively.

_____   **m.** I study the law constantly.

n. I write on the blackboard neatly.

o. I act diplomatically.

EXERCISE 3

How are the speakers saying the sentences below? Match each sentence with the best adverb. Write the adverb in the blank.

▶ **EXAMPLE:** "Shhh, don't say a word." she said <u>quietly</u>.

politely	sadly	nervously	quickly	shyly
incorrectly	impolitely	happily	angrily	kindly

1. "I just got engaged!" she said _____.

2. "My dog just died," he said _____.

3. "I'm in a hurry," she said _____.

4. "I no make mistakes," he said _____.

5. "May I make a telephone call?" she asked _____.

6. "Bring me a menu, fast!" he said _____.

7. "This is the last time I'm telling you! Clean up your room!" she said

_____.

8. "WWWWWWWWWWill yyyyou mmmmmmmmmarry mmmmmm-mmmmme?" he asked _____.

9. "Please, don't ask me to speak in front of the class," she said

_____.

10. "Can I help you?" he asked _____.

EXERCISE 4

Read each statement. Use the adjective in parentheses to make another statement with an adverb.

▶ **EXAMPLE:** My son is a safe driver. (careful)

<u>My son drives carefully.</u>

1. Baryshnikov is an excellent dancer. (graceful)

_____

2. Uta Pippig is a great runner. (fast)

_____

3. My father is a good teacher. (patient)

_____

4. The President is a good speaker. (effective)

_____

5. Andrea Bocelli is a wonderful singer. (beautiful)

_____

6. Teachers are hard workers. (diligent)

_____

7. He is a well-behaved child. (polite)

_____

8. Some students are fast learners. (quick)

_____

9. These painters are messy workers. (sloppy)

_____

10. She is a good thinker. (quick/clear)

_____

EXERCISE 5

Work with a partner. Take turns asking and answering the questions below. The first one has been done for you.

1. Why is Carrie an excellent teacher?

   (a) speak/slow
     She speaks slowly.

   (b) pronounce words/clear

   (c) prepare/careful

2. Why is Mark a good secretary?

   (a) type/fast

   (b) answer the phone/ polite

   (c) take message/accurate

3. Why is Mike a good truck driver?

   (a) drive/slow

   (b) respond/quick

   (c) drive/defensive

4. Why is Gloria Estefan a popular performer?

    (a) sing/good

    (b) dance/energetic

    (c) perform (enthusiastic)

5. Why is Miyuki a good language learner?

    (a) study/hard

    (b) guess/intelligent

    (c) ask questions/constant

FOCUS **3**

▶ Talking about a Person or an Action

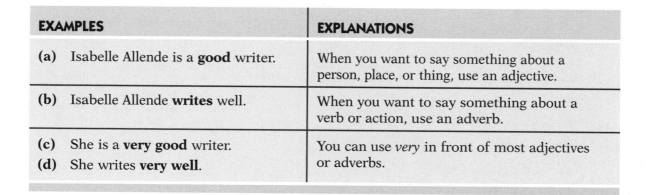

EXAMPLES	EXPLANATIONS
(a) Isabelle Allende is a **good** writer.	When you want to say something about a person, place, or thing, use an adjective.
(b) Isabelle Allende **writes** well.	When you want to say something about a verb or action, use an adverb.
(c) She is a **very good** writer. **(d)** She writes **very well**.	You can use *very* in front of most adjectives or adverbs.

EXERCISE 6

Do these sentences focus on the person or the action? Check the correct column.

	Person	Action
1. Meryl Streep is a fantastic actress.		
2. My students learn easily.		
3. Steven reads slowly.		
4. Karl's a fast runner.		
5. My children are good cooks.		
6. Bill Rogers drives carelessly.		
7. My accountant is an honest person.		
8. Anh speaks to his parents impolitely.		
9. Linda dresses beautifully.		
10. Your friend is a generous person.		

EXERCISE 7

Read the statements below. Write one sentence that focuses on the person and another that focuses on the action.

▶ **EXAMPLE:** Can you believe it! Jeryl is the winner of the race! (runner)

  She is a great runner. She runs very fast.

1. Just look at Joe! He finishes one cigarette and then lights up another. (smoker)

   _____

2. My mom cooks a great meal every night. She loves to make new dishes. (cook)

   _____

3. Gloria goes to work at 8:00 in the morning and leaves at 6:00 in the evening. She never takes a break. (worker)

   _____

4. Nancy manages a large ESL program. She has a staff of over 50 people. (manager)

   _____

5. Bob can sing, dance, and play the piano too. (performer)

   _____

EXERCISE 8

Read each sentence and give two or three reasons why the sentence is true. Use adverbs in your reasons.

▶ **EXAMPLE:**   I don't want Henry to drive me downtown.

   Reasons: He doesn't drive very carefully.

   He drives very fast.

   He's a careless driver.

1. I'm already late. I don't want Harold to drive me to school.
2. I can't understand Bruce when he speaks.
3. Patricia is now the chef at that expensive restaurant downtown.
4. Rose is a great friend.
5. Lucia is a good language learner.
6. Ms. Wu is a great boss.

EXERCISE 9

Correct the mistakes in the following sentences.

1. Sarah comes to work in a suit every day. She dresses elegant.
2. Melanie speaks fluently French.
3. Sam studies three hours every night. He studies hardly.
4. Dinner starts at 8:00. They always arrive at 9:30. They always come very lately.
5. Johan plays the piano very good.
6. She speaks slow.
7. She sings lovely.
8. The city traffic is heavily.

Use Your English

ACTIVITY 1: SPEAKING

Work in a group. One person in the group chooses an adverb of manner, but does not tell the other students the adverb. The students in the group tell the person to do something "in that manner." The person mimes the action and the other students guess the adverb.

▶ **EXAMPLE:** 1. The first student chooses the adverb *slowly*.

2. Students in the group say: "Walk to the door in that manner."

3. The first student mimes.

4. Students in the group guess: *slowly*.

(Example adverbs: *slowly, fast, nervously, happily, angrily, loudly, sadly, romantically, passionately*.)

ACTIVITY 2: SPEAKING

Work in a group. Are you a good student? A good mother? A good friend? A good worker? Choose one and give your group five reasons to explain why or why not.

▶ **EXAMPLE:** I'm a very good student. I study hard. . .

ACTIVITY 3: SPEAKING

Think about the Opening Task on pages 188–189. Interview your partner. Role-play a conversation between an insurance agent and a person like Bill Rogers. The person tries to convince the agent to give him/her insurance. Then explain to the class why your partner can or cannot get insurance easily.

ACTIVITY 4: LISTENING/ SPEAKING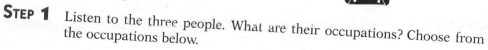

STEP 1 Listen to the three people. What are their occupations? Choose from the occupations below.

    waiter   salesperson   flight attendant   doctor   receptionist

STEP 2 Describe an occupation to the class. The class guesses the occupation.

DIRECT AND INDIRECT OBJECTS, DIRECT AND INDIRECT OBJECT PRONOUNS

UNIT GOALS:

- To use direct objects and direct object pronouns correctly
- To use indirect objects correctly
- To form two sentence patterns with indirect objects
- To know where to place the indirect object in a sentence to focus on new information
- To know which verbs do not omit *to* with indirect objects

▶ **O PENING TASK**

Giving Gifts

STEP 1   You need to give gifts to the people on your list below.
Look at the gifts you have and decide which gift you want to give to each person.

Gifts

A.
Camera

B.
Flowers

C.
Toaster

D.
Doll

E.
Earrings

F.
Running Shoes

G.
Compact Disc Player

People

1. a single thirty-five-year-old athletic male friend
2. your sixty-three-year-old grandmother
3. your friend's four-year-old daughter
4. an artistic twenty-seven-year-old friend
5. your mother
6. your music-loving boyfriend/girlfriend
7. a newlywed couple

STEP 2   Tell a partner which gift you want to give each person and why.

▶ **EXAMPLE:**   I want to give the earrings to my mother because she loves jewelry.

▶ **Direct Objects**

EXAMPLES			EXPLANATIONS
Subject	Verb	Direct Object	
(a) My friend	sings.		Some sentences have only a subject and a verb.
(b) He	loves	music.	Some sentences have a subject, a verb, and an object.
(c) He	buys	compact discs.	A direct object answers the question "What?" *Compact discs* is the direct object.
(d) He	loves	the Beatles.	A direct object also answers the question "Who(m)?" *The Beatles* is the direct object.

EXERCISE 1

Underline the direct object in each sentence below.

▶ **EXAMPLE:** My friend loves <u>sports.</u>

1. My grandmother loves flowers. She always has fresh flowers on the dining room table.

2. Andrea and Bob have a new home.

3. My mother adores jewelry.

4. My friend's daughter has a doll collection. She owns ten different dolls.

5. Akiko takes beautiful pictures.

6. My friend enjoys classical music. She prefers Mozart.

7. In my family, we always celebrate our birthdays together.

▶ **Direct Object Pronouns**

EXAMPLES	EXPLANATIONS
Subject **Verb** **Direct Object** **(a)** My mother loves my father. **(b)** My mother loves him.	The direct object can also be a pronoun.
(c) My mother loves **my father.** She thinks about **him** all the time. **(d)** My father loves **my mother.** He thinks about **her** all the time.	Object pronouns refer to a noun that comes before. In (c), *him* refers to "my father." In (d), *her* refers to "my mother."

SUBJECT	VERB	OBJECT	SUBJECT	VERB	OBJECT PRONOUN
I You	need	a friend.	She	likes	me. you. him. her. it. us. you. them.
He She It	needs				
We You They	need				

EXERCISE 2

Fill in the correct subject or object pronouns.

1. My grandmother is a very special person. (a) _____ has a vegetable garden in her backyard. (b) _____
plants tomatoes, cucumbers, eggplant, leeks, and carrots. She picks
(c) _____ fresh every day. We love her fresh vegetables.
(d) _____ taste delicious. We eat (e) _____
in salads and soup. Her vegetable garden gives (f) _____
great pleasure.

2. Mariela and Juan are newlyweds. (a) _____ have a new

home, and (b) _____ really love (c) _____ .

Their appliances are on order, but they don't have (d) _____

yet, so Mariela and Juan have a lot of work to do. He helps

(e) _____ with the cooking. She helps

(f) _____ with the laundry.

3. Sally: Billy, do you like heavy metal music?

   Billy: (a) _____ love (b) _____!

   Sally: Really? I hate heavy metal. (c) _____ bothers

   (d) _____ . I hate all that noise.

EXERCISE 3

This is a story about three people in a love triangle. Maggie has a steady boyfriend, Ted. She also has a male friend, Jim. Read the text below. Cross out the incorrect pronouns and write the correct pronouns above them.

Maggie

Ted   Jim

Maggie loves her boyfriend, Ted. She also likes Jim. (1) Jim works with ~~she~~ <u>her</u>. (2) She sees he every day. (3) She sometimes invites he to dinner. (4) She likes to talk with he. (5) Maggie doesn't love Jim, but Jim loves she. (6) Jim thinks about she all the time. Jim knows about Ted, but Ted doesn't know about Jim. Ted is very jealous. (7) So, Maggie can't tell he about Jim. (8) Maggie doesn't want to leave he. But she cares for both Ted and Jim. She doesn't know what to do. (9) She doesn't want to hurt they. She says to herself, "What's wrong with me? (10) Ted loves I and I love he. (11) Jim is my friend and I like to be with he. So what can I do?"

EXERCISE 4

Ted finds out about Jim. He talks to Maggie on the phone late one night. Fill in the correct object pronouns.

1. **Ted:** Hello, Maggie. Do you remember (a) _____ me _____ ?

   Maggie: Of course, I remember (b) _____ , Ted. You're my boyfriend!

2. **Ted:** I know about Jim, Maggie.

   Maggie: What? You know about (a) _____ ?

3. **Ted:** That's right, Maggie. I know everything about (a) _____ .

   Maggie: How do you know?

   Ted: John—your secretary—told me. I meet (b) _____ for lunch sometimes. He knows about (c) _____ and Jim.

4. **Ted:** Jim can't come between (a) _____ , Maggie.

   Maggie: I know, Ted. Don't worry. I don't love (b) _____ . We're just friends.

   Ted: Do you love (c) _____ ?

   Maggie: Of course, I love (d) _____ , Ted. I want to marry (e) _____ .

5. **Ted:** Then you can't see (a) _____ so much, Maggie.

   Maggie: Ted, please trust (b) _____ .

EXERCISE 5

Ask your partner questions with *how often*. Your partner answers with object pronouns.

▶ **EXAMPLE:** **You:** How often do you call your parents?

   Your Partner: I call them every week.

1. clean your room?
2. do your laundry?
3. see your dentist?
4. buy the newspaper?
5. cut your nails?

6. wash your hair?
7. visit your friends?
8. drink coffee?
9. do the grocery shopping?
10. watch the news?

► **Indirect Objects**

	EXAMPLES				EXPLANATION
	Subject	Verb	Direct Object	Indirect Object	
(a)	I	want to give	the toaster	to **the newlyweds.**	Some sentences have two objects: a direct object and an indirect object. *The toaster* is the direct object. It tells **what** I want to give. *The newlyweds* is the indirect object. It tells **to whom** I want to give the toaster.
(b)	I	buy	flowers	for **my grandmother.**	*My grandmother* is the indirect object. It tells **for whom** I buy flowers.
(c)	I	want to give	the toaster	to **the newlyweds.**	The indirect object can be a noun or a pronoun.
(d)	I	want to give	the toaster	to **them.**	
(e) I cook **for** my grandmother. **(f)** I want to give the earrings **to** my mother.					***For* and *To*** *For* tells us one person does the action to help or please another person. *To* tells us about the direction of the action: The earrings go from you to your mother.

EXERCISE 6

Write sentences telling what you want to give to each of the people in the Opening Task. Underline the direct object and circle the indirect object. Then tell why you want to give that item to that person.

► **EXAMPLE:** I want to give the toaster to the (newlyweds.) They have a new home

and don't have any appliances.

EXERCISE 7

New Year's Resolutions. Every January 1st, North Americans decide to change their lives and do things differently. Read the following resolutions. Change each underlined noun to a pronoun. Then add the information in parentheses. Read the statements aloud.

► **EXAMPLE:** Every year, I give my father a tie. (golf clubs)

This year, I want to *give him golf clubs.*

1. Used car salesman:
   I always sell <u>my customers</u> bad cars. (good cars)
   This year, I want to . . .

2. Child away at college:
   I always write to <u>my parents</u> once a month. (once a week)
   This year, I want to . . .

3. People with money problems:
   Every year, the bank sends <u>my husband and me</u> a big credit card bill.
   (a very small bill)
   This year, I want the bank to . . .

4. Boyfriend:
   I usually buy <u>my girlfriend</u> flowers for her birthday. (a diamond ring)
   This year, I want to . . .

5. Teenager:
   Sometimes I lie to <u>my mother</u>. (tell the truth)
   This year, I want to . . .

6. Mother:
   I never have time to read to <u>my children</u> at night. (every night)
   This year, I want to . . .

7. Student:
   I always give my homework to <u>the teacher</u> late. (on time)
   This semester, I want to . . .

8. Friend:
   Every year, I lend money to <u>you and your brother</u>. (lend money)
   This year, I don't want to . . .

Now say three things you want to do differently this year.

▶ **Position of the Indirect Object**

All verbs that take indirect objects can follow Pattern A.

Pattern A

SUBJECT	VERB	DIRECT OBJECT	INDIRECT OBJECT
(a) I	give	presents	to my mother on her birthday.
(b) I	give	presents	to her.
(c) I	give	them	to her.
(d) We	make	a party	for our twin daughters on their birthday.
(e) We	make	a party	for them.
(f) We	make	it	for them.

Some of these verbs also follow Pattern B. In Pattern B, put the indirect object before the direct object. Do not use *to* or *for*.

Pattern B

SUBJECT	VERB	INDIRECT OBJECT	DIRECT OBJECT
(g) People	send	their friends	birthday cards.
(h) People	send	them	birthday cards.
(i) I	make	my friends	birthday cakes.
(j) I	make	them	birthday cakes.

> NOTE: Do not put an indirect object pronoun before a direct object pronoun.
>
> I make my friend a cake.
>
> I make her a cake.
>
> NOT: I make her it.

Some verbs that follow both Pattern A and B

bake	do	hand	offer	sell	tell
bring	find	lend	pass	send	throw
buy	get	mail	pay	show	write
cook	give	make	read	teach	

EXERCISE 8

Work with a partner. Write sentences about North American customs with the words below.

BIRTH: When a baby is born:

1. mother / flowers / the / to / give / friends
   Friends give flowers to the mother.

2. cigars / gives / friends / father / his / the

3. send / and / parents / friends / family / to / birth / announcements / their / the

4. baby / family / friends / gifts / the / buy / and

5. knit / for / grandmothers / sweaters / new / the / baby

6. grandfathers / for / toys / make / baby / the

7. child / the / the / parents / everything / give

ENGAGEMENT/MARRIAGE: When a couple gets engaged or married:

8. diamond / man / a / woman / the / gives / ring / the / to / sometimes

9. friends / couple / an / party / the / for / have / engagement

10. gifts / woman / give / friends / at the party / the

11. at the wedding / to / couple / gifts / give / the guests / the

DEATH: When someone dies:

12. send / family / some / flowers / people / the

13. people / special cards / the / send / family / to

14. some / to / give / people / money / charities

15. some / food / for / family / bring / people / the

▶ **Position of New Information**

New information comes at the end of a sentence. You can write these sentences in two different ways. Both are grammatically correct, but the emphasis is different.

EXAMPLES	EXPLANATIONS
(a) Whom do you give earrings to? I usually give earrings to **my mother.**	The emphasis is on **who(m)**. *My mother* is the new information.
(b) What do you usually give your mother? I usually give my mother **earrings**	The emphasis is on **what**. *Earrings* is the new information.

EXERCISE 9

Answer the following questions. The new information is in parentheses ( ).

▶ **EXAMPLES:** Who(m) do you usually give presents to at Christmas? (my family)

I usually give presents to my family.

What do you usually give your father? (a good book)

I usually give him a good book.

1. Who(m) do you want to give presents to at work? (three of my co-workers)

2. What do you usually give your parents for their anniversary? (tickets to a play)

3. Who(m) do you tell jokes to? (my friend)

4. What do you send your sister every year? (some photographs)

5. Does she teach English to your brother or sister? (my brother)

6. Which story do you usually read to your little sister—"Cinderella" or "Snow White"? ("Cinderella")

7. Who(m) do you need to mail the application to? (the admissions office)

8. What do you usually buy for your son on his birthday? (compact discs)

EXERCISE 10

Choose the best sentence.

▶ **EXAMPLE:** You are waiting for a friend in front of a restaurant.

You do not have your watch. You want to know the time.

You see someone coming. You ask him:

((a)) Could you please tell me the time?

(b) Could you please tell the time to me?

1. You are alone at a restaurant. You finish your meal. You see the waiter. You ask him:
   (a) Could you please give the check to me?
   (b) Could you please give me the check?

2. You are celebrating someone's birthday with a group of friends. You finish your meal. You want to be sure you pay the check. You tell the waiter:
   (a) Please give the check to me.
   (b) Please give me the check.

3. What do your children usually do for you on Mother's Day?
   (a) They usually serve breakfast in bed to me.
   (b) They usually serve me breakfast in bed.

4. You are at a friend's house for dinner. The food needs salt. You say:
   (a) Please pass me the salt.
   (b) Please pass the salt to me.

5. You realize you don't have any money for the bus. You ask a friend:
   (a) Could you lend a dollar to me?
   (b) Could you lend me a dollar?

6. You are in class. It is very noisy. You say to a classmate:
   (a) Do me a favor. Please close the door.
   (b) Do a favor for me. Please close the door.

7. Why does your class look so sad on Mondays?
   (a) because our teacher gives us a lot of homework on weekends.
   (b) because our teacher gives a lot of homework to us on weekends.

8. You want to apply to the City University. You have the application form in your hand. The Director is helping you.
   Director: (a) Please send the application form to the City University.
   (b) Please send the City University the application form.

9. You come home from the supermarket. Your car is full of groceries. You need help. You say to your roommate:
   (a) Can you please give a hand to me?
   (b) Can you please give me a hand?

10. There are three children at a table. They are finishing a box of cookies. A fourth child sees them and runs toward them. The child says:
    (a) Wait! Save me one!
    (b) Wait! Save one for me!

FOCUS **6**

▶ **Verbs that Do Not Omit**
To with Indirect Objects

EXAMPLES	EXPLANATION
S + **V** + **D.O.** + **I.O.** (a) My mother reads stories to us. **S** + **V** + **I.O.** + **D.O.** (b) My mother reads us stories.	Many verbs follow both Pattern A and B. (See Focus 4)
D.O. + **I.O.** (c) The teacher explains the grammar to us. (d) NOT: The teacher explains us the grammar.	Some verbs only follow Pattern A.
carry *fix* *repeat* *clean* *introduce* *report* *describe* *open* *shy* *do* *prepare* *solve* *explain* *repair* *spell*	Verbs that follow Pattern A ONLY. Do not omit *to/for*.

EXERCISE 11

Read the following sentence or question pairs aloud. Check any sentence that is not possible. In some pairs, both patterns are possible.

▶ **EXAMPLE 1:**
Pattern A: My husband sends flowers to me every Valentine's Day.
Pattern B: My husband sends me flowers every Valentine's Day.
(Both patterns are possible.)

▶ **EXAMPLE 2:**
Pattern A: The teacher always repeats the question to the class.
NOT: **Pattern B**: The teacher always repeats the class the question.

Pattern A	Pattern B
1. Tell the truth to me.	Tell me the truth.
2. Please explain the problem to me.	Please explain me the problem.
3. Spell that word for me, please.	Spell me that word, please.
4. I need to report the accident to the insurance company.	I need to report the insurance company the accident.
5. My father usually reads a story to my little brother every night.	My father usually reads my little brother a story every night.
6. He always opens the door for me.	He always opens me the door.
7. Let me introduce my friend to you.	Let me introduce you my friend.
8. Cynthia gives her old clothes to a charity.	Cynthia gives a charity her old clothes.
9. The students write letters to their parents every week.	The students write their parents letters every week.
10. Please repeat the instructions to the class.	Please repeat the class the instructions.
11. Can you describe your hometown to me?	Can you describe me your hometown?
12. Can you carry that bag for me?	Can you carry me that bag?

Use Your English

ACTIVITY 1: SPEAKING

Think of the different things people have. Then give clues so that your classmates can guess the objects.

▶ **EXAMPLE:** **Clues:** The Japanese make a lot of them. We drive them. What are they?

Answer: Cars!

ACTIVITY 2: SPEAKING

STEP 1 Write down the names of ten occupations on ten pieces of paper.

STEP 2 Choose one piece of paper and make sentences for the class so they can guess what the occupation is. You get one point for each sentence you make.

STEP 3 When the class guesses the occupation, another student picks a piece of paper. The person with the most points at the end wins.

▶ **EXAMPLE:** (You choose "firefighter.")

You say: *This person wears a hat.*

He or she drives a big vehicle.

He or she saves people's lives.

ACTIVITY 3 : WRITING/SPEAKING

STEP 1 Each person in the class writes down a personal habit—good or bad.

STEP 2 Each person reads his or her statement to the class.

STEP 3 The class asks questions to find out more information. (Possible habits: playing with your hair, tapping your feet.)

▶ **EXAMPLE:** **You:** *I bite my fingernails.*

Class: *Why do you bite them?*

You: *Because I'm nervous!*

ACTIVITY 4 : SPEAKING

What customs do you have in your country for events such as birth, engagement, marriage, death? Tell the class what people do in your country.

▶ **EXAMPLE:** In Chile, when a baby is born . . .

when a couple gets married . . .

when someone dies . . .

when a person turns thirteen . . .

OTHER . . .

ACTIVITY 5: SPEAKING

Work in a small group. On small slips of paper, write the numbers 1 to 16 and put them in an envelope. One person in the class is the "caller" and only he or she looks at the grid below. The first student picks a number from the envelope. The caller calls out the command in that square for the student to follow. Then a second student picks out a number and the caller calls out the command. Continue until all the commands are given.

▶ **EXAMPLE:**   You pick the number 7.
  Caller: Lend some money to Maria.

1. Whisper a secret to the person next to you.	2. Give a penny to the person on your left.	3. Write a funny message to someone in your group.	4. Hand your wallet to the person on your right.
5. Make a paper airplane for the person across from you.	6. Tell a funny joke to someone.	7. Lend some money to a person in your group.	8. Describe a friend to someone.
9. Explain indirect objects to a person near you.	10. Tell your age to the person on your right.	11. Introduce the person on your left to the person on your right.	12. Offer a piece of gum to someone.
13. Teach your classmates how to say "I love you" in your language.	14. Open the door for someone in the class.	15. Throw your pen to the person across from you.	16. Pass a secret message to one person in your group.

ACTIVITY 6: LISTENING/ SPEAKING

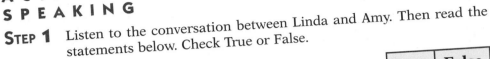

STEP 1 Listen to the conversation between Linda and Amy. Then read the statements below. Check True or False.

	True	False
1. Linda is giving her mother perfume on Mother's Day.		
2. Linda's mother tells her what gift she wants.		
3. Amy's mother always tells her daughter what gift she wants.		
4. Linda's father only takes Linda's mother to a restaurant on Mother's Day.		
5. Linda's father does not buy his wife a gift.		

STEP 2 Compare your answers with a partner's. If a statement is false, make a true statement.

STEP 3 Tell your classmates what you do and give to a person on a special day like Mother's Day or a birthday.

CAN, KNOW HOW TO, BE ABLE TO, CONNECTORS: AND/BUT/SO/OR

UNIT GOALS:

- To use *can* to express ability
- To ask questions with *can*
- To ask for help with English using *can*
- To understand the difference between *can/know how to/be able to* for expressing learned or natural ability
- To use sentence connectors: *and, but, so,* and *or* correctly

▶ OPENING TASK

Find Someone Who Can . . .

STEP 1 Find someone in your class who can do these things:

1. dance **2.** swim **3.** draw

4. sing

5. cook

6. use a computer

7. drive a car

8. play a
musical instrument

9. speak three
languages

STEP 2 Report to the class what you know about your classmates. Who is
the most versatile person in the class? Who can do the most?

▶ *Can*

Can expresses ability.

AFFIRMATIVE	NEGATIVE	NEGATIVE CONTRACTION
I You He She **can** speak English. We You They	I You He She **cannot** We speak Chinese. You They	I You He She **can't** speak French. We You They
(a) She can DANCE. **(b)** He can SING.	In the affirmative, we pronounce *can* as /kən/ and stress the base form of the verb.	
(c) He CAN'T DANCE. **(d)** She CAN'T SING.	In the negative, we stress both *can't* and the base form of the verb.	

EXERCISE 1

Go back to the Opening Task on pages 216-217. With a partner, take turns saying what you can or can't do.

▶ **EXAMPLES:**   I can cook.

               I can't play a musical instrument.

EXERCISE 2

Make affirmative or negative statements about the pictures. The first one has been done for you.

 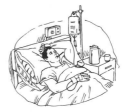 

1. He/hear his mother
He can't hear his mother.

2. She/swim

3. They/play basketball

4. She/open the jar

5. He/walk

6. He/go to work

7. They/see the screen

8. They/speak Korean

EXERCISE 3

What can you do in English? Check *Yes* or *No*.

	Yes	No
1.		
2.		
3.		
4.		
5.		
6.		
7.		

1. I can introduce someone.
2. I can ask about prices.
3. I can describe people and places.
4. I can make a polite request.
5. I can give directions.
6. I can give advice.
7. I can ask for information about English.

Now, exchange books with a partner. Tell what your partner can or can't do in English.

▶ **EXAMPLE:** My partner can introduce someone.

▶ **Questions with *Can***

(a)	**Can** you use a computer? Yes, I can. No, I can't.
(b)	**Can** he cook? Yes, he can. No, he can't.
(c)	What **can** he cook? He can boil water!
(d)	Who **can** cook in your family? My mother can. My father can't.

EXERCISE 4

STEP 1 Write *yes/no* questions with *can*. Then, under *Your Response*, check *Yes* or *No* to give your opinion about each question. Leave the columns under *Total* blank for now.

<table>
<tr><th colspan="2">Your Response</th><th colspan="2">Total</th></tr>
<tr><th>Yes</th><th>No</th><th>Yes</th><th>No</th></tr>
<tr><td></td><td></td><td></td><td></td></tr>
<tr><td></td><td></td><td></td><td></td></tr>
<tr><td></td><td></td><td></td><td></td></tr>
<tr><td></td><td></td><td></td><td></td></tr>
<tr><td></td><td></td><td></td><td></td></tr>
</table>

1. a woman/work as a firefighter

<u>Can a woman work as a firefighter?</u> ?

2. women/fight bravely in wars

_____ ?

3. a man/be a good nurse

_____ ?

4. men/raise children

_____ ?

5. women/be good police officers

_____ ?

	Your Response		Total	
	Yes	**No**	**Yes**	**No**

6. a woman/be a construction worker

_____?

7. a man/keep house neatly

_____?

8. a woman/be a good president of a country

_____?

9. men/communicate successfully with women

_____?

STEP 2 Go back to Step 1. Read the questions aloud. Do a survey in your class. Count how many students say "yes" and how many say "no." Write the *total* number of Yes and No answers in the *Total* column. Do you agree or disagree with your classmates? Give reasons for your answers.

▶ **EXAMPLE:** Women can be good police officers.

They can help people in trouble. They can use guns when necessary.

EXERCISE 5

Work in a group of four to six people. Take turns asking the following questions.

▶ **EXAMPLES:** **a.** Who/type?　　　**b.** How fast/type?

　　　Who can type?　　　How fast can you type?

1. a. Who/cook?　　　　　　　　　**b.** What/cook?
2. a. Who/speak three languages?　　**b.** What languages/speak?
3. a. Who/play a musical instrument?　**b.** What/play?
4. a. Who/sew?　　　　　　　　　**b.** What/sew?
5. a. Who/fix a car?　　　　　　　**b.** What/fix?
6. a. Who/draw?　　　　　　　　**b.** What/draw?
7. a. Who/run a marathon?　　　　**b.** How fast/run a marathon?

▶ **Asking for Help with English**

EXAMPLES	EXPLANATIONS
(a) **Can I say,** "She can to swim" **in English?**	When you are not sure your English is correct, use the expression: *Can I say . . . in English?*
(b) **How can I say,** ". . ." **in English?**	When you don't know how to say something in English, ask the question: *How can I say, ". . ." in English?*
	And then explain your meaning: Use your hands to show "tremendous."
	Use your face to show "sour."
	Use your whole body to show actions like "sweeping."

EXERCISE 6

Look at the pictures. First mime each action and then ask your classmates questions to find out how to say each word.

▶ **EXAMPLE:** How can I say (*mime the action*) in English?

1.

2.

3.

4.

5.

6.

FOCUS **4**

FORM MEANING
USE

▶ **Expressing Ability:** *Can, Know How to,* **and** *Be Able to*

EXAMPLES	EXPLANATIONS
(a) She **can** cook. **(b)** She **knows how to** cook. **(c)** She **is able to** cook.	To express learned ability, use *can, know how to,* **or** *be able to*.
(d) A blind person **can't** see. **(e)** A blind person **isn't able to** see. **(f)** **NOT:** A blind person **doesn't know how to** see.	To express natural ability, use *can* **or** *be able to* only. *Be able to* is more formal than *can*. Use *be able to* in all tenses; not *can*.

EXERCISE 7

Make affirmative or negative statements with the words below. To express learned ability, make one statement with *can* and one statement with *know how to*. To express natural ability, make only one statement with can.

▶ **EXAMPLES:** **a.** fix/a flat tire

I can fix a flat tire.

I know how to fix a flat tire.

b. see/without glasses

I can see without glasses.

1. A blind person/see
2. A dog/live for twenty-five years
3. Infants/walk
4. A deaf person/hear
5. Fish/breathe on land

6. Mechanics/fix cars
7. Men/take care of babies
8. A man/have a baby
9. Doctors/cure some diseases
10. Roses/grow without water

EXERCISE 8

Fill in the blanks with the affirmative or negative forms of *can* or *be able to*.

Fran: Hello, Vanna. How are you today?

Vanna: I'm sorry to say I'm still not well, Fran. My back still hurts. I (1) __can__ sit up now, but I (2) __am not able to__ walk very well.

Fran: What? You mean you (3) _____ come in to work today? Vanna, I (4) _____ do my work without you. I (5) _____ use my computer. I (6) _____ find any of my papers. I (7) _____ remember any of my appointments. This office is a mess. I (8) _____ do all this work myself.

Vanna: What about your temporary secretary? What (9) _____ he do?

Fran: This temporary secretary is terrible. He (10) _____ do anything. He (11) _____ even make a good cup of coffee! I need you here, Vanna. Only you (12) _____ do everything in this office.

Vanna: Well, Fran, do you remember our conversation about my pay raise?

Fran: O.K., O.K., Vanna. You can have your raise. But please come in today!

Vanna: O.K., calm down, Fran, and listen to me. I (13) _____ come in to the office this morning, but I (14) _____ come in this afternoon.

Vanna: Oh . . . thank you, Vanna . . . See you later.

EXERCISE 9

Test your knowledge. Make *Yes/No* questions and discuss your answers.

▶ **EXAMPLES:** people/live without food for six months

Can people live without food for six months?

Yes, they can.

No, they can't.

Are people able to live without food for six months?

Yes, they are.

No, they aren't.

1. a computer/think
2. smoking/cause cancer
3. an airplane/fly from New York to Paris in four hours
4. a person/run twenty-five miles an hour
5. a river/flow uphill
6. we/communicate with people from other planets
7. a person/learn a language in one week
8. modern medicine/cure AIDS
9. a two-year old child/read
10. the United Nations/stop wars
11. you/think of any more questions

▶ Sentence Connectors:
And/But/So/Or

And, but, so, and **or** are sentence connectors. We use them to connect two complete sentences.

EXAMPLES	EXPLANATIONS
(a) I can rollerskate, **and** I can ski.	**And** adds information.
(b) I can dance, **but** I can't sing. He can swim, **but** his brother can't.	**But** shows contrast.
(c) I can't cook, **so** I often go out to eat.	**So** gives a result.
(d) You can go, **or** you can stay.	**Or** gives a choice.
(e) I can speak English, but I can't speak Spanish. **(f)** I can speak Spanish, and my sister can speak Japanese.	When you connect two complete sentences, use a comma (,) before the connector.
(g) I can say it in English, or I can say it in French. **(h)** I can say it in English or French.	When the subject is the same for the two verbs, it is not necessary to repeat the subject or *can*. Do not use a comma.

EXERCISE 10

What can you do? Write sentences about yourself with *can* or *know how to* with *and* or *but*.

▶ **EXAMPLE:** use a typewriter/use a computer

I can use a typewriter, but I can't use a computer.

I can use a typewriter and a computer.

1. rollerskate/rollerblade
2. ride a bicycle/drive a car
3. use a camera/use a video camera
4. use a telephone/use a fax machine
5. cook rice/cook Chinese food
6. sew a button/sew a dress
7. walk fast/run fast
8. swim/dive

Now make three statements of your own:

9. _____

10. _____

11. _____

EXERCISE 11

Look back at the pictures in Exercise 2. Fill in the blanks with *and, but,* or *so.*

1. (Look at Picture 7 in Exercise 2)

Bob and Andrea love the movies, (a) __but__ they are often too busy to go to the movies on Saturdays. They usually go to the first show on Sundays. On Sunday afternoon, the tickets are half-price, (b) _____ the theater is very crowded. There is one woman in the audience who is always a problem. Today, Bob and Andrea are behind her. The woman has very bushy hair, (c) _____ Bob and Andrea can't see the movie screen. She loves popcorn (d) _____ eats it non-stop during the movie. Popcorn is delicious, (e) _____ it is also very noisy, (f) _____ Bob and Andrea can't hear the movie. Sometimes they think it's better to stay home and rent a movie!

2. (Look at Picture 6 in Exercise 2)

Larry is in the hospital. He has a high fever, (a) _____ he is very sick. The doctor wants him to stay in the hospital, (b) _____ Larry wants to go home. The doctor says he needs to rest, (c) _____ Larry wants to go back to work. He is bored in the hospital, (d) _____ he misses his family. He is unhappy, (e) _____ he decides to leave.

3. (Look at Picture 1 in Exercise 2)

Tommy loves to listen to loud music, (a) _____ his mom hates his music. Tommy's mom has a headache, (b) _____ she asks Tommy to use his walkman. Tommy has a walkman, (c) _____ he can't use it. It's broken.

EXERCISE 12

You want to spend a Saturday with a classmate. Choose a partner. Ask each other questions to decide what kind of day you want to have.

STEP 1   Ask each other the six questions given.

▶ **EXAMPLE:**   **You:** Do you want to meet early for breakfast or wait until later to meet?

Your Partner: Let's meet early for breakfast.

1. meet early for breakfast/wait until later to meet
2. skip lunch/have a picnic lunch
3. go to a museum/spend some time outdoors (in a park or at the beach)
4. go on the Internet/play soccer
5. cook dinner together/eat out
6. rent a video/go to a movie

STEP 2   Now add three questions of your own.

Use Your English

ACTIVITY 1: SPEAKING

Read the job advertisement in the newspaper for a baby sitter. Interview your partner for the job. Ask questions with *can, know how to,* and *be able to.*

▶ **EXAMPLES:** Do you know how to cook?

Can you work full-time?

142 Employment

WANTED: Baby sitter ★
Responsible person. Full-time work five days a week 8:00-5:00, some evenings and weekends. Must speak English and be able to drive. Laundry, light housekeeping, and cooking required. Experience with children necessary. References requested.

Chemist ★
Stable, fast-growing company seeks chemist for formulation of industrial

ACTIVITY 2: WRITING

What can you do that your parents or other people you know cannot do? Write six sentences.

▶ **EXAMPLES:** My mother can't ride a bicycle, but I can.

My sister knows how to sew, but I don't.

ACTIVITY 3: WRITING/SPEAKING

Do you think it's better to be a man or a woman? Write as many reasons as you can for your opinion and then discuss them.

▶ **EXAMPLE:** It's better to be a woman. A woman can have children.

A C T I V I T Y   4 :   S P E A K I N G

Make a list of ten jobs.

Say what you can or are able to do. The class decides what job is good for you. Use *and* and *but*.

▶ **EXAMPLE:** **You say:** I can help sick people, and get along with them. I am able to follow directions.

Your group: Then you can be a nurse!

A C T I V I T Y   5 :   S P E A K I N G

STEP 1 Ask a classmate if he or she can do one of the activities in the box below.

▶ **EXAMPLE:** Can you touch your toes without bending your knees?

STEP 2 If the person says *yes*, write his/her name in the box. Then go to another student and ask another question.

If the person says *no*, ask the other questions until he or she says *yes*. Then write his or her name in the box.

STEP 3 Each student who answered *yes* must perform the action in the box!

touch your toes without bending your knees _____	dance _____	whistle _____
sing a song in English _____	say "Hello" in four languages _____	tell a joke in English _____
draw a horse _____	pronounce the word "Psychology" _____	juggle _____

ACTIVITY 6: LISTENING/ SPEAKING

STEP 1 Listen to Ken's interview for a job. Then answer the questions. Check *Yes* or *No*.

	Yes	No

1. Ken can speak French, Spanish, and German.
2. Ken can stay in another country for a year.
3. Ken can drive.
4. Ken can use computers.
5. Ken can sell computers.
6. Ken can repair computers.

STEP 2 Discuss with your classmates.

1. What kind of job is the interview for?
2. Can Ken get the job? Why or why not?

U N I T 15

P R E S E N T   P R O G R E S S I V E   T E N S E

UNIT GOALS:

- To make affirmative and negative statements in the present progressive tense
- To know how to spell verbs ending in *-ing*
- To choose between the simple present and the present progressive
- To know which verbs are not usually used in the progressive
- To ask *yes/no* questions in the present progressive

▶ O P E N I N G   T A S K
A Bad Day at the Harrisons'

Robin's babysitter cannot come today, so her husband Regis is staying at home and taking care of the children and the house.

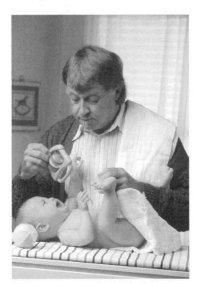

Why is Regis having a bad day today?

Talk about what is happening in the picture using the subjects on the left and the verbs in the box.

the food

Suzy

the telephone

the baby and the dog

the baby

Jimmy

the dog

Regis

bark
play cowboy on his father's back
burn on the stove
go crazy
watch TV
cry
ring
fight over a toy

▶ **P**resent Progressive: Affirmative Statements

EXAMPLES	EXPLANATIONS
(a) The food **is burning.** (b) The baby **is crying.** (c) The dog and the baby **are fighting.**	Use the present progressive to talk about an action that is happening right now; an action in progress.
now *right now* *at the moment*	Use these time expressions with the present progressive.

SUBJECT	BE	BASE FORM OF THE VERB + *-ING*
I	am	
You	are	
He She It	is	working.
We You They	are	

Affirmative Contractions

SUBJECT + *BE* CONTRACTION	BASE FORM OF THE VERB + *-ING*
I'm	
You're	
He's She's It's	working.
We're You're They're	

EXERCISE 1

Underline all the present progressive verbs in the text.

▶ **EXAMPLE:** Regis <u>isn't having</u> a good day.

Today is not a normal day at the Harrisons'. Usually, Robin's babysitter comes at 3:00 when Robin leaves for work. But today, Robin is attending an all-day meeting at the college, and her babysitter can't come. So Regis is spending the day at home. He's taking care of the children and the house. He's trying very hard, but everything is going wrong. Regis isn't having a good day. Actually, poor Regis is going crazy. He's thinking about Robin. He's learning something today. It's not easy to stay home with the children. He's beginning to understand this.

▶ Spelling of Verbs Ending in -ing

VERB END	RULE	EXAMPLES	
1. consonant + e	Drop the -e, add -ing.	write	writing
2. consonant + vowel + consonant (one syllable verbs)	Double the consonant, add -ing.	sit	sitting
Exception: verbs that end in -w, -x, and -y.	Do not double w, x, and y.	show fix play	showing fixing playing
3. consonant + vowel + consonant. The verb has more than one syllable, and the stress is on the last syllable.	Double the consonant, add -ing.	beGIN forGET	beginning forgetting
If the stress is not on the last syllable	Do not double the consonant.	LISten HAPpen	listening happening
4. -ie	Change -ie to y, add -ing.	lie die	lying dying
5. All other verbs	Add -ing to the base form of verb.	talk study do agree	talking studying doing agreeing

EXERCISE 2

Fill in the blanks with the present progressive.

Today's a normal day at the Harrisons'. It is 4:00. Robin (1) _____ (prepare) dinner in the kitchen. She (2) _____ (slice) onions and (3) _____ (wipe) the tears from her eyes. The house is quiet, so she (4) _____ (listen) to some music. She (5) _____ (think) about her class tonight. She (6) _____ (wait) for her babysitter to arrive. The baby (7) _____ (sleep). The dog (8) _____ (lie) on the floor and (9) _____

(chew) on a bone. Jimmy (10) _____ (play) with his toys. Suzy
(11) _____ (clean) her room. Nothing unusual (12) _____
(happen). Everything is under control.

EXERCISE 3
Who's talking? Fill in the blanks with the present progressive of the verb.
Then match each statement to a picture.

▶ **EXAMPLE:** "You're _____*driving*_____ (drive) me crazy.
            Turn off the TV!"

1. "That crazy dog _____ (bite) me!"

a.

2. "I _____ (walk) into a zoo!"

b.

3. "Quiet! You _____ (make) a lot of
       noise. I can't hear the TV."

c.

4. "Stop that, Jimmy. You _____
       (hurt) me."

d.

5. "Oh no! The food _____ (burn)!"

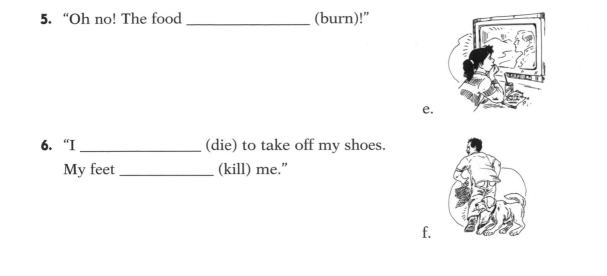

e.

6. "I _____ (die) to take off my shoes.
My feet _____ (kill) me."

f.

FORM

▶ **Present Progressive:
Negative Statements**

SUBJECT + *BE* + *NOT*		NEGATIVE CONTRACTION		BE CONTRACTION + *NOT*	
I am		*		I'm	
You are		You aren't		You're	
He She is It	not working.	He She isn't It	working.	He's She's It's	not working.
We You are They		We You aren't They		We're You're They're	
*There is no standard English contraction with *I am not*.					

EXERCISE 4
Make negative statements using contractions.

▶ **EXAMPLE:** Robin/take care of the children today

Robin isn't taking care of the children today.

1. Robin/wear comfortable shoes today
2. Robin's babysitter/come today
3. The baby and the dog/get along
4. Regis/relax
5. The children/listen to Regis
6. Suzy/do her homework
7. Suzy/help Regis
8. Regis/pay attention to the dinner on the stove
9. Regis/laugh
10. Regis/enjoy his children today

EXERCISE 5
Look at the picture. Make affirmative or negative statements.

▶ **EXAMPLES:** Mrs. Bainbridge _____is having_____
(have) a party at her home
this evening.

Mrs. Bainbridge _____isn't talking_____
(talk) to her guests at the moment.

Mrs. Bainbridge is having a party at her home this evening. The guests
(1) _____ (talk) in the living room. But Mr. and Mrs. Parker
(2)_____ (talk) to the other guests. They (3) _____
(enjoy) the party. They (4) _____ (feel) very bored right now.
They (5) _____ (think of) a way to escape. Mrs. Bainbridge
(6) _____ (stand) in the doorway. She (7) _____
(turn) her back to the Parkers. The Parkers (8) _____ (leave),
but they (9) _____ (leave) by the front door. Mr. and Mrs.
Parker (10) _____ (climb) out of the bedroom window. Mr.
Parker (11) _____ (hold) his hat between his teeth. He
(12) _____ (help) Mrs. Parker climb out. Mr. and Mrs. Parker
(13) _____ (say) good-bye to the other guests.

▶ **Choosing Simple Present or Present Progressive**

The simple present and the present progressive have different uses.

USE THE SIMPLE PRESENT FOR:	USE THE PRESENT PROGRESSIVE FOR:
• **habits and repeated actions** **(a)** Suzy usually does her homework in the afternoon. • **things that are true in general** **(c)** Women usually take care of children.	• **actions in progress now** **(b)** Suzy's watching TV right now. • **actions that are temporary, not habitual** **(d)** Regis is taking care of the children to-day • **situations that are changing** **(e)** These days, men are spending more time with their children.

Time Expressions		**Time Expressions**	
always	*rarely*	*right now*	*now*
often	*never*	*today*	*at the moment*
usually	*every day*	*this week*	*this evening*
sometimes	*once a week*	*this year*	*this month*
seldom	*on the weekends*	*these days*	*nowadays*

EXERCISE 6

Read each statement on the next page. If the statement is in the simple present, make a second statement in the present progressive. If the statement is in the present progressive, make a second statement in the simple present. Discuss the differences in meaning.

Simple Present	Present Progressive
1a. Suzy usually does her homework in the evening.	1b. <u>Tonight she isn't doing her homework. She's watching cartoons.</u>
2a. _____	2b. Tonight, Robin isn't cooking dinner.
3a. Robin usually takes care of the children.	3b. _____
4a. _____	4b. Today, Regis is spending the day at home.
5a. The babysitter usually takes care of the children when Robin goes to work.	5b. _____
6a. _____	6b. Right now, the baby and the dog are fighting.
7a. The babysitter doesn't usually go crazy.	7b. _____

EXERCISE 7

Make sentences with *these days, nowadays,* or *today* to show changing situations in the United States.

▶ **EXAMPLE:** women/get more education

These days, women are getting more education.

1. Women/get good jobs
2. Fifty percent of American women/ work outside the home
3. Women/earn money
4. Women/become more independent
5. Men/share the work in the home
6. Husbands/help their wives
7. Fathers/spend more time with their children
8. The roles of men and women/ change

Add two sentences of your own.

9. _____

10. _____

▶ Verbs Not Usually Used in the Progressive

There are some verbs we usually do not use in the present progressive. These verbs are *not* action verbs. They are called nonprogressive (or stative) verbs.

EXAMPLES	NONPROGRESSIVE (STATIVE) VERBS
(a) Robin **loves** her job. **(b) NOT:** Robin is loving her job. **(c)** The children **need** help. **(d) NOT:** The children are needing help.	**FEELINGS AND EMOTIONS** *(like, love, hate, prefer, want, need)*
(e) Regis **understands** his wife.	**MENTAL STATES** *(think, believe, understand, seem, forget, re-member, know, mean)*
(f) Regis **hears** the telephone ringing.	**SENSES** *(hear, see, smell, taste, feel, sound)*
(g) Robin and Regis **own** a house.	**POSSESSION** *(belong, own, have)*

There are some stative verbs you can use in the present progressive, but they have a different meaning.

SIMPLE PRESENT	PRESENT PROGRESSIVE
(h) I **think** you're a good student. (*Think* means "believe.")	**(i)** I **am thinking** about you now. (Here *thinking* shows a mental action.)
(j) I **have** two cars. (*Have* means "possess.")	**(k)** I'm **having** a good time. (*Have* describes the experience.)
(l) This soup **tastes** delicious. (*Taste* means "has a delicious flavor.")	**(m)** I'm **tasting** the soup. (*Taste* here means the action of putting soup in one's mouth.)

EXERCISE 8

Fill in the blanks with the present progressive or simple present form of the verb. Read the dialogues aloud. Use contractions.

▶ **EXAMPLE:** **Regis:** _____I'm going_____ (go) crazy in this house.

Robin: _____I think_____ (think) you need a vacation!

1. **Regis:** Suzy, I need your help here.

   Suzy: But, Dad, you (a) _____ (need) my help every five minutes! I (b) _____ (watch) TV right now!

2. It is 3:00. The telephone rings.

   Regis: Hello.

   Laura: Hello, Regis. What are you doing home in the middle of the afternoon?

   Regis: Oh, hi, Laura. I know I (a) _____ (be) never home in the afternoon, but today I (b) _____ (try) to be a househusband!

   Laura: Oh really? Where's Robin?

   Regis: Robin (c) _____ (attend) a meeting at the college, so I (d) _____ (take care of) the kids.

3. Jimmy interrupts Regis's telephone conversation:

   Regis: Hold on a minute, Laura . . . Jimmy (a) _____ (pull) on my leg! Jimmy, I (b) _____ (talk) to Mommy's friend Laura right now. You (c) _____ (know) Laura. She (d) _____ (come) to see Mommy every week. Now, just wait a minute, please . . .

   Laura: Is everything O.K., Regis?

   Regis: Oh, yes, Laura, don't worry. We (e) _____ (do) just fine. Talk to you later; bye!

4. It is 5:30. The telephone rings.

   Regis: Hello.

   Robin: Hi, honey! The meeting (a) _____ (be) over. I (b) _____ (be) on my way home. What (c) _____ (happen)? I hope the children (d) _____ (behave).

Regis: They (e) _____ (behave) like wild animals, Robin. I
(f) _____ (yell) at them all the time, but they don't listen to me. I
(g) _____ (not/have) a very good day today. Please come home
soon!

Robin: You (h) _____ (sound) terrible! Can I bring anything
home, dear?

Regis: Yes, a bottle of aspirin!

EXERCISE 9

Work with a partner. Choose any picture (do not go in order). Describe the picture by
making one statement with *seem*, *look*, or *feel* and an adjective from the box. Make
another statement with the present progressive to say what the person is doing. Your
partner must guess the number of the picture you are talking about. Take turns.

▶ **EXAMPLE:** **You say:** The woman looks nervous. She's smoking five cigarettes at one
time.

Your partner says: Picture Number 5.

sad	sick	scared	tired
angry	happy	cold	hot
bored	surprised	nervous	confused

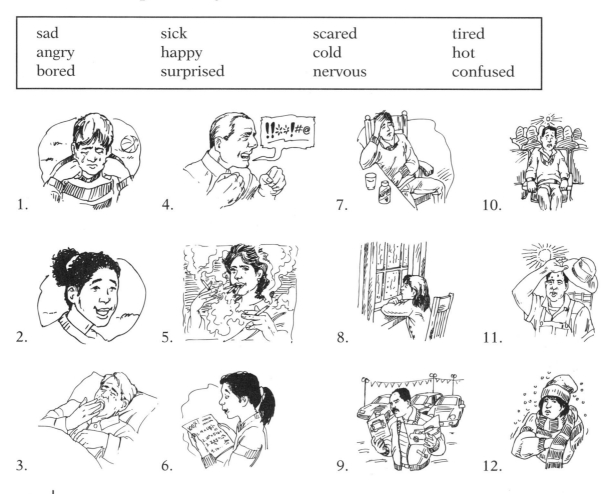

▶ **Present Progressive: *Yes/No*
Questions and Short Answers**

YES/NO QUESTIONS				SHORT ANSWERS					
Am	I			Yes,	you	are.	No,	you	aren't
Are	you			Yes,	I	am.	No,	I'm	not.
Is	he she it		working?	Yes,	he she it	is.	No,	he she it	isn't.
Are	you we they			Yes,	we you they	are.	No,	we you they	aren't.

EXERCISE 10

Refer to the picture in the Opening Task on page 233. With a partner, take turns asking and answering questions about the Harrisons. Give short answers. Use the verbs from the box below.

▶ **EXAMPLE:**   Suzy/ . . . /her father

    You: Is Suzy helping her father?

    Your Partner: No, she isn't.

watch	ring	play	bite	come
enjoy	burn	help	fight	smile

1. children / their father
2. the baby and the dog/ . . .
3. Suzy / TV
4. their dinner/ . . .
5. the phone/ . . .

6. Jimmy / cowboy
7. the dog / Regis
8. Robin / home
9. Robin
10. Regis/his children

EXERCISE 11

Work with a partner. Ask each other *yes/no* questions about your lives these days. Check *Yes* or *No*.

▶ **EXAMPLES:** a. enjoy English class

        Are you enjoying your English class?

      b. your English/improve

        Is your English improving?

You		Your Partner	
Yes	No	Yes	No

1. enjoy English class?
2. your English/improve?
3. take any other classes?
4. learn a lot?
5. get good grades?
6. make progress?
7. do a lot of homework?
8. cook for yourself?
9. go out with friends?
10. meet lots of new people?
11. eat well?
12. sleep well?
13. exercise?
14. work after school?

► Present Progressive: Wh-Questions

WH-WORD	BE	SUBJECT	VERB + -ING	ANSWERS
What	am	I	doing?	(You're) getting ready for the beach.
When Where Why How	are	you	going?	(I'm going) at 2:00. (We're going) to Malibu Beach. (We're going) because we don't have school today. (We're going) by car.
Who(m)	is	she	meeting?	(She's meeting) her friends.
Who	is			Clara (is going with us).

Who is asking about the subject.

EXERCISE 12

Write the question that asks for the underlined information.

1. Q: Who is watching television?

   A: <u>Suzy</u> is watching television.

2. Q: Who(m) is Regis taking care of tonight?

   A: Regis is taking care of <u>the children</u>.

3. Q: _____

   A: The baby and the dog are fighting <u>because they both want the toy.</u>

4. Q: _____

   A: Robin is meeting <u>her colleagues</u> at the college.

5. Q: _____

   A: Robin's thinking that <u>she's lucky to be at work!</u>

6. Q: _____

   A: They're eating peanut butter and jelly sandwiches for dinner <u>because Regis' dinner is burnt.</u>

7. **Q:** _____

    A: <u>Regis</u> is watching the children today.

8. **Q:** _____

    A: Regis is taking two aspirin <u>because he has a terrible headache.</u>

9. **Q:** _____

    A: Robin's meeting is taking place <u>at the college.</u>

10. **Q:** _____

    A: Robin is coming home <u>right now.</u>

11. **Q:** _____

    A: Regis is feeling <u>very tired</u> right now.

12. **Q:** _____

    A: <u>The children</u> are making a lot of noise.

EXERCISE 13

Correct the mistakes in the following sentences.

▶ **EXAMPLE:** Is the pizza tasting good?

             Does the pizza taste good?

1. The baby and the dog are fight.

2. He's having a new TV.

3. Why you are working today?

4. Are you needing my help?

5. What Robin is thinking?

6. Is she believing him?

7. Right now, he plays cowboy on his father's back.

8. The soup is smelling delicious.

9. Where you are going?

10. People no are saving money nowadays.

11. You working hard these days.

12. How you doing today?

Use Your English

Your teacher will divide the class into two groups.

STEP 1 Group A should look at the statements in Column A. One student at a time will mime an action. Students in Group B must guess the action. Group B students can ask questions of Group A. Then Group B mimes statements from Column B and Group A guesses the actions.

Column A

1. You are opening the lid of a jar. The lid is on very tight.
3. You are watching a very funny TV show.
5. You are trying to sleep and a mosquito is bothering you.
7. You are crossing a busy street. You are holding a young child by the hand and carrying a bag of groceries in the other hand.
9. You are trying to thread a needle, but you're having trouble finding the eye of the needle.

Column B

2. You are reading a very sad story.
4. You are watching your country's soccer team playing in the final game of the World Cup.
6. You are sitting at the bar in a noisy disco. At the other side of the bar, there is someone you like. You are trying to get that person's attention.
8. You are a dinner guest at a friend's house. Your friend is not a good cook. You don't like the food!
10. You are cutting up onions to cook dinner.

STEP 2 Make up three situations like those above. Write each situation on a separate piece of paper and put all the situations in a hat. Every student will then pick a situation and mime it for the others to guess.

ACTIVITY 2: WRITING

In this unit, we see that family life is changing in the United States. Is family life changing in your home country or in a country that you know? Write sentences expressing habits and things that are generally true or things that are changing. Discuss your statements in a group or with the whole class.

Mothers . . .   Grandparents . . .
Fathers . . .   Couples . . .
Children . . .   Men . . .
Teenagers . . .   Women . . .

ACTIVITY 3: LISTENING/ SPEAKING

LISTEN AND DECIDE

STEP 1 Look at the three pictures. Listen to the conversation. Decide which picture fits the description. Check A, B, or C.

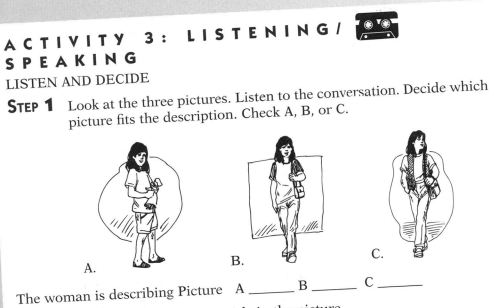

A.   B.   C.

The woman is describing Picture   A _____ B _____ C _____

STEP 2 Describe the other two girls in the picture.

ACTIVITY 4: WRITING/SPEAKING

STEP 1 Look at the picture. Give this person a name, nationality, occupation, age, and so on. Write a story about this person. What is the woman doing? Where is she? How does she look? What is she thinking about? Why is she there?

STEP 2 Tell the class your story.

UNIT 16

ADJECTIVE PHRASES

Another, The Other, Other(s), The Other(s), and Intensifiers

UNIT GOALS:

- To understand and know how to use adjective phrases
- To ask questions with *which*
- To understand and use *another, the other, other(s),* and *the other(s)*
- To use intensifiers with adjectives

▶ **OPENING TASK**

Meeting the Staff at P.S. 31

Identify the people below only by describing them. Do not point to the picture or say the letter. Say what each person does at P.S. 31.

A.

B.

C.

D.

E.

F.

1. <u>The man in the suit and tie</u> is the school principal.

2. _____ teaches science.

3. _____ is the school nurse.

4. _____ is the girls' basketball coach.

5. _____ works in the school cafeteria.

6. _____ teaches art.

▶ Adjective Phrases

EXAMPLES			EXPLANATIONS
Noun	Adjective Phrase	Verb	
(a) The man	**in the suit**	is the school principal.	Adjective phrases are groups of words that describe nouns.
(b) The food	**on the table**	is delicious.	
The woman is in a white coat. The woman is the school nurse.			Adjective phrases combine two sentences.
(c) The woman	**in the white coat**	is the school nurse.	
(d) The **man** with the books **is** the science teacher.			The verb agrees with the subject, not with the noun in the adjective phrase.

EXERCISE 1

Put parentheses around the adjective phrases. Underline the subject and the verb in each sentence.

▶ **EXAMPLE:**   The man (in the suit) works in an office.

1. The man in the suit and tie is the school principal.
2. The man with the books and microscope is the science teacher.
3. The woman in the white coat is the school nurse.
4. The woman with the stopwatch is the girls' basketball coach.
5. The man with the white hat works in the school cafeteria.
6. The woman with the easel and paints is the art teacher.
7. The people on page 252 work at P.S. 31.

EXERCISE 2

The ten people below sit in specific chairs on the next page. Match each person to a chair. Then write a sentence with an adjective phrase. The first one has been done for you.

1.

2.

3.

4.

5.

6.

7.

8.

9.

10.

A.

B.

C.

D.

E.

F.

G.

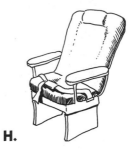

H.

I.

J.

	Chair	Person	
1.	B	1	The man with the megaphone sits in chair B.
2.		2	
3.		3	
4.		4	
5.		5	
6.		6	
7.		7	
8.		8	
9.		9	
10.		10	

EXERCISE 3

Combine each of the sentence pairs into one sentence using an adjective phrase. Then find the person in the picture and write the number of your sentence on the person.

Kindergarten Chaos

1. The girl has a bow in her hair. She is kicking her partner.
   The girl with the bow in her hair is kicking her partner.

2. The boy has a striped shirt and black pants. He is throwing a paper airplane across the room.

   _____

3. The girls are near the window. They are waving to their friends outside.

   _____

4. The boy is in a baseball uniform. He is standing on the teacher's desk.

   _____

5. The boys are in the back of the room. They are fighting.

_____

6. The boy is in the corner. He is reading.

_____

7. The boy is in the closet. He is crying.

_____

8. The girl has a Walkman. She is singing.

_____

9. The man has a rope around him. He is the new teacher.

_____

10. The man is in a suit and tie. He is the school principal.

_____

▶ **Questions with *Which***

EXAMPLES	EXPLANATIONS
(a) **Which** woman is wearing a white coat? the school nurse **(b)** **Which** teachers are women? the coach and the art teacher	Use *which* when there is a choice between two or more people or things.
(c) **Which** coat do you like, Mom? I like the black **one**. **(d)** **Which** shoes do you like, Dad? the brown **ones**	Substitute the words *one* or *ones* for nouns so you do not repeat the noun.
(e) **Which** shoes do you want? the ones **in the window**	You can also use adjective phrases after *one* and *ones*.

EXERCISE 4

Julie's house was robbed. She is very upset, and is talking to her husband on the phone, describing the damage. Work with a partner. Find the differences between the pictures. You say Julie's statements. Your partner is the husband, and asks questions to get more specific information.

▶ **EXAMPLE:** **Julie:** The window is broken.

Husband: Which window?

Julie: The one over the kitchen sink.

BEFORE

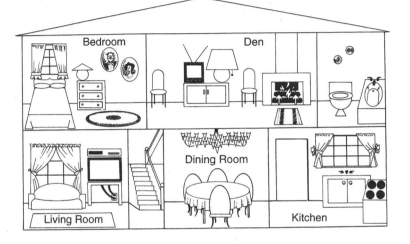

AFTER

1. The floor is dirty.
2. The curtains are torn.
3. The TV is missing.
4. The door is open.
5. The lamp is broken.
6. The VCR is missing.
7. The cabinet is empty.
8. The rug is missing.
9. The chandelier is gone.

▶ **A**nother, The Other, Other(s),
The Other(s)

	ADJECTIVE	PRONOUN	MEANING
A: I'm hungry. B: Here. Have a cookie. A: I am still hungry. Can I have **another** cookie? (Can I have **another**?)	**another** cookie	**another**	one more cookie; one more from a group
B: There are no more cookies in the box. A: There are two **other boxes** in the closet. (There are two **others** in the closet.)	**other** boxes	**others**	more than one more
A: I found one box. Where is **the other box**? (Where is **the other**?) B: **The other box** is behind it.	**the other** box	**the other**	the one you spoke about; the last one in a group
A: How many more cookies can I have? B: You can have one more. **The other cookies** are for me! (**The others** are for me!)	**the other** cookies	**the others**	the ones you spoke about; the last ones in a group

EXERCISE 5

Thor is visiting Earth from another planet. Ed Toppil interviews Thor on television. Fill in the blanks with *another, the other, other(s),* or *the other(s)*.

Ed: We on Earth are really excited to know there is (1) _____ planet out there, Thor. Many of us know there are (2) _____ , but we are not able to find them. Do you know of any (3) _____ planets?

Thor: Yes, we do. We know two (4) _____: Limbix and Cardiax. I have photos of the people from both of (5) _____ planets.

The Limbix are the ones on the left. The Cardiax are (6) _____ ones. We also now know the planet Earth. We are sure there are (7) _____ out there, but (8) _____ are very far away.

Ed: I am surprised that you speak English so well, Thor. Do the Thoraxes have (9) _____ language too?

Thor: Yes, of course. We speak Thoracic, but English is a universal language, you know, so we all learn it in school. People on (10) _____ two planets speak English too!

Ed: So what brings you to Earth?

Thor: Well, Ed, we are looking for (11) _____ intelligent beings in the universe.

Ed: On Earth?!! I don't know if you can find many intelligent beings on Earth, Thor! But we can discuss this at (12) _____ time. Right now, let's stop for a station break.

EXERCISE 6

Thor tours America. Fill in *another, other(s),* or *the other(s).*

1. **Ed:** You only have one tie, Thor. You need to buy (a) _____
   one.

   Thor: Why?

   Ed: Because Americans are consumers. They like to buy
   things.

   Thor: But I don't like any (b) _____ ties here.

   Ed: O.K. Look at (c) _____ over there. Maybe
   you can find (d) _____ one.

2. Thor is in a candy store with a child:

   Thor: Which candy is good here?

   Child: This one is good, but first taste

   (a) _____ one in the brown and green paper.

   It's out of this world!

   Thor: Hmmmm, excellent. Is it O.K. to take

   (b) _____ one?

3. **Soaprah:** So, Thor, tell us about your family. Are you married?

   Thor: Yes. I am, and I have two children. One is a specialist in interplanetary
   communication and (a) _____ owns a spaceship factory.

   Soaprah: And what does your wife do?

   Thor: My wife is a spaceship pilot.

   Soaprah: What about (b) _____
   people on Thorax? What do they do?

   Thor: (c) _____ do different jobs.
   We have doctors, teachers, artists, and so on. We
   don't have any tax collectors.

   Soaprah: Are there any (d) _____ professions you don't have?

   Thor: We don't have any lawyers, I'm happy to say.

   Soaprah: That sounds great to me too!

   Thor: Do you have any (e) _____ questions?

   Soaprah: I have a million (f) _____ questions! But our time is
   up. It was nice meeting you, Thor. Thanks so much for coming.

FOCUS **4**

▶ **Intensifiers**

Intensifiers are words that make adjectives more or less strong.

SUBJECT	*BE*	INTENSIFIER	ADJECTIVE
(a) Earth	is	very	beautiful.
(b) The people on Thorax	are	quite	similar.
(c) The people on Earth	are	rather/pretty* fairly	different.
(d) Thorax	isn't	very**	beautiful.

Pretty has the same meaning as rather, but is very informal.
**Very* is the only intensifier we use in negative sentences.

SUBJECT	*BE*	ARTICLE	INTENSIFIER	ADJECTIVE	NOUN
(e) Earth	is	a	very	special	place.
(f) Thorax	is	a	rather/pretty* fairly	small	planet.
(g) Thorax	isn't	a	very**	attractive	place.

SUBJECT	*BE*	INTENSIFIER	ARTICLE	ADJECTIVE	NOUN
(h) Thorax	is	quite	a	small	planet.

EXERCISE 7

Test Thor's knowledge. How many of the objects can Thor (and you) guess?

1. This is fairly long and thin.

    People eat it.

    It is very popular in Italy.

    What is it? _____

2. This is a liquid.

    People usually drink it hot.

    They like its rather strong, rich smell.

    It's brown.

    What is it? _____

3. This is an electrical appliance.

    It is quite common in people's homes.

    Sometimes it is very hot.

    You put bread into it.

    What is it? _____

4. This is very cold.

    It's also pretty hard.

    People put it in drinks on hot days.

    It's quite slippery.

    What is it? _____

5. This is quite a big metal box.

    It's electrical and pretty practical.

    It's very useful in tall buildings.

    People go inside the box.

    The box goes up and down.

    What is it? _____

6. This is a very popular piece of plastic.

    It isn't very big.

    With it, we can buy rather expensive things without cash.

    What is it? _____

7. There are different kinds of candy.

All of them are good.

But this one is very special.

It comes in brown or white.

It's pretty fattening.

It's quite delicious.

What is it? _____

8. This thing is quite colorful.

It isn't very common.

It sometimes follows rainstorms.

It is quite a beautiful sight.

What is it? _____

EXERCISE 8

Ed Toppil continues his interview with Thor. Write an intensifier in each blank. There is more than one possible answer.

Ed: So tell me, Thor, what do you think of our planet?

Thor: Well, Earth is a beautiful planet, but it's (1) _____quite_____ a strange place. Many of your leaders are not doing a (2) _____ good job. Some people on Earth are (3) _____ rich. Others are (4) _____ poor. There can be a (5) _____ big difference between people. On Thorax, we are all equal. Money isn't (6) _____ important. Learning is (7) _____ important. That's why we're visiting Earth. Your knowledge can be (8) _____ useful to us. Also, your art and music are (9) _____ beautiful.

Ed: That's (10) _____ interesting. I'm sure we can learn many (11) _____ useful and exciting things from you, too, Thor.

EXERCISE 9

How necessary or important is each item to you? Give your opinion using intensifiers. Explain your answers.

▶ **EXAMPLE:**   a cellular phone

A cellular phone is very important to me. I can call my friends anytime I want.

1. a computer
2. a life partner
3. a driver's license
4. a university degree
5. children
6. good health

7. a beautiful planet
8. the Internet
9. art and music
10. friends
11. free time
12. a good leader for my country

EXERCISE 10

Read the statements and comments. Fill in an intensifier in each blank. Sometimes, there can be more than one possible answer.

Statement	**Comment**
1. I want to see the movie "Psycho."	Don't! That's a _____ scary movie!
2. She's planning a birthday party for me.	That's _____ a nice thing to do.
3. Do you still watch talk shows on TV?	Yes, I do. They're _____ interesting programs.
4. I like this restaurant very much.	Me too! This is _____ a delicious dinner.
5. My friends want to stay up all night.	That's not a _____ good idea.
6. He's working in Vietnam.	Really! That's _____ a fascinating place!
7. They have eight children.	Wow! That's a _____ large family.
8. Eric and Tina are doing well in my class.	In mine too. They're _____ bright students.
9. I'm bored again today.	I'm afraid this is not a _____ exciting vacation.
10. Do you know Newport, Rhode Island?	Oh, yes. The mansions in Newport are _____ big—just like castles.

Use Your English

ACTIVITY 1: WRITING/SPEAKING

STEP 1 Write ten sentences that give information about your home country or city.

▶ **EXAMPLES:** The beaches in the south are very beautiful.

The market in the center of the city is always crowded.

The coffee in Brazil is delicious.

STEP 2 Now tell the class about your country or city.

ACTIVITY 2: WRITING/SPEAKING

STEP 1 In a group, write sentences about ten students in the class. Use adjective phrases. Do not use names.

STEP 2 Read your sentences to the class. The class guesses the person you are talking about.

▶ **EXAMPLES:** The student from Bogotá has pretty eyes.

The student next to Miyuki wears glasses.

The student with the big smile is from Ecuador.

ACTIVITY 3: SPEAKING/WRITING

STEP 1 Check (✔) the adjectives that describe you, and write *very/quite/rather/ pretty/fairly/not very* under **You** in the chart below.

STEP 2 Ask your partner questions to find out which adjectives describe him or her. Then ask questions with how and write *very/quite/rather/pretty/ fairly/not very* under **Your Partner** in the same chart.

▶ **EXAMPLE:** **You ask:** Are you shy?

Your partner answers: Yes, I am.

You ask: How shy are you?

Your partner answers: I'm very shy.

Adjective	You	very quite rather pretty fairly not very	Your Partner	very quite rather pretty fairly not very
				very
shy				
lazy				
quiet				
romantic				
friendly				
old-fashioned				
organized				
jealous				
talkative				
athletic				
healthy				

ACTIVITY 4: WRITING

Use the information in Activity 3 to write five sentences about you or about your partner using *very/quite/rather/pretty/fairly/not very*.

▶ **EXAMPLE:** My partner is a very romantic person. He is pretty old-fashioned, and he is very jealous.

ACTIVITY 5: SPEAKING

Imagine you are starting life on a new planet. Look at the list of people. Then choose only ten people to move to the new planet. Say how necessary each one is and why. Say why the others are not necessary and why

▶ **EXAMPLE:** A doctor is very necessary because we need to stay healthy.

an actor
a scientist
a historian
a farmer
a doctor
a military person

an artist
a religious leader
a writer
a teacher
a mechanic
a stockbroker

a police officer
a young man
a musician
a journalist
a computer specialist
an elderly person

a political leader
a young woman
a lawyer
a pilot
a dancer
an engineer

ACTIVITY 6: WRITING/SPEAKING

Write descriptions of objects using intensifiers like those in Exercise 7. Test your classmates' knowledge of these objects.

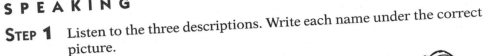

ACTIVITY 7: LISTENING/ SPEAKING

STEP 1 Listen to the three descriptions. Write each name under the correct picture.

STEP 2 Work in a group. Each student draws a face. Then, the student describes the face to the rest of the group. The rest of the group draws what the student describes.

PAST TENSE OF BE

UNIT GOALS:

- To make affirmative and negative statements with the verb *be* in the past tense
- To ask and answer *yes/no* and *wh*-questions with *be* in the past tense

▶ **OPENING TASK**

Test Your Memory

Look at the photos and the information about famous people from the past. Make statements about each person. Correct any facts that are not true.

		Nationality	Occupation
	1. Martin Luther King, Jr.	African	civil rights leader
	2. The Beatles	British	hairdressers
	3. Diana	American	actress

	Nationality	Occupation
4. Mahatma Gandhi	Indian	rock singer
5. Pierre and Marie Curie	French	fashion designers
6. Mao Zedong	Chinese	political leader
7. Jacqueline Kennedy Onassis	Greek	millionaire
8. George Washington, Thomas Jefferson, Abraham Lincoln, Theodore Roosevelt	Canadian	presidents

▶ **P**ast Tense of *Be:*
Affirmative Statements

SUBJECT	VERB	
I	was	
You	were	
He She It	was	famous.
We You They	were	
There There	was were	a famous actress in that film. many political leaders at the meeting.

EXERCISE 1

Use the past tense of *be* to make correct statements about the famous people in the Opening Task.

1. The Beatles _____ a famous British rock group in the 1960s.

2. Mahatma Gandhi _____ a nationalist and Hindu religious leader in India.

3. Marie and Pierre Curie _____ French scientists.

4. Mao Zedong _____ a revolutionary and political leader in the People's Republic of China.

5. George Washington, Thomas Jefferson, Abraham Lincoln, and Theodore Roosevelt _____ presidents of the United States.

6. Martin Luther King, Jr. _____ an American civil rights leader.

7. Diana _____ a British princess, the wife of Prince Charles.

8. Jacqueline Kennedy Onassis _____ the wife of president John F. Kennedy, and then, of Aristotle Onassis, a Greek millionaire.

EXERCISE 2

Fill in the blanks in the postcard. Use *be* in the simple past.

Dear Grandma and Grandpa,

Here we are in Florida. What a place! Yesterday

we (1) _____ at Disneyworld all day. The sun

(2) _____ really strong and it (3) _____ very hot.

The lines (4) _____ long, but the rides and the shows

(5) _____ fun. Disneyworld (6) _____ crowded,

but all the people (7) _____ friendly and polite. Our favorite

place (8) _____ Cinderella's palace! The fireworks at night

(9) _____ beautiful! It (10) _____

great for us, but Dad (11) _____ really

hot and tired at the end of the day!

    We miss you! See you soon.

      Love, Melanie and Michele

USA 33

Grandma and Grandpa Henner
Homestead Lane
Harvard, MA 01451

► Past Tense of *Be*: Negative Statements

SUBJECT	BE + NOT		NEGATIVE CONTRACTIONS		
I	was not	famous.	I	wasn't	famous.
You	were not		You	weren't	
He She It	was not		He She It	wasn't	
We You They	were not		We You They	weren't	
There	was	no time to eat	There	wasn't	any time to eat.
There	were	no good restaurants	There	weren't	any good restaurants.

EXERCISE 3

How do Michael and Carol remember their trip to Disneyworld? Fill in the blanks with the affirmative or negative of *be* in the simple past. Then read the dialogue aloud.

Alice: Oh, hi, Michael. Hi, Carol. How (1) _____was_____ your trip to Disneyworld last week?

Carol: Hi, Alice. Oh, it (2) _____ fun.

Michael: Fun! That vacation (3) _____ (not) fun, it (4) _____ terrible!

Carol: But Michael, how can you say that? I think the children and I (5) _____ very satisfied with our vacation.

Michael: Carol, the weather (6) _____ boiling hot.

Carol: It (7) _____ (not) boiling hot, it (8) _____ very comfortable.

Michael: The food (9) _____ (not) very good . . .

Carol: The food (10) _____ fine, Michael.

Michael: The people (11) _____ (not) friendly.

Carol: Of course, they (12) _____ friendly.

Michael: The kids (13) _____ very difficult.

Carol: The kids (14) _____ (not) difficult, Michael. Come on, they (15) _____ great.

EXERCISE 4

A positive person sees the world in a positive way and believes that good things will happen. A negative person usually sees only the bad things in life. Make sentences using *was/were* for the situations below. These adjectives may help you. Use other adjectives you know.

terrible	ugly	romantic	small
rude	friendly	sunny	rainy
delicious	beautiful	polite	spacious
fantastic	loud	ordinary	extraordinary

Situation	A positive person says:	A negative person says:
1. Yesterday evening, you were at a restaurant with friends.	a. The place was romantic. c. The food _____. e. The waiters _____.	b. The place was ugly. d. The food _____. f. The waiters _____.
2. Last Saturday, you went to a disco.	a. The music _____. c. The dance floor _____.	b. The music _____. d. The dance floor _____.
3. Last summer, you were on vacation with your friends.	a. The weather _____. c. The scenery _____.	b. The weather _____. d. The scenery _____.

EXERCISE 5

Do you remember the story *Cinderella?* Fill in the blanks with the affirmative or negative form of *be*.

Once upon a time, there (1) _____ a young woman named Cinderella. She (2) _____ rich, but she (3) _____ very beautiful and kind. Her two stepsisters (4) _____ beautiful. They (5) _____ jealous of Cinderella. Cinderella's stepmother (6) _____ good to her.

One day, there (7) _____ a ball for the Prince at the King's palace. . . .

FOCUS 3

▶ Yes/No Questions and Short Answers with *Be* in the Simple Past

YES/NO QUESTIONS			SHORT ANSWERS			
Verb	Subject		Affirmative		Negative	
Was	I			you were.		you were not. you weren't.
Were	you			I was.		I was not. I wasn't.
Was	he she it	right?	Yes,	he she was. it	No,	he/she/it was not he/she/it wasn't.
Were	we you they			you we were. they		you/we were not. they you/we weren't. they
Was there any good food at Disneyworld?			Yes,	there was.	No, No,	there was not. there wasn't.
Were there long lines at Disneyworld?			Yes,	there were.	No, No,	there were not. there weren't.

EXERCISE 6

Detective Furlock Humes is questioning a police officer about a crime. Fill in the blanks with *there + be* in the simple past.

▶ **EXAMPLES:** ___Was there___ a crime last night?

___Yes, there were___ several police officers at the house.

Police Officer: The body was here, Detective Humes.

Furlock: (1) _____ a weapon?

Police Officer: Yes, (2) _____ a gun next to the body.

Furlock: (3) _____ any fingerprints on the gun?

Police Officer: No, sir, (4) _____ .

Furlock: (5) _____ any motive for this crime?

Police Officer: We don't know, sir.

Furlock: How about witnesses? (6) _____ any witnesses to the crime?

Police Officer: Yes, sir. (7) _____ one witness—a neighbor. She said (8) _____ loud noises in the apartment at midnight.

Furlock: Where is she? Bring her to me . . .

EXERCISE 7

Ask your classmates *yes/no* questions about the events below. Give short answers. Correct the facts if necessary.

▶ **EXAMPLE:** Margaret Thatcher/the first female Prime Minister of Great Britain.

Was Margaret Thatcher the first female Prime Minister of Great Britain?

Yes, she was.

1. Tom Hanks/the first man to walk on the moon
2. AIDS/a known disease in 1949
3. Yugoslavia/a country in 1980
4. Europeans/the first people on the American continent
5. Nelson Mandela/in prison for many years in South Africa
6. The Wright Brothers/the first men to cross the Atlantic Ocean by plane
7. a big earthquake/in Kobe, Japan in 1995
8. any women/in the Olympic Games in 1920

▶ *Wh*-Questions with *Be*

WH-QUESTION	BE	SUBJECT	ANSWERS
When Where Who What How	was	JFK's assassination? the assassination? the assassin? his motive? the day?	November 22, 1963 It was in Dallas, Texas. Lee Harvey Oswald, we think. There were different theories. very sad
Why	were	people sad?	because Kennedy was a popular president
Whose gun	was	it?	Lee Harvey Oswald's

EXERCISE 8

Fill in the *wh*-question word and the correct form of *be* to complete each question.

Andrea: (1) _____ you on the day of Kennedy's assassination?

Helene: I was in school. There was an announcement over the loud speaker.

Andrea: (2) _____ you with at the time?

Helene: I was with my friend Patty.

Andrea: (3) _____ it in school that day?

Helene: It was terrible. We were all very upset and silent.

Andrea: (4) _____ you all silent?

Helene: because it was hard to believe he was dead.

Andrea: And at home? (5) _____ things at home?

Helene: At home, things were very bad. My parents were in shock too.

Andrea: (6) _____ their feelings after the assassination?

Helene: They were angry, sad, confused, and afraid.

EXERCISE 9

Look at the photo and write a *wh*-question for each answer.

1. _____?
These people were mountain climbers.

2. _____?
They were in the Himalayas.

3. _____?
They were there for the adventure and the challenge.

4. _____?
They were there in 1996.

5. _____?
The name of the mountain was Mount Everest.

6. _____?
It was their idea to take this trip.

7. _____?
The trip was a disaster; eight people died on this trip.

EXERCISE 10

Work in a group. Take turns. One student makes a statement about last weekend. The other students ask questions. Use *wh*-questions and the past tense of *be*.

▶ **EXAMPLE:**   **Statement:** I was at the movies on Saturday.

   Questions: What was the movie? Who were you with?

   Who was in the movie? How was the movie?

EXERCISE 11

Correct the mistakes in the following sentences.

1. Do was Mahatma Gandhi a Prime Minister?
2. The Beatles wasn't fashion designers.
3. Was hot the weather at Disneyworld last week?
4. Where the earthquake was in 1996?
5. Why the people were on Mount Everest?
6. Was good the service at the restaurant?
7. No was any good restaurants in Disneyworld.
8. How it was the trip to Disneyworld?

Use Your English

ACTIVITY 1: WRITING/SPEAKING

Work with a partner. Finish writing the story of Cinderella in Exercise 5 (page 278). Then tell your stories to each other.

ACTIVITY 2: SPEAKING

Work with a partner. Ask your partner the questions below and other questions to find out about a special place he or she knows.

QUESTIONS: Where were you last summer? When were you there?

Why were you there? What was special about this place?

How was the weather? Were the people friendly? How was the food?

ACTIVITY 3: SPEAKING/WRITING

With the information from Activity 2, tell the class about your partner's special place, or write a paragraph about it.

▶ **EXAMPLE:** Last summer, my partner was in Greece. She was there with her friend. Greece was very beautiful and interesting.

ACTIVITY 4: SPEAKING

Work in a group.

STEP 1 Write the dates below on pieces of paper. Mix all the papers together.

STEP 2 Pick a piece of paper and say something about your life at that time and your life now. Take turns with the classmates in your group.

▶ **EXAMPLE:** In 1994, I was a doctor in the Philippines, but now I am an ESL student in the United States.

In the summer of 1999	In the 90's		1998
On November 22, 1963	In the 80's		1994
On December 31, 1999	In the 70's	In	1990
	In the 60's		1985

ACTIVITY 5: LISTENING /  SPEAKING

STEP 1 Listen to the beginning of the stories on tape. Decide what kind of story type each one is. Write the number of the story you hear next to the story type.

A horror story _____   A murder mystery _____
A love story _____   A children's story/fairy tale _____

STEP 2 Finish one of the stories. Tell the story to the class.

U N I T 18

P A S T   T E N S E

UNIT GOALS:

- To make affirmative and negative statements with regular and irregular past tense verbs
- To know how to spell and pronounce regular past tense verbs
- To understand the meaning and position of past time expressions
- To ask and answer *yes/no* and *wh*-questions in the past tense

▶ **O P E N I N G   T A S K**

Solve the Mystery: Who took the VCR?

STEP 1   Read the mystery.

For most students, Ms. Ditto was the best ESL teacher in the English Language Center. Three years ago, she began to use a VCR in her classes. She brought in interesting videotapes for her students to watch every week. The students enjoyed her classes and really liked her.

Only one student, Harry, didn't like Ms. Ditto. Harry's writing wasn't very good, so he failed Ms. Ditto's class twice. Last summer, he got a job in the language lab to help pay the tuition for her class again this semester. Yes, Harry felt angry at Ms. Ditto.

Just before the new semester started, the Director of the English Language Center heard the university didn't have money to pay the teachers. They were not able to give Ms. Ditto a job this semester. Everyone was sad. Harry just laughed!

On the first day of class, Professor Brown wanted to use the VCR. He asked Harry to open the language lab. But when Harry opened the door to the lab, the VCR was not there. In its place, there was a typed note with a signature on it. The note said:

Today, I very sad. I no can work in English Language Center because there no have money to pay me. What I can do now? How I can live? I take this VCR because I have angry. Please understand my. I sorry . . .

C. Ditto

STEP 2   Read the sentences and check True or False.

	True	False
1. Ms. Ditto's students didn't like her.		
2. Harry needed money.		
3. Harry worked in the language lab.		
4. Ms. Ditto didn't have a job this semester.		
5. Harry disliked Ms. Ditto.		
6. Harry did well in Ms. Ditto's class.		

STEP 3   Solve the mystery. Discuss your answers with the class. Who took the VCR? How do you know?

▶ Forming and Spelling Regular Past Tense Verbs

SUBJECT	BASE FORM + -ED
I You He She It We You They	started three years ago.

Regular verbs can change spelling in the simple past tense.

IF THE VERB ENDS IN:	SPELLING RULE
(a) a consonant **want** **need**	Add -ed **wanted** **needed**
(b) a vowel + *y* **enjoy** **play**	Add -ed **enjoyed** **played**
(c) a consonant + *e* **like** **smile**	Add -d **liked** **smiled**

IF THE VERB ENDS IN:	SPELLING RULE
(d) a consonant + *y* **study** **worry**	Change -*y* to -*i*, add -*ed* **studied** **worried**
(e) consonant + vowel + consonant (one syllable verbs) **stop** **drop**	Double the consonant, add -*ed* **stopped** **dropped**
(f) -*x*, -*w* (one syllable verbs) **show** **fix**	Do not double the consonant, add -*ed* **showed** **fixed**
(g) two-syllable verbs with the stress on the last syllable **oCCUR** **preFER**	Double the consonant, add -*ed* **occurred** **preferred**
(h) two-syllable verbs with the stress on the first syllable **LISten** **VISit**	Do not double the consonant, add -*ed* **listened** **visited**

EXERCISE 1

Go back to the Opening Task on page 287 and underline all the regular past tense verbs in the mystery.

▶ **EXAMPLE:** They <u>enjoyed</u> her classes and really <u>liked</u> her.

EXERCISE 2

Fill in the blanks with the past tense of the verbs.

1. Ms. Ditto ___*enjoyed*___ (enjoy) her classes.
2. Ms. Ditto _____ (use) interesting videotapes in her classes.
3. She _____ (help) her students to understand the tapes.
4. The students _____ (study) new vocabulary.
5. They _____ (learn) about American life.
6. They _____ (discuss) the tapes in class.
7. The students _____ (play) language learning games in class.
8. Many students _____ (register) for her class every semester.
9. All the students really _____ (love) her.
10. Ms. Ditto _____ (stop) teaching because the university didn't have money to pay her.
11. Ms. Ditto's students _____ (cry).
12. One day, a robbery _____ (occur) at the English Language Center.
13. A VCR _____ (disappear) from the language lab.

▶ Pronunciation of the -*ed* Ending

VERB END	EXAMPLES
Group I After voiceless sounds,* the final -*ed* is pronounced /t/.	**/t/** *asked* *kissed* *stopped*
Group II After voiced sounds,** the final -*ed* is pronounced /d/.	**/d/** *robbed* *killed* *played*
Group III After /t/ and /d/, the final -*ed* is pronounced /Id/. *Voiceless sounds: p, k, f, s, sh, ch **Voiced sound: b, g, v, z, l, m, n, r, or a vowel	**/Id/** *pointed* *wanted* *waited*

EXERCISE 3

STEP 1 Put each verb in the simple past and read each sentence aloud. Check the column that shows the pronunciation of each verb.

Bookworm Benny was an excellent student.

	/t/	/d/	/Id/
1. Teachers always ___liked___ (like) Bookworm Benny.	✔		
2. He _____ (work) hard in school.			
3. He always _____ (finish) his work first.			
4. The teacher always _____ (call) on him.			
5. He always _____ (answer) questions correctly.			

	/t/	/d/	/ɪd/

6. He _____ (remember) all his lessons.

7. He never _____ (talk) out of turn.

8. The other students _____ (hate) Benny.

9. One day, they _____ (decide) to get him into trouble.

10. They _____ (roll) a piece of paper into a ball.

11. They _____ (wait) for the teacher to turn his back.

12. They threw the paper ball at the teacher. It _____ (land) on the teacher's head.

13. The teacher was really angry. He _____ (yell) at the class.

14. "Who did that?" he _____ (ask).

15. All the students _____ (point) to Benny.

16. But the teacher _____ (trust) Benny.

17. The teacher _____ (punish) the other students.

STEP 2 The pictures about Bookworm Benny on the next page are not in the correct order. Number the pictures in the correct order. Then use the pictures to retell Bookworm Benny's story.

A. Number _____   B. Number _____   C. Number _____

D. Number _____   E. Number _____

EXERCISE 4

The solution to the Ms. Ditto story is in this exercise. Fill in the blanks with the past tense of the verbs in the box.

discuss	look	remember	fire	notice	learn ✔
type	confess	believe	lock	ask	sign

When the Director of the English Language Center

(1) ____learned____ about the robbery, she was sad. She

(2) _____ Ms. Ditto was an honest person.

To solve the mystery, the Director (3) _____ herself in
her office alone. She (4) _____ the problems between
Harry and Ms. Ditto. Then, the Director (5) _____ at the
note again. She (6) _____ all the grammar mistakes!
And the signature on the note was not Ms. Ditto's signature.

The Director (7) _____ Harry to come to her office.
She (8) _____ the problem with him. Finally, Harry
(9) _____ to the crime. Harry said, "I
(10) _____ the note and (11) _____
Ms. Ditto's name." In the end, the Director (12) _____
Harry and kicked him out of the school.

FORM

▶ **Irregular Past-Tense Verbs:
Affirmative Statements**

Many verbs in the past tense are irregular. They do not have the *-ed* form.

SUBJECT	VERB	
I You He She It We You They	went	to Miami last year.

You can learn irregular past tense forms in groups.

BASE FORM	SIMPLE PAST
/I/ sound	**/æ/ sound**
begin	began
drink	drank
ring	rang
sing	sang
sink	sank
swim	swam

BASE FORM	SIMPLE PAST
	ought/aught
buy	bought
bring	brought
catch	caught
fight	fought
teach	taught
think	thought

BASE FORM	SIMPLE PAST
	Base form and past-tense forms are the same
cost	cost
cut	cut
hit	hit
hurt	hurt
put	put
quit	quit
shut	shut
let	let
-ow	**-ew**
blow	blew
grow	grew
know	knew
throw	threw
/iy/ sound	**/ɛ/ sound**
feed	fed
feel	felt
keep	kept
lead	led
leave	left
meet	met
read	read
sleep	slept
-d	**-t**
lend	lent
send	sent
spend	spent
bend	bent
build	built

BASE FORM	SIMPLE PAST
	Change of vowel
become	became
come	came
dig	dug
draw	drew
fall	fell
forget	forgot
get	got
give	gave
hold	held
hang	hung
run	ran
sit	sat
win	won
	/o/ sound
break	broke
choose	chose
sell	sold
tell	told
speak	spoke
steal	stole
drive	drove
ride	rode
wake	woke
write	wrote

BASE FORM	SIMPLE PAST
	Other
be	was
bite	bit
do	did
eat	ate
find	found
fly	flew
go	went
have	had
hear	heard
hide	hid
lose	lost
make	made
pay	paid
say	said
see	saw
shake	shook
shoot	shot
stand	stood
take	took
tear	tore
understand	understood
wear	wore

(See Appendix 8 for an alphabetical list of common irregular past tense verbs.)

EXERCISE 5

Go back to the Opening Task on page 287. Circle the irregular past tense verbs.

▶ **EXAMPLE:** For most students, Ms. Ditto ⟨was⟩ the best ESL teacher in the English Language Center.

EXERCISE 6

Liisa and Kate are from Finland. They had a dream vacation in New York last fall. Fill in the blanks with the past tense of the verbs in parentheses.

1. Liisa and Kate _____flew_____ (fly) to New York on Sunday, November 4.

2. They _____ (find) many interesting things to do in the city.

3. They _____ (eat) great food every day.

4. They _____ (go) to the Statue of Liberty.

5. They _____ (take) a ferry to the Immigration Museum at Ellis Island.

6. They _____ (stand) at the top of the World Trade Center.

7. They _____ (spend) an evening at a jazz club.

8. Liisa _____ (buy) gifts for her friends in Finland.

9. They _____ (see) an exhibit at the Museum of Modern Art.

10. They _____ (meet) a nice woman at the museum.

11. They _____ (speak) English with her all afternoon.

12. They _____ (think) New York was a beautiful, friendly city.

EXERCISE 7

Monique and Daniel are from France. Their vacation in New York was a nightmare. Fill in the blanks with the past tense of the verbs in parentheses.

1. On Sunday, November 4, Monique and Daniel's flight to New York was late, so they _____sat_____ (sit) in the airport in Paris for four hours.

2. The airline company _____ (lose) all their luggage, so on Monday they _____ (go) shopping for new clothes.

3. On Tuesday, they _____ (get) stuck in the subway when their train _____ (break) down.

4. On Wednesday, they _____ (pay) ninety dollars to rent a car, and _____ (drive) to the Aquarium.

5. They _____ (leave) the car on the street and _____ (get) a fifty-dollar parking ticket!

6. A thief _____ (throw) a rock through the car window and _____ (steal) Monique's camera.

7. On Thursday, they _____ (buy) a new camera downtown.

8. On Friday, they _____ (go) ice skating at Rockefeller Center. Monique had the new camera around her neck.

9. Monique _____ (fall) on the ice _____ (hurt) her knee.

10. She _____ (break) her new camera.

11. Monique was wet and frozen, so she _____ (catch) a cold.

12. On Saturday night, they _____ (eat) some unusual food in a restaurant.

13. On Sunday morning, they each _____ (wake) up and _____ (feel) sick.

14. Later that Sunday, they _____ (take) a taxi to the airport and finally _____ (leave) for home.

FOCUS 4

▶ Time Expressions in the Past

Time expressions tell us when the action occurred in the past.

yesterday	morning afternoon evening	night week last month year summer	an hour two days six months a year	ago	in 1988 on Sunday at 6:00 the day before yesterday

EXAMPLES	EXPLANATIONS
(a) **On Sunday,** they flew to New York. (b) Liisa and Kate went to Spain **two years ago.**	Time expressions can come at the beginning or at the end of a sentence.
(c) **Yesterday morning,** a VCR disappeared from the English Language Center.	Use a comma after the time expression if it is at the beginning of the sentence.

EXERCISE 8

On Tuesday, November 13, Monique and Daniel meet their friend Colette in Paris to talk about their trip. Complete the sentences with time expressions.

Colette: When did you get home?

Monique: 1. We left New York _____.

2. We got home _____ 8:00 yesterday morning.

Colette: So, how was your trip?

Daniel: Well, pretty bad.

3. _____ week was a week to remember!

4. Our plane arrived in New York four hours late _____ Sunday.

5. Today's Tuesday, right? Well, exactly a week _____ , we got stuck in the subway for two hours!

6. Then, _____ Wednesday, we rented a car and got a parking ticket.

7. What else? Oh, _____ Thursday, we bought a new camera and Monique broke it.

Monique: 8. So you see, we had bad luck every day _____ week.

9. We were happy to come home _____ .

10. Our trip to New York four years _____ was much better!

EXERCISE 9

Make true statements about yourself. Use each of the time expressions below.

▶ **EXAMPLE:** Six months ago

Six months ago, *I took a trip to Mexico.* _____ .

1. Two months ago, _____ .
2. In 1988, _____ .
3. Last year, _____ .
4. Last summer, _____ .
5. Two days ago, _____ .
6. On Sunday, _____ .
7. The day before yesterday, _____ .
8. Yesterday morning, _____ .
9. At six o'clock this morning, _____ .
10. An hour ago, _____ .

FOCUS **5**

Past Tense: Negative Statements

SUBJECT	DID + NOT/DIDN'T	BASE FORM OF VERB
I You He She It We You They	**did not** **didn't**	work.

EXERCISE 10

Make affirmative or negative statements aloud about the people in this unit.

▶ **EXAMPLE:**   the teacher/like Benny

The teacher liked Benny.

the teacher/get angry at Benny.

The teacher didn't get angry at Benny.

1. The other students/like Bookworm Benny
2. The teacher/trust Benny
3. The students/try to get Benny into trouble
4. The students' plan for Benny/succeed
5. Liisa and Kate/lose their luggage
6. Liisa's camera/break
7. Liisa and Kate/get stuck on the subway
8. Liisa and Kate/enjoy their vacation in New York
9. Harry/notice the grammar mistakes in his note
10. Ms. Ditto/sign the note
11. Harry/steal the VCR
12. The Director/believe Harry
13. Monique and Daniel/spend an evening at a jazz club
14. Monique and Daniel/visit the Statue of Liberty
15. Monique and Daniel/enjoy their vacation in New York

Past Tense: *Yes/No* Questions and Short Answers

Yes/No Questions

DID	SUBJECT	BASE FORM OF THE VERB	
Did	I you he she we you they	visit	New York last year?

Short Answers

AFFIRMATIVE			NEGATIVE		
Yes,	I you he she we you they	did.	No,	I you he she we you they	did not. didn't.

EXERCISE 11

Ask a partner *yes/no* questions about Ms. Ditto and the missing VCR.

▶ **EXAMPLES:** **Q:** understand the mystery

Did you understand the mystery?

A: Yes, I did.

1. like the Ms. Ditto story
2. enjoy being a detective
3. think Ms. Ditto took the VCR
4. guess that Harry was the thief
5. find the grammar mistakes in Harry's note
6. correct the mistakes in the note
7. feel sorry for Harry
8. want to give Harry any advice

EXERCISE 12

Look at the cartoon about Jinxed Jerry, a man with very bad luck. He left on a two-week Caribbean cruise last winter and there was a big storm at sea.

STEP 1   Ask a partner *yes/no* questions with the words below. The pictures can help you answer the questions.

▶ **EXAMPLE:**   Jerry/go on a cruise last winter

Did Jerry go on a cruise last winter?

Yes, he did.

1. Jerry's ship/get to the Caribbean
2. Jerry/know how to swim
3. Jerry/die
4. he/find an island
5. he/meet anyone on the island

6. the island/have stores
7. he/have enough food
8. he/write postcards home
9. he/make tools
10. he/build a good boat

STEP 2   Remember, Jerry has very bad luck. Ask each other *yes/no* questions and guess the end of the story.

11. Jerry's luck/change
12. a helicopter/find Jerry
13. Jerry/find his way back home

14. the story/have a happy ending
15. Jerry/ever take another cruise again

See the Appendix for the conclusion to Exercise 12 (page A-20).

▶ Past Tense: *Wh-* Questions

WH-WORD	DID	SUBJECT	BASE FORM OF VERB	ANSWERS
What		I	do last summer?	You went to Paris.
When		you	make plans?	(I made plans) last month.
Where		he	go last summer?	(He went) to Scotland.
Why		the ship	sink?	(It sank) because there was a storm.
How	did	she	get to Paris?	(She got there) by plane.
How long		they	stay in New York?	(They stayed there for) two weeks.
How long ago		you	visit Alaska?	(I visited Alaska) ten years ago.
Who(m)		Liisa and Kate	meet in New York?	(They met) a nice woman.

WH-WORD AS SUBJECT	PAST TENSE VERB	ANSWERS
What	happened to Jerry's ship?	It sank.
Who	had a terrible vacation?	Monique and Daniel (did).

EXERCISE 13

Write *wh*-questions about Jerry. Then ask your partner the questions. Your partner gives an answer or says "I don't know."

▶ **EXAMPLES:**   Jerry/eat on the island?

   Q: What <u>did Jerry eat on the island</u> ?

   A: <u>(He ate) fruit from the trees and fish from the sea</u> .

1. Jerry/want to go on vacation

   Q: Where _____ ?

   A: _____

2. Jerry/go on vacation

   Q: When _____?

   A: _____

3. Jerry/leave home

   Q: How long ago _____?

   A: _____

4. Jerry's ship/sink

   Q: Why _____?

   A: _____

5. Jerry/do after the ship sank

   Q: What _____?

   A: _____

6. Jerry/meet on the island

   Q: Who(m) _____?

   A: _____

7. Jerry/build the boat

   Q: How _____?

   A: _____

8. Jerry/put on the boat

   Q: What _____?

   A: _____

9. Jerry/feel when he finished the boat

   Q: How _____?

   A: _____

10. the story end (in your opinion)

   Q: How _____?

   A: _____

EXERCISE 14

Make questions that ask for the underlined information. Use *who, whom,* or *what.*

▷ **EXAMPLES:** **Q:** ___What did the students enjoy___ ?

  A: The students enjoyed Ms. Ditto's classes.

1. Q: _____ ?
  A: The students loved Ms. Ditto.

2. Q: _____ ?
  A: Ms. Ditto used a VCR in her classes.

3. Q: _____ ?
  A: Harry wanted to hurt Ms. Ditto.

4. Q: _____ ?
  A: Harry got hurt in the end.

5. Q: _____ ?
  A: Professor Brown found the note.

6. Q: _____ ?
  A: The Director fired Harry.

7. Q: _____ ?
  A: Harry stole the VCR.

8. Q: _____ ?
  A: The Director fired Harry.

9. Q: _____ ?
  A: The moral of the story was *"crime doesn't pay."*

EXERCISE 15

Information Gap. This is a true story about a very special woman named Doina. Work with a partner. You look at Text A, below. Your partner looks at Text B on page A-20. Take turns asking questions to get the information in the blanks.

▷ **EXAMPLE:** **Your Partner:** (Look at Text B) 1. Where did Doina grow up?

  You: (Look at Text A) 1. She grew up in Romania.

TEXT A:

1. Doina grew up in Romania.

2. She married _____ (who/m)

3. She had a daughter.

4. Doina was unhappy because she was against the government in Romania.

5. She thought of _____ (what) every day.

6. She taught her daughter how to swim.

7. On October 9, 1988, she and her daughter swam across the Danube River. They swam to _____ (where)

8. The police caught them.

9. Doina and her daughter went _____ (where)

10. They tried to escape several months later.

11. Finally, they left Romania _____ (how)

12. They flew to New York in 1989.

13. Doina went to school _____ (why)

14. She wrote the story of her escape from Romania in her ESL class.

EXERCISE 16

Correct the mistakes in the following sentences.

1. This morning, I waked up early.

2. I saw him yesterday night.

3. Harry didn't felt sad.

4. They don't met the Mayor of New York last week.

5. What Harry wanted?

6. Harry didn't noticed his mistakes.

7. Who did signed the note?

8. What did the Director?

9. What did happen to Harry?

10. Where Liisa and Kate went on vacation?

11. Who did go with Lisa to New York?

12. How Jerry built a boat?

13. They no had dinner in a Greek restaurant.

14. Whom did trust the teacher in the Bookworm Benny story?

15. The ship sank before a long time.

Use Your English

ACTIVITY 1: SPEAKING

STEP 1 Get into groups. One person in the group thinks of a famous person from the past.

STEP 2 The others in the group can ask up to twenty *yes/no* questions to guess who the person is. After twenty questions the group loses if they haven't guessed.

▶ **EXAMPLES:** Did this person sing?

Did this person live in North America?

Was this person a woman?

ACTIVITY 2: WRITING/SPEAKING

Write your own ending for the story about Jinxed Jerry. Compare your ending with your classmates'. Who has the best ending? When you are finished, look at the cartoons that tell the end of Jerry's story on page A-20. Discuss how your ending compares with the ending in the cartoon.

ACTIVITY 3: SPEAKING

Who is telling the truth?

STEP 1 Work in groups of three. Each person tells a true personal story. The group chooses one story. Then each of you must learn as much as you can about that story.

STEP 2 Each person tells the same beginning to the class. Your classmates ask each of you questions to find out who is telling the truth. Your job is to make the class believe this is your story. (See Example on next page.)

▶ **EXAMPLE:** **Student 1 says:** When I was ten years old, I went on a long trip.

Student 2 says: When I was ten years old, I went on a long trip.

Student 3 says: When I was ten years old, I went on a long trip.

The Class asks each person questions: Student #1, where did you go?

Who(m) did you go with? etc.

A C T I V I T Y   4 :   S P E A K I N G

Interview a partner about a past vacation. Ask as many *wh*-questions as you can. Report back to the class about your partner's trip.

▶ **EXAMPLE:** Where did you go?   How long did you stay?

When did you go?   With whom did you go?

How did you get there?   Why did you go there?

What did you do there?

A C T I V I T Y   5 :   L I S T E N I N G / S P E A K I N G

STEP 1 Listen to the three students talking about their vacations. Match the students to the titles of the essays they wrote about their vacations.

Names	**Essay Titles**
Pedro	A Great Vacation
Hakim	My Terrible Trip
Angela	A Boring Vacation

STEP 2 In a group discuss why each vacation was good or bad. What is your opinion of each vacation?

ACTIVITY 6: SPEAKING

Jeopardy Game. Your teacher will choose one student to be the host. Only the host can look at the complete game board (page A-21). The rest of the class will be divided into two teams. Team 1 chooses a category and an amount of money from the blank game board below. The host reads the answer. Team 1 has one minute to ask a correct question. If Team 1 can't, Team 2 gets a chance to ask a question. There may be more than one correct question for each answer. The team with the most money wins.

▶ **EXAMPLE:**   **Team 1 chooses:** People for $10.

   Host reads: Ms. Ditto

   Team 1 asks: Who lost her job?

   Who(m) did Harry hate?

GAME BOARD

$$$	Category 1 PEOPLE	Category 2 WH-QUESTIONS	Category 3 YES/NO QUESTIONS
$10 $20 $30 $40 $50			

ACTIVITY 7: WRITING/SPEAKING

The stories in this unit are about unfair or unlucky things that happen to people. Think about a time when something unfair or unlucky happened to you. Write your story and tell the class what happened. Your classmates can ask you questions.

REFLEXIVE PRONOUNS, RECIPROCAL PRONOUN:

Each Other

UNIT GOALS:

- To use reflexive pronouns correctly
- To know which verbs are commonly used with reflexive pronouns
- To know how to use *each other*

▶ OPENING TASK
Advice Columns

STEP 1 Read the letters to "Dear Darcy" in Part A. Match each one to a "Letter of Advice" in Part B. Fill in the name of the person who wrote each letter in the blanks in Part B.

PART A

Dear Darcy,

I'm married and have two children. I'm trying to be a super-woman. I work outside the home. I also do all of the housework, shopping, and the cleaning. I help my children with their school work. I never have time for myself. I am tired and unhappy. Please help!

—*Supermom in Seattle*

Dear Darcy,

My wife and I never go out anymore. We have a new baby, and my wife doesn't want to get a babysitter. I need a social life. I'm starting to talk to myself! Can you help me?

—*Bored in Boston*

Dear Darcy,

My mom and dad got divorced last month. They fought with each other a lot, and finally, my dad moved out. Maybe I wasn't a good daughter to them. Maybe the break-up was my fault. I can't forgive myself.

—*Guilty in Gainesville*

Part B

A. Dear _____ ,
Don't blame yourself. You did not cause these problems. Your parents need to learn to talk to each other.

B. Dear _____ ,
You need to explain how you feel to her. Tell her you want to go out once a week. Life is short. Find a babysitter. Go out and enjoy yourselves!

C. Dear _____ ,
You need to make time for yourself. Go out with your friends. Do yourself a favor and join a gym. Take care of yourself too. Buy yourself something special.

STEP 2 Now read the last letter from *Lonely in Los Angeles*. Read Darcy's response and circle the correct pronouns.

Dear Darcy:

I'm a rather shy and lonely high school student. I'm doing well in school, but I don't have many friends. The girls in my class always call each other, but they never call me. I don't go out. I don't enjoy myself. I don't even like myself very much anymore.

—*Lonely in Los Angeles*

Dear Lonely in Los Angeles:

Remember, the teenage years are difficult. At 16, many girls don't like (1) (they/them/themselves). You're doing well in school. Be proud of (2) (you/yourself). Try to like (3) (you/yourself) first. Then others will like (4) (you/yourself). Teenage girls need (5) (each other/themselves). Force (6) (you/yourself) to open up to other girls. Relax and try to enjoy (7) (you/yourself).

—*Darcy*

▶ Reflexive Pronouns

Use a reflexive pronoun when the subject and object are the same.

▶ **EXAMPLE:** Sara bought **herself** a new car.

   NOT: Sara bought Sara a new car.

EXAMPLES	REFLEXIVE PRONOUNS
(a) I bought **myself** a new car.	*myself*
(b) Look at **yourself** in the mirror.	*yourself*
(c) He doesn't take care of **himself.**	*himself*
(d) She blames **herself** for the accident.	*herself*
(e) A cat licks **itself** to keep clean.	*itself*
(f) We enjoyed **ourselves** at the theater.	*ourselves*
(g) Help **yourselves** to some food.	*yourselves*
(h) Babies can't feed **themselves.**	*themselves*

EXERCISE 1

Go back to Step 1 in the Opening Task on page 312. Underline all the reflexive pronouns and the subjects.

▶ **EXAMPLE:** <u>I</u> never have time for <u>myself</u>.

EXERCISE 2

Fill in each blank with a reflexive pronoun.

▶ **EXAMPLE:** I lost my wallet yesterday, and I wanted to kick _____myself_____ .

  1. Mary: Do you sometimes talk to _____ ?
     Bill: Well, sometimes, when I'm alone.

  2. Monica: Thanks for such a lovely evening. We really enjoyed (a)
     _____ .

     Gloria: Well, thanks for coming. And the children were just wonderful. They really behaved (b) _____ all evening. I hope you can come back soon.

  3. Jane: I can't believe my bird flew out the window! It's my fault. I forgot to close the birdcage.
     Margaret: Don't blame _____ . He's probably happier now. He's free!

4. **Cynthia:** What's the matter with Bobby's leg?
   Enrique: He hurt _____ at the soccer game last night.

5. **Jason:** My girlfriend Judy really knows how to take care of _____ . She eats well, exercises regularly, and gets plenty of sleep.

6. **Sylvia:** Hello Carol, hello Eugene. Come on in. Make (a) _____ at home. Help (b) _____ to some drinks.

7. **Mother:** Be careful! That pot on the stove is very hot. Don't burn _____ .

FOCUS **2**

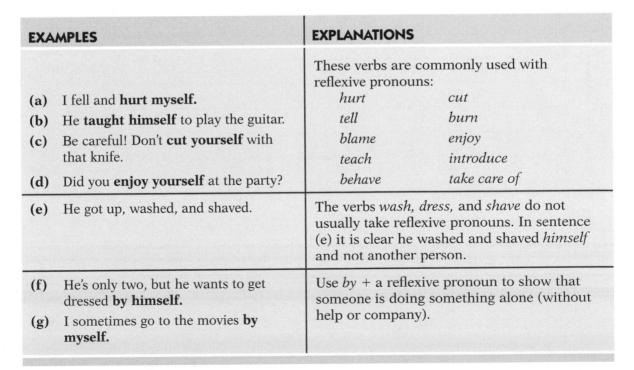

▶ **Verbs Commonly Used with Reflexive Pronouns/ *By* + Reflexive Pronoun**

EXAMPLES	EXPLANATIONS
(a) I fell and **hurt myself.** (b) He **taught himself** to play the guitar. (c) Be careful! Don't **cut yourself** with that knife. (d) Did you **enjoy yourself** at the party?	These verbs are commonly used with reflexive pronouns: *hurt* *cut* *tell* *burn* *blame* *enjoy* *teach* *introduce* *behave* *take care of*
(e) He got up, washed, and shaved.	The verbs *wash, dress,* and *shave* do not usually take reflexive pronouns. In sentence (e) it is clear he washed and shaved *himself* and not another person.
(f) He's only two, but he wants to get dressed **by himself.** (g) I sometimes go to the movies **by myself.**	Use *by* + a reflexive pronoun to show that someone is doing something alone (without help or company).

EXERCISE 3

Write a sentence describing the action in each picture.

▶ **EXAMPLES:** The woman is introducing herself to the man .

The woman introduced herself to the man .

1.

2.

3.

4.

5.

6.

7.

8.

cut	dry	enjoy	look at/admire
clean/lick	hurt	talk to	weigh

1. _____

2. _____

3. _____

4. _____

5. _____

6. _____

7. _____

8. _____

▶ **Reciprocal Pronoun:**
Each Other

The reciprocal pronoun *each other* is different in meaning from a reflexive pronoun.

(a) John and Ann blamed **themselves** for the accident.

(b) John and Ann blamed **each other** for the accident.

EXERCISE 4

Work with a partner. Draw pictures to show the differences in meaning between the following sentences.

1. (a) The weather was very hot. The runners poured water on themselves after the race.

    (b) The weather was very hot. The runners poured water on each other after the race.

2. (a) They love themselves.

    (b) They love each other.

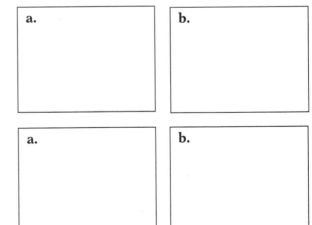

a.

b.

a.

b.

EXERCISE 5

Act out the following sentences to show the difference between *each other* and reflexive pronouns.

1. You and your classmate are looking at yourselves in the mirror.
2. You and your classmate are looking at each other.
3. You and your classmate are talking to yourselves.
4. You and your classmate are talking to each other.
5. You're playing ball with a friend, and you break a neighbor's window. Blame yourself for the accident.
6. You're playing ball with a friend, and you break a neighbor's window. Blame each other for the accident.
7. You introduce yourself to your partner.
8. You and your partner introduce each other to another person.

EXERCISE 6

Choose a reflexive pronoun or each other to complete the statements.

1. An egotistical person loves __himself/herself__ .
2. Divorced people can be friends if they forgive _____ .
3. Good friends protect _____ .
4. Close friends tell _____ their secrets.
5. A self-confident person believes in _____ .
6. In a good relationship, the two people trust _____ .
7. A realistic person doesn't lie to _____ .
8. Independent people take care of _____ .
9. Caring people help _____ .
10. Angry people say things to hurt _____ .
11. Young children can't always control _____ .
12. An insecure person doesn't have confidence in _____ .

EXERCISE 7

Circle the correct word in the "Dear Darcy" letters below.

▶ **EXAMPLE:** ((He,) Him, Himself) cares about (I, (me,) myself).

Dear Darcy,

(1) (I, My, Mine) boyfriend loves himself. (2) (He, His, Him) is very pleased with (3) (he, him, himself). He always looks at (4) (he, him, himself) in store windows when he passes by. (5) (Himself, He, Him) only thinks about (6) (his, himself, him). He never brings (7) (my, me, myself) flowers. The last time he told (8) (my, me, myself) that he loved me was two years ago. He's also very selfish with (9) (he, his, him) things. For example, he never lends me (10) (him, himself, his) car. He says that the car is (11) (himself, him, his), and he doesn't want me to use it. Do (12) (yourself, your, you) have any advice for me?

—"Unhappy"

Dear Unhappy:

(13) (You, Your, Yourself) boyfriend certainly is very selfish. (14) (You, Your, Yourself) can't really change (15) (he, himself, him). Get rid of (16) (he, himself, him)! Find (17) (you, yourself, yours) a new guy!

—Darcy

EXERCISE 8

Correct the mistakes in the following sentences.

1. I hurt me.
2. They're looking at theirselves in the mirror.
3. I shave myself every morning.
4. I have a friend in Poland. We write to ourselves every month.
5. We enjoyed at the circus.
6. Larry blamed Harry for the accident. Harry blamed Larry for the accident. They blamed themselves for the accident.
7. He did it hisself.

Use Your English

ACTIVITY 1: SPEAKING

Read the following riddle and try to find the answer. Discuss it with a partner.

A prison guard found a prisoner hanging from a rope in his prison cell. Did he hang himself or did someone murder him? There was nothing else in the prison cell but a puddle of water on the floor.

ACTIVITY 2: WRITING/SPEAKING

Who is the most independent person in your class?

Make up a survey with ten questions. Then go around to all the students in your class and ask your questions. Tell the class who the independent people are.

▶ **EXAMPLES:** Do you like to do things by yourself?

Do you usually travel by yourself?

Do you ever go to the movies by yourself?

ACTIVITY 3: SPEAKING

Interview another classmate, using the questions below.

1. Do you believe in yourself?
2. When you go shopping for clothes, do you like to look at yourself in the mirror?
3. Do you ever compare yourself to other people?
4. Do you ever buy yourself a present?
5. In a new relationship, do you talk about yourself or try to learn about the other person?
6. Do you ever talk to yourself?
7. Do you cook for yourself?
8. Do you blame yourself for your problems or do you blame others?
9. Do you take care of yourself? (Do you eat well? Do you get enough sleep?)
10. Do you ever get angry at yourself?

Add questions of your own.

ACTIVITY 4: LISTENING/ SPEAKING

Listen to the people talk about their problems.

STEP 1 Match the problems to the people.

Person #1 _____   (a) Serious

Person #2 _____   (b) Lonely

Person #3 _____   (c) Unhealthy

STEP 2 What advice can you give to each of these people? Tell your classmates.

ACTIVITY 5: WRITING

STEP 1 Write a letter to Dear Darcy about a problem you have.

STEP 2 Work with a partner. Exchange your letters and write a response to the problem.

U NIT 20

F UTURE TIME

Will **and** *Be Going To, May* **and** *Might*

UNIT GOALS:

- To talk about future time using *will, be going to, may,* and *might*
- To understand the meaning and position of future time expressions
- To choose between *will* and *be going* to when
  -talking about future intentions or plans
  -making predictions

What is Wanda the Fortune Teller saying about each person? Match the phrases to the correct person (or people). Then, make a statement about each person's future.

1. The bald man . . .   2. The homeless man . . .   3. The athlete . . .

4. The young boy . . .   5. The elderly couple . . .   6. The scientist . . .

7. The lifeguard . . .   8. The chef . . .   9. The movie director . . .

10. The writers . . .

a. ____ inherit one million dollars from an uncle

b. ____ win an Olympic gold medal

c. ____ have ten grandchildren

d. ____ open his own restaurant

e. ____ be very successful authors

f. ____ produce a new movie and win an Oscar

g. ____ find a cure for AIDS

h. ____ save someone's life

i. ____ grow hair on his head

j. ____ become a famous rock star

▶ **T**alking about Future Time

Use *will* and *be going to* to make predictions about the future or to say what you think will happen in the future.

EXAMPLES	EXPLANATIONS
(a) One day, he *will* be rich.	Use *will* for a prediction (what we think will happen).
(b) Look at those big black clouds. It **is going to** rain. **(c)** **NOT:** It will rain.	Use *be going to* for a prediction based on the present situation (what we can see is going to happen).
(d) Teacher to student: Your parents **will** be very upset about this.	*Will* is more formal.
(e) Father to daughter: Your mother**'s going to** be very angry about this.	*Be going to* is less formal.

EXERCISE 1
Match the sentences to the pictures.

 a.

 b.

 c.

 d.

 e.

 f.

g.

1. ____ Look at that waiter! He's going to fall!

2. ____ This marriage isn't going to last.

3. ____ You will find gold on the streets of America!

4. ____ She's going to get a headache.

5. ____ I will always love you.

6. ____ You will grow up and be famous.

7. ____ Be careful, Julian. You're going to fall!

▶ *Will*

AFFIRMATIVE STATEMENTS		NEGATIVE STATEMENTS	
I You He She It We You They	**will arrive** next week. **'ll arrive** next week.	I You He She It We You They	**will not arrive** next week. **won't arrive** next week.
There	**will be** peace in the world. **'ll be**	There **will not be** any wars. **won't be**	
Men **will be able** to stay home with their children.		Men **will not be able to** have children. **won't**	

YES/NO QUESTIONS			SHORT ANSWERS					
Will	I you he she it we you they	arrive next week?	Yes,	you I he she it we you they	**will**.	No,	you I he she it we you they	**won't**.

WH-QUESTIONS	ANSWERS
(a) **When will** the scientists discover a cure?	(They **will discover** a cure) in ten years.
(b) **Where will** the couple go on their honeymoon?	(They **will go**) to Hawaii.
(c) **What will** the homeless man do with the money?	He**'ll buy** a new house.
(d) **How will** the couple travel?	(They**'ll travel**) by plane.
(e) **How** long **will** they be on the plane?	(They**'ll be** on the plane) for five hours.
(f) **Who will** get an Olympic medal?	The athlete.
(g) **Who(m) will** the lifeguard save?	(He**'ll save**) a lucky person.

EXERCISE 2

Think about the people in the Opening Task on page 323. Make a second prediction for each.

▶ **EXAMPLE:** The scientist *will win a Nobel prize.*

1. The bald man . . .
2. The athlete . . .
3. The teenager . . .
4. The movie director . . .
5. The lifeguard . . .
6. The chef . . .
7. The homeless man . . .
8. The authors . . .
9. The elderly couple . . .

EXERCISE 3

How will our lives be different in fifty years? Make predictions with *will* or *won't*. Discuss your predictions with a partner.

1. The climate _____ change.
2. People _____ take vacations on the moon.
3. Couples _____ choose the sex of their babies.
4. All countries _____ share the world's money equally.

5. Most people _____ move back to the countryside.
6. The traditional family with a husband, wife, and two children _____ disappear.
7. Men and women _____ continue to marry.
8. All people of different races _____ learn to live together peacefully.
9. People _____ speak the same language.
10. Crime _____ stop.
11. People _____ drive electric cars.
12. We _____ discover life on other planets.
13. Science _____ continue to be very important.
14. People _____ live to be 130 years old.
15. A woman _____ be President of the United States.

EXERCISE 4

Think about the year 2025. Where will you be? What will you be able to do? Write *yes/no* questions with *will*. Interview your classmates and report their answers to the class.

	Classmate 1	**Classmate 2**
1. be in the United States **Will you be in the United States?**	_____	_____
2. speak English fluently	_____	_____
3. be back in your home country	_____	_____
4. have a good job	_____	_____
5. earn a living	_____	_____
6. have a big family	_____	_____
7. have a nice house	_____	_____
8. be content	_____	_____
9. want something different	_____	_____

Add two questions of your own.

| 10. _____ | _____ | _____ |
| 11. _____ | _____ | _____ |

EXERCISE 5

Work with a partner. You are Janice Williams and your partner is Wanda the Fortune Teller. Ask your partner *yes/no* and *wh*-questions with *will* and *will be able to*. Your partner looks into the crystal ball to answer your questions.

▶ **EXAMPLE:**   **You:** Will my husband lose his job?

   Your Partner: Yes, he will.

Wanda's Crystal Ball

Husband will find another job in 3 months

Daughter will get married to a computer specialist

Husband will lose job

Will have 5 grandchildren

You and your husband will retire to Tahiti!

Son will drop out of high school and get a job

Janice's Questions

1. my husband/lose his job?
2. my husband/be able to find another job?
3. when/my husband/find another job?
4. my daughter/get married?
5. who(m)/she/marry?
6. I/have grandchildren?
7. how many grandchildren/I/have?
8. my son/go to college?
9. what/he/do?
10. my husband and I/be able to retire?
11. where/we/retire?

▶ *Be Going To*

AFFIRMATIVE STATEMENTS			NEGATIVE STATEMENTS		
I	am 'm		I	am not 'm not	
You	are 're		You	are not aren't	
He She It	is 's	**going to** leave.	He She It	is not isn't	**going to** leave.
We You They	are 're		We You They	are not aren't	

YES/NO QUESTIONS			SHORT ANSWERS					
Am	I		Yes,	you	**are**.	No,	you	**aren't**.
Are	you			I am.			I'm	**not**.
Is	he she it	**going to** leave?		he she it	**is**.		he she it	**isn't**.
Are	we you they			we you they	**are**.		we you they	**aren't**.

WH-QUESTIONS			ANSWERS	
When		leave?		leave in two weeks.
Where		go?		go to Colorado.
What	**are you going to**	do there?	**I'm going to**	go skiing.
How		get there?		go by car.
How long		stay?		stay for one week.
Who(m)		visit?		visit my cousin.
Who**'s**	**going to**	drive?	My friend (is **going to** drive).	

Remember: *Going to* is often pronounced "gonna" when we speak. We do not usually write "gonna."

EXERCISE 6

Look at the pictures. Then fill in the blanks with the affirmative or negative form of *be going to*.

1. "Watch out! That bag _____ fall!"

2. "Hurry up! We _____ miss the bus."

3.

"This _____ hurt you one bit."

4.

"I am so tired! I _____ take a nap."

5.

"Hello, dear. I _____ be home on time tonight."

6.

George: What are you _____ have, Fred?

Fred: I _____ have a pizza, as usual.

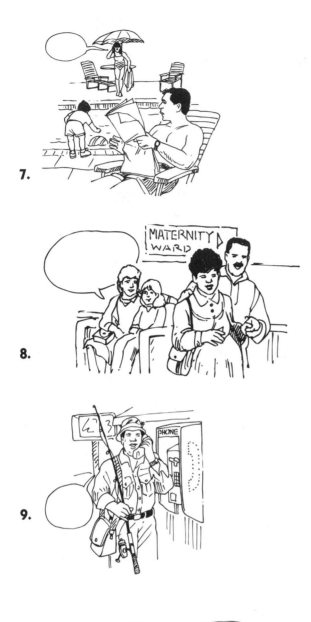

7.

"Watch her, Jack! She _____ fall into the pool!"

8.

"They _____ have a baby today."

9.

"Hello, boss. I'm sorry, I _____ be able to come in today. I have a terrible backache and I can't get out of bed."

10.

Ben: I have a test tomorrow. I _____ study.

Roommate: I have a test tomorrow too, but I _____ study. I _____ watch the game on TV!

EXERCISE 7

Read the answers. Write a *yes/no* or *wh-* question with *be going to*.

▶ **EXAMPLE:** **Richard:** My doctor says I need to leave my job and get away somewhere.

Robert: _Where are you going to go?_ ?

Richard: To California.

Robert: (1) _____ ?
Richard: I don't know (what I'm going to do there).

Robert: (2) _____ ?
Richard: (I'm going to stay) with some old friends.

Robert: (3) _____ ?
Richard: For about a month.

Robert: (4) _____ ?
Richard: By plane.

Robert: (5) _____ ?
Richard: I don't know (if I'm going to come back to my job).

EXERCISE 8

Use your imagination to answer these questions about the people in the Opening Task on page 323. Use *be going to* in writing your answers. Compare your answers with your classmates'.

▶ **EXAMPLE:** What is going to happen to the elderly people?

They're going to live to a ripe old age.

1. What is the poor person going to do with the million dollars?
2. Who is the lifeguard going to save?
3. What kind of movie is the director going to make?
4. What kind of food is the chef going to serve in his restaurant?
5. How are the authors going to celebrate their success?
6. What is the athlete going to do after the Olympics?
7. What kind of life is the rock star going to have?

► **T**ime Expressions in the Future

EXAMPLES	EXPLANATIONS
(a) I'm going to visit you **tomorrow evening.** **(b)** **A month from now,** Wanda will be on a tropical island.	Future time expressions can come at the beginning or at the end of the sentence. Put a comma (,) after the time expression when it is at the beginning of the sentence.

Future Time Expressions

(Later) this	morning afternoon evening	next	week month year Sunday weekend	tomorrow	morning afternoon evening night	soon later the day after tomorrow a week from today tonight

EXAMPLES		EXPLANATIONS
I'll see you	**(c)** **in** fifteen minutes. general two weeks. March. 2015. **(d)** **on** Tuesday. May 21st. **(e)** **at** 4:00. midnight. specific	We also use prepositional phrases of time to talk about future time.
(f) We are going to go to the Bahamas **for** three weeks.		*For* shows how long the action will last.
(g) I'll be there **until** 3:00 (At 3:00, I will leave. I will not be there after 3:00.) **(h)** I won't be there **until** Monday. (Before Monday, I won't be there. After Monday, I'll be there.)		*Until* shows the specific time in the future when the action will change.

EXERCISE 9

Make statements about yourself. Use *be going to*.

▶ **EXAMPLE:** <u>In a few days, I'm going to move out of my apartment.</u>

1. In a few days, _____ .

2. Next summer, _____ .

3. The day after tomorrow, _____ .

4. This evening, _____ .

5. Tomorrow night, _____ .

6. This weekend, _____ .

7. At 9:00, _____ .

8. In December, _____ .

9. On Wednesday night, _____ .

10. On New Year's Eve, _____ .

EXERCISE 10

Anthony and Sally are planning a vacation in Europe. They are going to visit four countries in seven days. Sally is telling Anthony about their travel plans. Fill in the blanks with *in, on, at, for,* or *until*.

1. We are going to arrive in London (a) __at__ 6:00 P.M.
    (b) __on__ Sunday.

2. We'll stay in London _____ two days.

3. Then, we'll fly to Paris _____ Tuesday morning.

4. We'll stay in Paris _____ Wednesday afternoon.

5. Then, we'll fly to Rome _____ the evening.

6. We won't leave Rome _____ Friday morning.

7. _____ 10:00 A.M. on Friday morning, we'll fly to our final destination, Athens, Greece.

8. We'll stay in Greece _____ two days.

9. We'll return home _____ Sunday. Then, we'll need a vacation!

EXERCISE 11

Look at Wanda's calendar. Imagine it is now 2 P.M. on Wednesday, April 10. Read the sentences about Wanda's plans and fill in the blanks on the next page with a time expression or a preposition of time. There may be more than one correct answer.

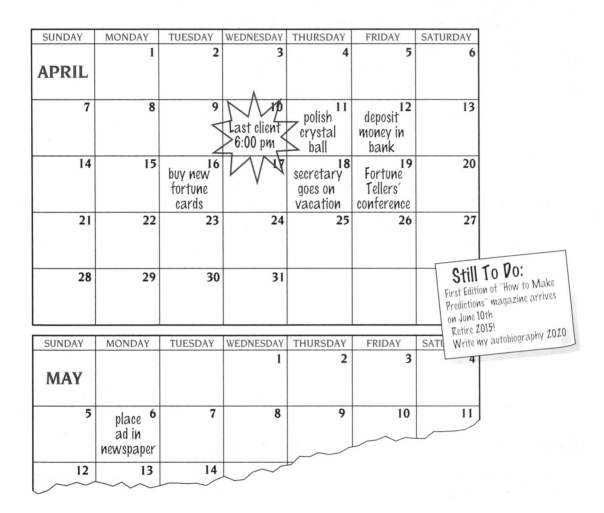

1. Wanda is going to see her last client <u>at 6:00 this evening/in</u> <u>four hours</u>.

2. She's going to attend the Fortune Tellers' Conference _____ _____.

3. She's going to polish her crystal ball _____.

4. She's going to deposit all her money in the bank _____ _____.

5. Her secretary is going to go on vacation _____.

6. She is going to buy new fortune cards _____.

7. She's going to put an advertisement about herself in the newspaper _____.

8. She will read her first *How To Make Predictions* magazine _____.

9. She will retire to a tropical island _____.

10. She will write a book called *How to Be a Successful Fortune Teller in 10 Easy Lessons* _____.

▶ **Talking about Future Intentions or Plans**

EXAMPLES	EXPLANATIONS
(a) **A:** The phone is ringing. **B:** O.K. I**'ll get** it.	Use *will* when you decide to do something **at** the time of speaking.
(b) Mother: Where are you going? Daughter: I**'m going to** take a drive with Richard tonight. Remember, Mom? You said it was okay . . . Mother: I did?	Use *be going to* when you made a plan to do something **before** the time of speaking.

EXERCISE 12

Work with a partner. You read the first five statements in Column A aloud. Your partner chooses an answer from Column B. After the first five, your partner reads from Column A and you choose the answer from Column B.

▶ **EXAMPLE:**   Do you have any plans for tonight?

A. Yes, we will go to the theater.

(B.) Yes, we're going to the theater.

Column A

1. Christine called. She's coming over for dinner.

2. What are you doing with that camera?

3. Do you need a ride home today?

4. We don't have a thing to eat in the house.

5. Help! The car died again.

6. Why are you meeting Jenny in the library tonight?

7. Look, those thieves are robbing the bank!

8. Mom, can you brush my hair?

9. Are you off the phone yet?

10. Why did Maria cancel her date for Saturday night?

Column B

A. Great! I'll cook.
B. Great! I'm going to cook.

A. I'll take your picture.
B. I'm going to take your picture.

A. No, thanks. Jason will take me home.
B. No, thanks. Jason's going to take me home.

A. I'll call up and order a pizza.
B. I'm going to call up and order a pizza.

A. Calm down. I'll be right there.
B. Calm down. I'm going to be right there.

A. She'll help me with my homework.
B. She's going to help me with my homework.

A. I'll call the police.
B. I'm going to call the police.

A. I'll do it in a minute, sweetie.
B. I'm going to do it in a minute, sweetie.

A. I'll be off in a minute!
B. I'm going to be off in a minute!

A. Her parents will take her away for the weekend.
B. Her parents are going to take her away for the weekend.

▶ *May* and *Might*

Use *may* or *might* to say something is possible in the future.

EXAMPLES	EXPLANATIONS
(a) I **will go** to Mexico next year.	**(a)** Shows certainty. The speaker is 100% sure.
(b) I **may/might go** to Mexico next year.	**(b)** Shows possibility. The speaker is 50% sure.

AFFIRMATIVE STATEMENTS			NEGATIVE STATEMENTS		
I You He She We You They	**may** **might**	study abroad next year. be able to stay abroad for two years.	I You He She We You They	**may not** **might not**	take a vacation be able to stay for two years.
It		rain later.	It		rain later.
There		be cheap flights to Mexico.	There		be any discounts on flights.

NOTE:
• There are no contractions for *may* or *might*.

EXERCISE 13

Fill in the blanks with *may* or *might* in the affirmative or negative.

▶ **EXAMPLE:** **Peter:** How are you going to go to Boston next weekend?

Al: I <u>may</u> drive or I <u>may</u> take the train. I won't fly because it's expensive.

1. **Joanne:** Is Ilene going to come to your New Year's Eve party?

   Paula: She (a) _____ be able to come. She went out of town on business and she (b) _____ be back in time for the party.

2. **Tamara:** Where are you and Jeff going to go on vacation this summer?

   Susan: Jeff (a) _____ start a new job in July, so we (b) _____ be able to go on vacation. We (c) _____ stay home and go to the beach.

3. **Eugene:** What's Jason going to major in at the university?

   Carol: Well, he really loves the ocean, so he (a) _____ major in marine biology, or he (b) _____ major in environmental science.

4. **Priscilla:** Will you go back to your country after you finish college here?

   Arnaldo: I don't know. I (a) _____ want to go back to visit my family, but I (b) _____ want to go back to live. There (c) _____ be more job opportunities for me here in the United States.

EXERCISE 14

What are your plans for the future? Complete your chart with a base verb.
Exchange charts with your partner. Report your partner's plans to the class.

▶ **EXAMPLES:** He**'s going to/might/may/will go to** see a movie this evening.

He **may/might** study at home this weekend.

	Base Verb	Will/Be Going to	May/Might
1. This evening,	see a movie	x	
2. This weekend,	study at home		x
3. Tomorrow night,			
4. A week from today,			
5. In 3 months,			
6. Next summer,			
7. In 5 years,			

EXERCISE 15

What is our future in the computer age? Make statements with affirmative or
negative forms of *will, be going to, may,* or *might.*

▶ **EXAMPLE:** Computers/always be part of our lives

Computers will always be part of our lives.

1. People/want to go back to a time before computers
2. The number of computers in the world/increase
3. We/all have pocket computers
4. The Internet/connect people in every home all over the world
5. Students in classrooms all around the world/be able to "talk" to each
   other
6. People/learn languages easily with computers
7. People/prefer to communicate by computer
8. Books/disappear completely
9. People who cannot use computers/be able to find jobs
10. Computers/take away our privacy.

Use Your English

ACTIVITY 1: WRITING/SPEAKING

What do you think the world will be like in 2050? Think about changes in travel, the home, food, technology, and people, etc. With your group, write down ten changes. Discuss your group's ideas with the rest of the class.

ACTIVITY 2: SPEAKING

Imagine that you and your partner win $10,000 in the lottery. You have one day to spend it. What are you going to do together? Give details of your activities. For example, if you rent a car, say what kind of car you are going to rent (a sports car, a limousine, a jeep?). Share your plans with the class. Decide which pair has the most interesting plans.

ACTIVITY 3: SPEAKING

Make a weekly calendar and fill in your schedule for next week. Write different activities for each day. Try to make a date to do something with your partner in the future.

▶ **EXAMPLES:**   What are you going to do on Sunday?

I'm going to go jogging along River Walk.

ACTIVITY 4: LISTENING/SPEAKING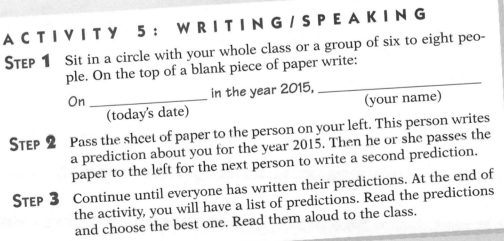

You are a group of tourists going to Europe. You are at the airport and the tour guide is giving you some information.

STEP 1 Listen to the tour guide, and complete the travel plan below.

Day	Place	Number of Days/Nights
Sunday	Paris	
		3 nights
	Milan	
Saturday		
	Vienna	
Thursday		
Saturday		

STEP 2 Compare your plan with a partner's.

STEP 3 Tell the class your travel plans, real or imaginary. Say when you are going to go, how you are going to go there, where you are going to stay, etc.

▶ **EXAMPLE:** In June, I'm going to go to Vancouver. I'm going to fly there. I'm going to visit my uncle.

ACTIVITY 5: WRITING/SPEAKING

STEP 1 Sit in a circle with your whole class or a group of six to eight people. On the top of a blank piece of paper write:

On _____ in the year 2015, _____
       (today's date)   (your name)

STEP 2 Pass the sheet of paper to the person on your left. This person writes a prediction about you for the year 2015. Then he or she passes the paper to the left for the next person to write a second prediction.

STEP 3 Continue until everyone has written their predictions. At the end of the activity, you will have a list of predictions. Read the predictions and choose the best one. Read them aloud to the class.

U N I T 21

PHRASAL VERBS

UNIT GOALS:

- To understand the meaning of common phrasal verbs
- To use separable and inseparable phrasal verbs
- To know how to use direct objects with phrasal verbs
- To learn phrasal verbs that do not take objects

▶ OPENING TASK
Nervous Nelly Gives a Lecture

Nelly is nervous about the lecture she is going to give.

STEP 1 Look at the pictures and describe the steps in Nelly's lecture.

STEP 2 Nelly has index cards to help her remember what to do. Complete each index card with appropriate expressions from the box. Then read each card aloud.

sit down	calm down	take out
call up	call on	stand up
put on		slow down

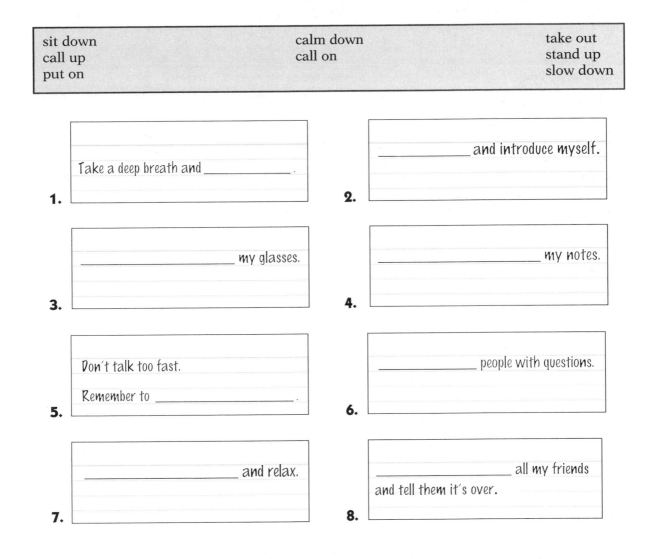

1. Take a deep breath and _____.

2. _____ and introduce myself.

3. _____ my glasses.

4. _____ my notes.

5. Don't talk too fast.
   Remember to _____.

6. _____ people with questions.

7. _____ and relax.

8. _____ all my friends and tell them it's over.

► **Phrasal Verbs**

EXAMPLES	EXPLANATIONS

(a) **Turn on** the lights.	A phrasal verb is:
	     a verb + a particle
	     turn + on
	     sit + down
	     stand + up

(b) Plants grow. (grow = to increase in size) Children **grow up.** (grow up = to become an adult)	The verb + particle together have a specific meaning

EXERCISE 1

Look at Nelly's index cards from the Opening Task on page 345 and circle all the phrasal verbs.

1. Take a deep breath and calm down.
2. Stand up and introduce myself.
3. Put on my glasses.
4. Take out my notes.
5. Don't talk too fast. Remember to slow down.
6. Call on people with questions.
7. Sit down and relax.
8. Call up all my friends and tell them it's over!

EXERCISE 2

Read each statement on the left to your partner. Your partner chooses a response from the right.

Statement

1. I don't want to cook tonight.
2. It's hot in here.
3. It's so quiet in here.
4. I can't read the map. The print's too small.
5. I can't do my homework with the TV on.
6. I'm bored.
7. My feet hurt.
8. I'm sleepy.
9. I'm really upset about our argument today.
10. I'm tired of sitting on this plane.

Response

a. Calm down.
b. Call up a friend.
c. Stand up for a few minutes.
d. Sit down for a while.
e. Lie down and take a nap.
f. Take off your jacket.
g. Put on your glasses.
h. Turn off the TV.
i. Let's eat out.
j. Turn on the radio.

▶ **Phrasal Verbs**

EXAMPLES	EXPLANATIONS
(a) I **hung up** the picture.	Sometimes the meaning of a phrasal verb is clear from the verb + particle combination.
(b) I **ran into** Joe on the street the other day.	Sometimes it is difficult to guess the meaning of a phrasal verb. The meaning of *ran into* is not the combination of *ran* and *into*. *Run into* means "to meet someone by chance."
	In informal English, phrasal verbs are more frequent than one-word verbs with the same meaning.
(c) Please **put out** your cigarette, Jake.	In (c), you are talking to a friend.
(d) Please **extinguish** your cigarettes, ladies and gentlemen.	In (d), an announcer is speaking to passengers at a train station.

EXERCISE 3

Circle the phrasal verbs. Then match each phrasal verb with a one-word verb.

Sentences with phrasal verbs

One-word verb with same meaning

1. I called 911 Emergency. The firefighters will be here soon to put out the fire. __*d*__

2. Don't just stand at the door. Come in. _____

3. Fill out the application. _____

4. We're going to practice some phrasal verbs. Henry, can you please hand out this exercise? _____

5. I left my book at school. I don't remember the homework for tonight. I'll call up Manny and ask him. _____

6. I can't talk to you now. Come back in fifteen minutes. _____

a. raise

b. remove

c. telephone

d. extinguish

e. enter

f. distribute

7. I can't concentrate! Would you please turn down the music! _____   **g.** complete

8. I am freezing in this house. Please turn up the heat. _____   **h.** wait

9. Please take off your wet shoes. _____   **i.** lower

10. Hold on a minute. I'm not ready yet. _____   **j.** return

EXERCISE 4

Fill in the blanks with the phrasal verbs below.

put away	turn on	pick up	throw away	turn off

DIRECTIONS FOR LANGUAGE LAB ASSISTANTS

When you leave the language lab, there are several things you must do. First, (1) _____ all the trash from the floor. Then (2) _____ all the equipment—tape recorders, VCRs, etc. (3) _____ all the cassettes students used. (4) _____ any coffee cups or trash students left in the room. Finally, (5) _____ the alarm system before you lock the doors.

► **S**eparable and Inseparable Phrasal Verbs

Separable Phrasal Verbs

EXAMPLES	EXPLANATIONS
Verb **Particle** **(a)** The teacher **handed out** the exercise. **Verb** **Direct Object** **Particle** **(b)** The teacher **handed** the exercise **out.**	When the direct object is a noun, it can go: • after the particle (*out*) • between the verb (*handed*) and the particle (*out*)
(c) The teacher handed **it** out. **(d)** NOT: The teacher handed out **it.**	When the direct object is a pronoun, it always goes between the verb and the particle.

Inseparable Phrasal Verbs

EXAMPLES	EXPLANATIONS
(e) I **ran into** an old friend on the street. **(f)** I **ran into** her on the street. **(g)** **NOT:** I **ran** an old friend **into** on the street. **(h)** **NOT:** I **ran** her **into** on the street.	The direct object—noun or pronoun—goes after the particle.

EXERCISE 5

Sergeant Strict is giving orders to his new soldiers. He's losing his patience. Repeat the Sergeant's orders in a different way each time.

1. (a) "Take off your civilian clothes."
   (b) *"I said,* __take your civilian clothes off__."
   (c) *"Come on,* __take them off__!"

2. (a) "Hand out these uniforms."
   (b) "I said, _____."
   (c) "Come on, _____!"

3. (a) "Put on your new Army clothes."
   (b) "I said, _____."
   (c) "Come on, _____!"

4. (a) "Turn down that radio."
   (b) "I said, _____."
   (c) "Come on, _____!"

5. (a) "Put away your old clothes."
   (b) "I said, _____."
   (c) "Come on, _____!"

6. (a) "Throw out that junk food from home."
   (b) "I said, _____."
   (c) "Come on, _____!"

7. (a) "Clean up this mess."
   (b) "I said, _____."
   (c) "Come on, _____!"

8. (a) "Turn off the lights!"
   (b) "I said, _____."
   (c) "Come on, _____!"

▶ **C**ommon Separable and Inseparable Phrasal Verbs

Separable Phrasal Verbs

SEPARABLE PHRASAL VERBS	MEANING	EXAMPLES
calm down	relax	**(a)** She is very upset about the accident. We can't **calm** her **down.**
call up	telephone	**(b)** I **called** my friend **up** the other night to ask about the homework.
cheer up	become happy, make someone happy	**(c)** My friend failed her final exam, so I brought her flowers to **cheer** her **up.**
clean up	clean	**(d)** **Clean** your room **up** before you watch TV!
figure out	solve, understand	**(e)** This puzzle is very confusing. I can't **figure** it **out.**
fill out	complete	**(f)** **Fill out** the application for a new license.
fill up	fill	**(g)** **Fill** it **up** with regular gas, please.
hand out	distribute	**(h)** The teacher **handed** the tests **out** to the the class.
hang up	place on a hanger or hook	**(i)** My husband never **hangs** his clothes **up.** **(j)** Please **hang up** the phone.
look up	search for in a reference book	**(k)** I didn't know his telephone number, so I **looked** it **up** in the phone book.
pick up	collect, lift	**(l)** In my neighborhood, they **pick up** the garbage every Tuesday. **(m)** I **picked** my pen **up** and started to write.
put away	put in its usual place	**(n)** My kids are neat! They always **put** their toys **away.**
put on	dress yourself	**(o)** It's really cold outside, so **put** a coat **on.**
put out	extinguish	**(p)** It took firefighters a few hours to **put** the fire **out.**

SEPARABLE PHRASAL VERBS	MEANING	EXAMPLES
take off	remove	**(q)** **Take** your shoes **off** before you come into the house.
take out	put something outside	**(r)** Will you please **take** the garbage **out**?
throw out/ away	put in the garbage	**(s)** I have a lot of old things in the garage. I need to **throw** them **out**.
turn down	lower the volume	**(t)** It's 2:00 in the morning. **Turn** that stereo **down!**
turn off	stop the power	**(u)** There aren't any good programs on TV tonight. **Turn** it **off**.
turn on	start the power	**(v)** I always **turn on** the radio in the morning.
turn up	increase the volume	**(w)** When I hear my favorite song, I **turn** the volume **up**.
wake up	to open your eyes; to finish sleeping; to interrupt someone's sleep	**(x)** Be quiet! Don't **wake** the baby **up**.

Inseparable Phrasal Verbs

INSEPARABLE PHRASAL VERBS	MEANING	EXAMPLES
get in *get out of**	enter and leave a vehicle (car, taxi, truck)	**(y)** I **got in** my car and drove away. **(z)** I dropped my bag when I **got out of** the cab.
get on *get off*	enter and leave other forms of transportation (bus, plane, train)	**(aa)** I **got on** the train at 42nd Street. **(bb)** I **got off** the bus in front of the school.
go over	review	**(cc)** I **went over** my notes before the test.
run into	meet by chance	**(dd)** I **ran into** an old friend the other day.

*Sometimes phrasal verbs have three parts.

EXERCISE 6

Fill in the blanks with the phrasal verbs below. Use a pronoun in the second blank of each dialogue.

▶ **EXAMPLE:** (clean up)

Mother: Danny, don't forget to (a) __clean up__ the mess in your bedroom.

Danny: Mom, I (b) ___cleaned it up___ this morning.

pick up	cheer up	hand out	throw out	fill out

1. **Counselor:** You need to (a) _____ this application for college.

   Abdul: Can I (b) _____ at home?

2. **Susie:** Danny, I think it's time to (a) _____ all these old newspapers.

   Danny: I'm (b) _____ right now.

3. **Jackie:** Could you please (a) _____ that paper on the floor for me?

   Mark: I'll (b) _____ in a minute!

4. **Ms. Wagner:** Can you help me (a) _____ these exams, John?

   John: Sure, I'll (b) _____ right now.

5. **Mom:** Please try to (a) _____ your sister. She's in a bad mood!

   Bobbie: No one can (b) _____ . She's always in a bad mood.

EXERCISE 7

Sylvia is working late tonight. She's calling her husband, Abe, to see if he has done all the things on her list. Role-play the dialogue with a partner.

▶ **EXAMPLE:**   **Sylvia:** Did you pick up the children at school?

Abe: Yes, dear. I picked them up.

1. pick up your shirts at the cleaners
2. clean up the kitchen
3. put away the clean laundry
4. take out the dog
5. throw out the old flowers in the vase
6. fill up the car with gas
7. pick up a pizza for dinner
8. turn on the movie for the children
9. call up Warren to invite him to dinner

Common Phrasal Verbs without Objects

Some phrasal verbs do not take an object.

PHRASAL VERBS WITHOUT OBJECTS	MEANING	EXAMPLES
break down	stop working	**(a)** My car **broke down** last night, so I walked home.
come back	return	**(b)** He left home and never **came back**.
come in	enter	**(c)** **Come in** and make yourself comfortable.
eat out	eat in a restaurant	**(d)** I hate to cook, so I often **eat out**.
grow up	become an adult	**(e)** I **grew up** in the United States.
show up	appear	**(f)** After two hours, he finally **showed up**.
sit down	sit	**(g)** I feel tired, so I think I'll **sit down** for a while.
stand up	stand	**(h)** In some countries, students **stand up** to show respect when the teacher enters the room.

EXERCISE 8

Fill in the blanks with a phrasal verb from the box.

stand up	sit down	break down	eat out
show up	come in	come back	grow up

What do you say when . . . ?

1. you are very late for an important date:

"Oh, I'm so sorry. Please forgive me, my car _____."

2. your friend's dog runs away from home:

"Don't worry, Elliot; I'm sure she'll _____ home very soon."

3. a child is sitting and an elderly man is standing on the bus. The child's mother says: "_____ and give that man your seat."

4. your thirty-year-old friend is acting like a child: "Come on, Matt, _____ . You're not a child anymore."

5. you are a car salesperson and you are trying to get people into your showroom:

   "Please _____ , folks. We have many new models and great prices this year."

6. you and your roommate are hungry, but you're too tired to cook:

   "Let's _____ ."

7. your friend is crying about her date last night:
   Tammy: "What happened, Cheryl? Don't tell me your date didn't _____ last night."
   Cheryl: "Oh, he did! That's why I'm crying!"

8. you are a receptionist in a very busy doctor's office and an angry patient is complaining about waiting so long:

   "Please _____ , Mr. Brody. The doctor will be with you in a few minutes."

EXERCISE 9

Make a story by putting the pictures in the correct order. Write the number of each picture next to the letter. Then fill in each blank with a phrasal verb from the box below.

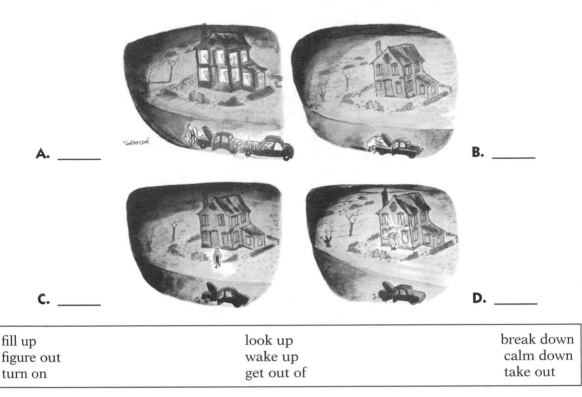

A. _____   B. _____

C. _____   D. _____

fill up	look up	break down
figure out	wake up	calm down
turn on	get out of	take out

It was a cold and lonely night. Forgetful Phil was on his way to visit his mother when his car suddenly (1) _____. He was angry and upset, but after a while, he (2) _____. It was dark, so Phil (3) _____ a flashlight from the glove compartment. Then he took out his car manual. He tried to (4) _____, "*What to do when your car breaks down in the middle of nowhere,*" but he didn't find anything in the manual. Next, he (5) _____ the car and looked under the hood. He wasn't able to (6) _____ what the problem was. Then Phil began to understand. He asked himself, "Did I (7) _____ my tank with gas?" The answer, of course, was no.

Luckily there was a house near by. He knocked on the door and shouted, but nobody answered. There were no other houses. There was no telephone. "What now??" thought Phil. Then, just as he turned around to go back to his car, another car crashed into the back of his car. Suddenly, the people in the house (8) _____ and (9) _____ the lights. Poor Phil felt like crying.

Use Your English

ACTIVITY 1: WRITING/SPEAKING

Work with a partner. Write a story or dialogue about the situation below, using the phrasal verbs in the box. Then role-play the situation for the class.

Situation: It is 11:00 P.M. You are sleeping very deeply. Suddenly, you hear some noise coming from the apartment downstairs. Your neighbor's stereo is very loud.

			turn off
wake up	throw out	turn down	call up
turn on	go back	calm down	

ACTIVITY 2: SPEAKING

Work in a group or as a whole class. The first person begins a story. He or she says, "I woke up . . ." and completes the sentence. The second person repeats the first sentence and adds a second sentence using a phrasal verb. The third person repeats the first two sentences and then adds a third, and so on. Try not to write anything down. Use your memory! Refer to the phrasal verbs in this unit.

▶ **EXAMPLES:** **Player #1:** I woke up early.

   Player #2: I woke up early, and turned off the alarm clock.

   Player #3: I woke up early, turned off the alarm clock, and took off my pajamas.

ACTIVITY 3: SPEAKING/WRITING

STEP 1 Work in a group. Put numbers 1 to 12 in a bag. Pick a number from the bag. Read the sentence in the box that corresponds to your number and then do the action.

STEP 2 After the group has done all the actions, write sentences about the things you did.

▶ **EXAMPLES:** Mario put on Marcela's cap.

José turned off the light.

1. Put on a piece of a classmate's clothing or jewelry.	2. Turn off the light.	3. You spill a cup of hot coffee on yourself and on the floor. Clean it up.
4. Call up a friend and tell him or her you are sick.	5. Draw a picture of yourself on a piece of paper and hang it up on the wall.	6. Stand up. Put your hands on your head. Then sit down.
7. Cheer a classmate up.	8. Hand your telephone number out to all the people in the group.	9. Take something out of your pocket and throw it away.
10. Take off an article of clothing and put it on someone else.	11. Turn on something electrical (tape recorder, radio, light, etc.) and then turn it off.	12. Pretend you find a word whose meaning you don't know. Look it up in the dictionary.

A C T I V I T Y   4 :   L I S T E N I N G / SPEAKING

Amy wants to buy a jacket. She goes to a store.

STEP 1 Listen to the conversation. Then look at the statements below. Check (✔) True or False.

		True	False
1.	The store doesn't have any size ten jackets.	____	____
2.	The jacket Amy tries on fits perfectly.	____	____
3.	Amy thinks the jacket is too expensive.	____	____
4.	Amy doesn't like the pink jacket she is wearing.	____	____
5.	Amy will return to the store.	____	____

STEP 2 Listen to the conversation again and complete the phrasal verbs you hear below:

take_____   put_____   throw_____   come_____   come_____

STEP 3 Compare the phrasal verbs you found with those your partner found. Now make a dialogue on a similar topic with your partner. Use the five phrasal verbs in the dialogue and others from this unit.

STEP 4 Role-play your dialogue in front of the class.

UNIT 22

COMPARISON WITH ADJECTIVES

UNIT GOALS:

- To use the (regular and irregular) comparative form of adjectives in statements
- To ask questions using comparative adjectives
- To express similarities and differences with adjectives using *as . . . as*
- To make polite comparisons

▶ **OPENING TASK**

Comparison Shopping for an Apartment

You are a college student and are looking for an apartment. You study during the day and have a part-time job at night.

FOR RENT
Studio Apartment. 200 square feet. Central location. Close to bus stop and market. Fully furnished. $500/month plus utilities.

FOR RENT
One-bedroom apartment. 900 square feet. Quiet. Lots of light. $800/month including utilities.

STEP 1 Look at the apartment ads. Read the statements below about the studio apartment. Check (✓) *Yes, No,* or *I Don't Know.*

			YES	NO	I DON'T KNOW
The studio apartment is	1. smaller	than the one-bedroom apartment.			
	2. closer to the bus stop				
	3. farther away from the downtown area				
	4. more expensive				
	5. more spacious				
	6. noisier				
	7. safer				
	8. more convenient				
	9. sunnier				
	10. quieter				

STEP 2 Which apartment is better? Give reasons for your choice.

I think the _____ is better because . . .

▶ **Comparative Form of Adjectives**

Regular Comparatives

There are two regular comparative forms of adjectives in English.

1. For adjectives with one syllable or those ending in *-y*:

X *is* _____ *er than* Y.

EXAMPLE	ADJECTIVE	COMPARATIVE	RULE
(a) This neighborhood is **safer than** that one.	*safe*	*safer than*	For adjectives ending in *-e*, add *-r*.
(b) The one-bedroom apartment is **bigger than** the studio.	*big*	*bigger than*	For adjectives that end in consonant-vowel-consonant, double the consonant, add *-er*.
(c) The studio is **noisier than** the one bedroom.	*noisy*	*noisier than*	For adjectives ending in *-y*, change the *-y* to *i*, add *-er*.
(d) The studio is **smaller than** the one-bedroom.	*small*	*smaller than*	For all other adjectives, add *-er*.

2. For adjectives with two or more syllables:

X *is (more/less)* _____ *than* Y.

EXAMPLE	ADJECTIVE	COMPARATIVE	RULE
(e) The studio is **more economical than** the one-bedroom.	*economical*	*more economical than*	Use *more* or *less* before the adjective.
(f) The studio is **less expensive than** the one-bedroom.	*expensive*	*less expensive than*	

NOTES:
- Some adjectives with two syllables can take either *-er* or *more/less*. For example: *quiet—quieter* or *more quiet*.
- In formal English we say: Joe is taller than **I** (am).
- In informal English we sometimes say: Joe is taller than **me**.
- Be sure to compare two like things: My hair is longer than Rita's (hair). NOT: My hair is longer than Rita.

Irregular Comparatives

EXAMPLES	EXPLANATIONS
(g) This neighborhood is **better than** that one. **(h)** This year's winter was **worse than** last year's (winter). **(i)** The one-bedroom is **farther** away from the bus stop **than** the studio is.	The comparative forms of good, bad, and far are irregular. *good—better* *bad—worse* *far—farther*
(j) This apartment is **much better than** that one. **(k)** This apartment is **much farther than** the other one.	Use *much* to make a comparison stronger.

EXERCISE 1

Make statements using the comparative form of each adjective in parentheses + *than*. Make a logical conclusion for each set of sentences.

▶ **EXAMPLES:** Dog lovers say:

        a. Dogs are (smart) <u>smarter than</u> cats.

        b. Dogs are (obedient) <u>more obedient than</u> cats.

        c. Therefore, dogs are (good) <u>better than</u> cats.

  1. a. A small car is (easy) _____ to drive _____ a big car.

    b. A small car is (economical) _____ a big car.

    c. A big car is (practical) _____ a small car.

  2. a. The weather in Spain is (hot) _____ the weather in Sweden.

    b. The food in hot countries is (spicy) _____ the food in cold countries.

    c. Therefore, the food in Sweden is (spicy) _____ the food in Spain.

  3. a. Outgoing people are often (nervous) _____ shy people.

    b. They are (talkative) _____ shy people.

    c. Therefore, they are (comfortable) _____ shy people in social situations.

  4. a. During a holiday season, airline tickets are (expensive) _____ they are off season.

    b. During a holiday season, hotels are (crowded) _____ they are off season.

    c. It's (difficult) _____ to travel during holidays _____ off season.

EXERCISE 2

Fill in the blanks with the comparative form of the adjective.

Jane: Kevin, I found these two apartment ads in the newspaper this morning. There's a studio and a one-bedroom. I think the one-bedroom sounds nice. What do you think?

Kevin: Well, the one-bedroom is definitely (1) (large) _____ than the studio, but the studio is (2) (cheap) _____ . You know you only have a part-time job. How can you afford to pay $800 a month for rent?

Jane: I know the one-bedroom is (3) (expensive) _____ , but I have so much furniture. The one-bedroom is (4) (big) _____ and I want to have guests visit and it will be much (5) (comfortable) _____ . Besides, maybe someday I'll have a roommate, and I'll need a (6) (spacious) _____ apartment, Kevin. Right?

Kevin: Well, maybe, but you need to be realistic. The studio is in the center of town. You'll be (7) (close) _____ to transportation, stores, the library, and the college.

Jane: You're much (8) (practical) _____ than I am, Kevin. But the studio is directly over a nightclub, so it will be (9) (noisy) _____ than the one-bedroom. I will need peace and quiet so I can study.

Kevin: Listen,—the studio is small, but it's much (10) (cozy) _____ than the one-bedroom and you'll spend much less time cleaning it!

Jane: True, but I think the one-bedroom will be much (11) (safe) _____ and (12) (good) _____ for me than the studio.

Kevin: It seems to me your mind is made up.

Jane: Yes, it is. By the way, Kevin, I'm going to see the one-bedroom later today. Can you come with me?

Kevin: Sure.

EXERCISE 3

Write an advertisement for each product on the left. Compare it to the product on the right. Use the adjectives below.

▶ **EXAMPLE:** *"Double Chocolate" cake tastes richer than "Chocolate Surprise."*

1. **Product:** Double Chocolate Cake Mix

   Compare with Chocolate Surprise Cake Mix.

   Adjectives: rich, creamy, delicious, sweet, thick, fattening

   _____

   _____

2. **Product:** Genie Laundry Detergent

   Compare with Bubbles Laundry Detergent.

   Adjectives: strong, effective, expensive, gentle, concentrated

   _____

   _____

3. **Product:** Save-a-Watt Space Heater

   Compare with Consumer Space Heater.

   Adjectives: efficient, safe, reliable, big, economical, practical

   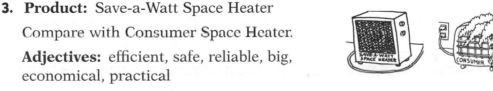

   _____

   _____

   _____

EXERCISE 4

Yoko wants to study English in the United States. She knows about an English program in Brattleboro, a small town in Vermont. She also knows about a program in Los Angeles, a big city in California. She needs to decide where she wants to live. Here is some information about the two places.

	Brattleboro, Vermont	Los Angeles, California
1. Rent for a one-bed apartment	$450 a month	$1,000 a month
2. Population	12,000	3 million
3. Weather	cold in winter hot in summer	warm in winter hot in summer
4. Public transportation	not good	good
5. Quality of life		
a. the environment	clean	not so clean
b. the crime rate	low	high
c. lifestyle	relaxed	busy
d. the streets	quiet	noisy

Make comparative statements about Brattleboro and Los Angeles.

1. crime rate (low/high) ___The crime rate is lower in Brattleboro___ than in Los Angeles. The crime rate is higher in Los Angeles than in Brattleboro.

2. (populated) _____

3. (cheap/expensive) _____

4. public transportation (good/bad) _____
   _____

5. winters (cold) _____

6. (dangerous/safe) _____

7. (clean/dirty) _____

8. (quiet/noisy) _____

9. (relaxed/busy) _____

10. In your opinion, which place is better for Yoko? Why?
    _____
    _____

▶ # Questions with Comparative Adjectives

EXAMPLES
(a) Is the one-bedroom **more expensive than** the studio?
(b) Are studios **better than** apartments?
(c) Are studios **less practical than** one bedroom apartments?
(d) **Who** is **older**, you or your brother?
(e) **Which** is **more difficult**, English or Chinese?
(f) **Whose** apartment is **more comfortable**, yours or hers?

EXERCISE 5

Refer to the Opening Task on pages 362–363 and ask a partner *yes/no* questions about the studio and the one-bedroom apartment. Answer the questions.

▶ **EXAMPLE:** economical

Is the studio more economical than the one-bedroom?

Yes, it is.

1. practical
2. far from the downtown area
3. small
4. cheap
5. sunny
6. comfortable
7. economical
8. roomy
9. quiet
10. convenient
11. close to the bus stop
12. pretty
13. large
14. good

EXERCISE 6

Interview your partner. Answer each other's questions.

▶ **EXAMPLE:** **Question:** Is a theater ticket more expensive than a movie ticket?

Answer: Yes, it is. No, it isn't. **OR** I'm not sure.

1. people in the United States/friendly/people in other countries
2. English grammar/difficult/the grammar of your native language
3. a house/good/an apartment
4. a single person's life/exciting/a married person's life
5. reading/interesting/watching TV
6. electric heat/economical/gas heat
7. men/romantic/women
8. a Japanese watch/expensive/a Swiss watch
9. the American population/diverse/the population in your native country

EXERCISE 7

Ask a partner questions with *who, which,* or *whose* and the words in parentheses. Answer each other's questions.

▶ **EXAMPLES:** (popular) Who is more popular, Elton John or Ricky Martin?

(practical) Which is less practical, a cordless phone or a regular phone?

1. (funny) Steven Martin or Jim Carrey?
2. (difficult) speaking English or writing English?
3. (hard) a man's life or a woman's life?
4. (bad) ironing or vacuuming?
5. (cheap) a public college or a private college?
6. (interesting) a taxi cab driver's job or a scientist's job?
7. (powerful) a four-cylinder car or a five-cylinder car?
8. (dangerous) a motorcycle or a car?
9. (sensitive) a man or a woman?
10. (good) Celine Dion's voice or Barbara Streisand's voice?
11. (delicious) Chinese food or Italian food?
12. (spicy) Indian food or Japanese food?

▶ **Expressing Similarities and Differences with *As . . . As***

EXAMPLES	EXPLANATIONS
(a) Mark is **as tall as** Sam. **(b)** Tokyo is **as crowded as** Hong Kong.	To say two things are equal or the same, use *as* + adjective + *as*.
(c) Mark is**n't as tall as** Steve. (= Steve is taller than Mark.) **(d)** The studio is**n't as expensive as** the one-bedroom.	To say there is a difference between two things, use *not as* + adjective + *as*.

EXERCISE 8

Here is a dialogue between teenage Tommy and his mother. Write the correct form of the comparative in the blanks. Use *-er, more than, less than,* and *as . . . as*.

Mother: Tommy, I don't want you to buy a motorcycle. Why don't you buy a car instead? A car is (1) __more convenient than__ (convenient) a motorcycle and it's (2) _____ (practical), too.

Tommy: Maybe it is, Mom, but a car isn't (3) _____ (economical) a motorcycle. I can get fifty miles to a gallon with a motorcycle! And a motorcycle's (4) _____ (cheap) a car.

Mother: Listen to me. You live in a big city. There are a lot of crazy people out there on the streets. A car is (5) _____ (safe) a motorcycle.

Tommy: Mom, I'm a good driver. I'm (6) _____ (good) you are! Besides that, it's (7) _____ (easy) to park a motorcycle in the city than it is to park a car.

Mother: Well, you're right about that. But I'm still your mother and you live in my house, so you will do as I say! When you are (8) _____ (old), you can do whatever you want.

Tommy: But all my friends are getting motorcycles, Mom. I won't look (9) _____ (cool) my friends.

Mother: I don't care, Tommy. Maybe their mothers aren't (10) _____ (nervous) I am, or (11) _____ (concerned) I am. My answer is "no" and that's final!

EXERCISE 9

Work with a partner. Make *yes/no* questions with *as . . . as*. Compare the city/town you are living in now with a city/town in your native country.

▶ **EXAMPLE:**   city/crowded

  Is Quito as crowded as Philadelphia?

1. capital city/big
2. foreign cars in . . . /expensive
3. the school year in . . . /long
4. soccer in . . . /popular
5. your hometown/safe
6. teenagers in your country/interested in rock music
7. beaches/crowded
8. foreign films/popular
9. air/polluted

FOCUS **4**

▶ **Making Polite Comparisons**

EXAMPLES	EXPLANATIONS
(a) Hamid is **shorter than** Marco. **(b)** Hamid is **not as tall as** Marco.	Sentence (b) is more polite. To make a polite comparison, use not *as* + adjective + *as*.

EXERCISE 10

You are "Blunt Betty." Your statements are very direct and a little impolite. Read a statement from Column A. Your partner, "Polite Polly," makes a statement with *not as* + *adjective* + *as* to make your statement more polite. The first one has been done for you.

Column A
Blunt Betty

Column B
Polite Polly

1. Marco is fatter than Jonathan.

(thin)
Marco is not as thin as
Jonathan.

2. London is dirtier than Geneva. (clean)
3. Science class is more boring than math. (interesting)
4. Your child is lazier than mine. (ambitious)
5. Your car is slower than ours. (fast)
6. Her eyesight is worse than mine. (good)
7. Your apartment is smaller than ours. (big)
8. Miguel's pronunciation is worse than Maria's. (good)
9. American coffee is weaker than Turkish coffee. (strong)
10. Your salary is lower than mine. (high)

EXERCISE 11

Make true statements about yourself. Use each of the categories below. Add more categories of your own.

▶ **EXAMPLES:**   My partner's older than I am. My partner's older than me.

I'm not as old as he is. I'm not as old as him.

Categories	Me	My Partner
1. Age	19	24
2. Height		
3. Hair length		
4. Hair color		
5. Personality		
6. Other		

EXERCISE 12

Correct the errors in the following sentences.

1. John is more tall than Mary.
2. Seoul is more safer than Los Angeles.
3. Paul is as intelligent than Robert.

4. Mary is not beautiful as Kim.

5. My test scores were more worse than Margaret's.

6. Lorraine's eyes are darker than me.

7. Jeff is more handsomer than Jack.

8. My parents' life was hard than mine.

9. Is New York exciting as Paris?

10. Is Lake Ontario cleaner that Lake Erie?

11. The Hudson River is not polluted as the Volga River.

12. Mexico's capital city is more crowded than the United States.

Use Your English

ACTIVITY 1: SPEAKING

How much do the following things cost in your country? Write the cost in United States dollars for each thing in your country. Ask a classmate the prices of the same things in his or her country. Add three items of your own. Present your comparisons to the class.

▶ **EXAMPLE:** A gallon of gas is more expensive in Malaysia than in Indonesia.

	Your Country	Your Classmate's Country
1. a gallon of gas		
2. a movie ticket		
3. bus fare		
4. a pair of jeans		
5. a cup of coffee		
6. rent for a one-bedroom apartment		
7. a newspaper		
8.		
9.		
10.		

ACTIVITY 2: WRITING/SPEAKING

Work in a group. Write six statements comparing cities, countries, or other places in the world. Make three statements that are true and three statements that are false. Read the statements to the class. The class guesses if they are true or false.

▶ **EXAMPLES:** Canada is larger than the People's Republic of China. (False)

The Pacific Ocean is bigger than the Atlantic Ocean. (True)

ACTIVITY 3: WRITING/SPEAKING

STEP 1 Look at the list of adjectives. Think about yourself and check *Very, Average,* or *Not Very* for each adjective.

STEP 2 Compare yourself with a partner. Write a comparative sentence for each adjective.

STEP 3 Tell the class about you and your partner.

▶ **EXAMPLES:** I'm more talkative than my partner.

He's less practical than I am.

I'm as athletic as he is.

	Very	Average	Not Very
1. talkative	_____	_____	_____
2. friendly	_____	_____	_____
3. shy	_____	_____	_____
4. neat	_____	_____	_____
5. practical	_____	_____	_____
6. optimistic	_____	_____	_____
7. moody	_____	_____	_____
8. lazy	_____	_____	_____
9. funny	_____	_____	_____
10. athletic	_____	_____	_____
11. jealous	_____	_____	_____
12. serious	_____	_____	_____
13. _____	_____	_____	_____
14. _____	_____	_____	_____
15. _____	_____	_____	_____

ACTIVITY 4: WRITING/SPEAKING

Work with a partner. Find a product or service you want to sell. Create a name for it. Then write a thirty-second radio or TV commercial for the product or service. Present your commercials to the class.

ACTIVITY 5: WRITING/SPEAKING

STEP 1 Compare life today with life fifty years ago. Read the first four sentences on the chart below and then add six statements of your own. Check *Agree* or *Disagree* under *You*. Then ask your partner and check *Agree* or *Disagree* under *Your Partner*.

	You		Your Partner	
	Agree	**Disagree**	**Agree**	**Disagree**
1. Life is more difficult.				
2. People are happier.				
3. Families are stronger.				
4. Children are more intelligent.				
5.				
6.				
7.				
8.				
9.				
10.				

STEP 2 Compare your answers with your partner's. Then write six sentences that compare life today with life fifty years ago.

▶ **EXAMPLE:** Today, children are more intelligent. They are more independent.

ACTIVITY 6: LISTENING/ SPEAKING

STEP 1 Look at the three different apartment ads below. Listen and say which apartment, A, B, or C, each person is talking about.

    A. FOR RENT: Studio apartment. 200 square feet. Close to bus stop and supermarket. Fully furnished. $500/month plus utilities.

    B. FOR RENT: One-bedroom apartment. 900 square feet. Quiet. Lots of light. $800/month including utilities.

    C. FOR RENT: Two-bedroom apartment. 1,500 square feet. Close to subway. Quiet area. $1,000/month plus utilities.

STEP 2 Which apartment is it? Work in a group. Each person gives two facts about one of the apartments and the others guess which apartment it is.

▶ **EXAMPLE:** It's more expensive than the studio. It's closer to the subway.

          Is it the _____ ?

          Yes, it is. No, it isn't.

UNIT 23

COMPARISON WITH ADVERBS

UNIT GOALS:

- To use the (regular and irregular) comparative form of adverbs in statements
- To express similarities and differences with adverbs using *as . . . as*
- To ask questions with *how*

What are your opinions about men and women? Check *Yes, No,* or *Maybe* for each question. Then talk about your answers with your classmates.

	Yes	No	Maybe
1. Do women work harder than men?			
2. Do men drive more safely than women?			
3. Do women communicate better than men?			
4. Do men dance less gracefully than women?			
5. Do women take care of children more patiently than men?			
6. Do men express their feelings more openly than women?			
7. Do women learn math less easily than men?			
8. Do men spend money more freely than women?			
9. Do women learn languages more easily than men?			
10. Do women think less clearly in emergencies than men?			

FOCUS **1**

▶ **Comparative Forms of Adverbs**

EXAMPLES	ADVERB/COMPARATIVE		RULE
(a) Women live **longer than** men.	*long*	*longer than*	For short adverbs, add *-er + than*.
(b) Do women drive **more safely than** men?	*safely*	*more/less safely than*	For adverbs with two or more syllables, use *more/less* + adverb + *than*.
(c) Do men drive **less carefully than** women?	*carefully*	*carefully than*	
(d) Eugene and Carol eat out much **more often than** Warren and Harriet.	*often*	*more/less often than*	With adverbs of frequency, use *more/less* + adverb + *than*.
(e) Do women **cook better than** men?	*well*	*better than*	With irregular adverbs, use the irregular form + *than*.
(f) Do boys do **worse** in school **than** girls?	*badly*	*worse than*	
(g) Can a man throw a ball **farther than** a woman?	*far*	*farther than*	

EXAMPLES	EXPLANATIONS
(h) Jason can climb higher than his brother **(can).** (i) She's better in school than I **(am).**	Sometimes, the auxiliary verb, for example *can, be,* or *will,* follows the subject after *than.*
(j) I type faster than my friend **(does).** (k) We speak Spanish better than they **(do).**	If there is no *be* or auxiliary verb, you can use *do.*
(l) I type faster than she **(does).** (m) I type faster than **her.**	In formal English, the subject pronoun follows *than.* In informal English, the object pronoun (*me, you, him, her, us, them*) follows *than.*

EXERCISE 1

Go back to the questions in the Opening Task on page 379 and underline the comparatives with adverbs.

▶ **EXAMPLE:** Do women live <u>longer than</u> men?

EXERCISE 2

Write sentences comparing yourself with your partner. Use the verbs and adverbs in the chart.

Verb	Adverb	Comparisons
1. cry	easily	My partner cries more easily than I (do).
2. drive	carefully	
3. speak English	fluently	
4. exercise	regularly	
5. travel	often	
6. study	hard	
7. laugh	loudly	
8. participate in class	actively	
9. take exams	calmly	
10. read	fast	

▶ Expressing Similarities and Differences with *As . . . As*

EXAMPLES	EXPLANATIONS
(a) A woman can work **as hard as** a man. **(b)** A man can dance **as gracefully as** a woman.	To show similarities, use *as* + adverb + *as*.
(c) He does**n't** speak **as clearly as** I	(do). **(d)** = I speak more clearly than he (does). **(e)** = He speaks less clearly than I (do).	To show differences, use *not as* + adverb + *as*. Remember that (c) is more polite, more tactful than (d) or (e). (See Focus 4 in Unit 22 on p. 372.)

EXERCISE 3

Sally Miller and Bill Benson are applying for a job as director of an art company. Decide who is better for the job. Make comparative statements about each person.

▶ **EXAMPLES:** Sally works as hard as Bill.

Bill draws better than Sally./Sally doesn't draw as well as Bill.

Work Habits	Sally Miller	Bill Benson
1. works hard	✔	✔
2. draws well		✔
3. thinks creatively	✔	✔
4. communicates openly	✔	
5. plans carefully		✔
6. works well with others	✔	✔
7. treats the staff fairly	✔	
8. solves problems calmly		✔
9. deals with clients successfully	✔	✔
10. works fast		✔

EXERCISE 4

Imagine you are the president of the art company. You want to compare Sally and Bill. Write some questions to ask about them.

▶ **EXAMPLES:**   Does Sally work as hard as Bill?

Does Bill draw better than Sally?

EXERCISE 5

Discuss these questions before you read.

1. Do you think boys and girls grow up differently?
   In what ways do they grow up differently?

2. Do you think boys and girls talk to each other differently?

3. In what ways do you think boys and girls play differently?

Now, read the following:

Boys and girls grow up in different worlds. Research studies show that boys and girls act very differently. For example, when boys and girls play, they don't play together. Some of their activites are similar, but their favorite games are different. Also, the language they use in games is different.

Boys usually play outside in large groups. The group has a leader. The leader gives orders. There are winners and losers in boys' games. Boys frequently brag about how good they are at something and argue about who is the best.

Girls, on the other hand, play in small groups or pairs. The most important thing for a girl is her best friend. Closeness is very important to girls. Girls like to sit together and talk. In their games, like jump rope, everyone gets a turn. In many of their activities, such as playing together with their dolls, there are no winners or losers. Girls don't brag about how good they are at something. They don't give orders. They usually make suggestions.

Docs this text say the same things you said in your discussion? What information is the same? What information is different?

EXERCISE 6

To test your understanding of the reading, check *True* or *False* for the statements below.

	True	False
1. Boys and girls play differently.		
2. Boys and girls usually play with each other.		
3. Girls act more aggressively than boys.		
4. Girls play more competitively than boys do.		
5. Boys brag about how good they are at something more frequently than girls.		
6. Girls talk to each other more intimately than boys do.		
7. Girls give suggestions more frequently than boys.		
8. Boys play more cooperatively than girls do.		

EXERCISE 7

For each statement you read, your partner says how he or she is similar or different.

▶ **EXAMPLE:** **You say:** I (can) cook well.

Your partner says: I can cook as well as you.

I can't cook as well as you.

I can cook better than you.

1. speak clearly

2. dance gracefully

3. sing sweetly

4. jump high

5. run far

6. add numbers quickly

7. meet new people easily

8. tell a joke well

9. study hard

10. learn English fast

EXERCISE 8

Write statements comparing men and women. Use *more/less/as . . . as*. Discuss your answers with the class.

1. think creatively

Men think more creatively than women.
Women think as creatively as men (do).

2. run fast

3. behave responsibly

4. act aggressively

5. ask for directions willingly

6. listen supportively

7. act independently

8. think logically

9. make friends quickly

10. cry easily

Add two statements of your own.

11. _____

12. _____

▶ **Questions with *How***

EXAMPLES	EXPLANATIONS
(a) **How old** are you? (b) **How well** do you speak English?	An adjective (*old, tall*) or an adverb (*well, far*) is often used in a *how* question.
(c) **How far** is it from here to the park? It's about five blocks.	*How far* asks about distance.
(d) **How long does it take** to fly from New York to Saigon? It takes about twenty-four hours. (e) **How long does it take** you to prepare dinner? It takes me an hour.	*How long does it take* asks about time.

EXERCISE 9

Ask a partner questions with *how*. Fill in your partner's answers on the right. Your partner asks you the same questions, and fills in your answers on the left.

▶ **EXAMPLES:**   How far do you live from school?

How well can you cook?

	You	Your Partner
1. how far/live from school	5 miles	4 blocks
2. how well/cook	very well	very well
3. how easily/fall asleep at night		
4. how far/run		
5. how hard/study		
6. how fast/type		
7. how late/stay up at night		
8. how early/get up in the morning		
9. how well/know your classmates		
10. how often/speak to your best friend		

EXERCISE 10

Compare yourself with your partner for each of the questions in Exercise 9.

1. <u>I live farther away from school than my partner (does).</u> .

2. <u>My partner cooks as well as I (do).</u> .

3. _____ .

4. _____ .

5. _____ .

6. _____ .

7. _____ .

8. _____ .

9. _____ .

10. _____ .

EXERCISE 11

Fill in the chart. Say how much time it takes you to do each of the activities below. Then interview a partner. Write statements with the comparative form of adverbs.

▶ **EXAMPLES:**   It takes me longer to do my homework.

I get dressed faster than you (do) in the morning.

	You	Your Partner
1. do your homework	1 hour	45 minutes
2. get dressed in the morning		
3. get to school		
4. clean your room/apartment/house		
5. have breakfast		
6. take a shower		
7. cook dinner		
8. fall asleep at night		

Use Your English

ACTIVITY 1: WRITING

Write sentences comparing two cities or places that you know.

▶ **EXAMPLE:** The trains run more smoothly in Montreal than in New York.

1. trains/run smoothly
2. buses/run efficiently
3. people/work hard
4. taxi drivers/drive recklessly
5. traffic/move slowly
6. people/talk quickly
7. people/talk to foreigners politely
8. stores/stay open late
9. people/drive fast
10. families/take vacations frequently

Add two sentences of your own:

11. _____

12. _____

ACTIVITY 2: SPEAKING/MIMING

STEP 1   Here is a list of adverbs and a list of actions. Write each adverb and each action on a separate card.

Adverbs	Actions
Slowly	Eat spaghetti
Sadly	Put on your clothes
Nervously	Make the bed
Angrily	Cook dinner
Fast	Type a letter
Carefully	Brush your teeth
Seriously	Comb your hair
Happily	Paint a picture
Loudly	Play tennis
Enthusiastically	Shake someone's hand
Shyly	Look at someone

STEP 2   Mix up each group of cards separately. With a partner, take one adverb card and one action card.

STEP 3   Both of you mime the same action and adverb. The class guesses the action and the adverb.

STEP 4   The class compares your two performances.

▶ **EXAMPLE:**   Angrily/Eat spaghetti

Paola ate spaghetti more angrily than Maria.

ACTIVITY 3: SPEAKING

Planning a Vacation

Here is a map of the southwestern United States. You and your friend want to take a two-week vacation to visit four national parks. You will start and end your trip in Las Vegas, Nevada.

Approximate Mileage Between National Parks and Las Vegas

	Las Vegas	Bryce Canyon	Death Valley	Grand Canyon	Zion National Park
Las Vegas		245	130	275	145
Bryce Canyon	245		365	300	100
Death Valley	130	365		405	275
Grand Canyon	275	300	405		250
Zion National Park	145	100	275	250	

STEP 1 Use the map and the mileage chart. Ask each other questions to find out the distances between parks. Fill in the information in the chart below.

▶ **EXAMPLE:** How far is it from Las Vegas to Death Valley?

It's 130 miles.

Depart from Las Vegas	Distance	Time
Stop 1: Death Valley	130 miles	2 hours
Stop 2: Zion National Park		
Stop 3: Bryce Canyon		
Stop 4: Grand Canyon		

STEP 2 Calculate the time required to go from one place to another and fill in the information in the chart. Remember you will travel by car and the average speed limit is 65 MPH. All distances are in miles.

▶ **EXAMPLE:** How long does it take to get from Las Vegas to Death Valley?

It takes about two hours.

ACTIVITY 4: WRITING

Compare yourself with someone you know—a family member, a friend, your boyfriend/girlfriend, etc. Write ten sentences.

▶ **EXAMPLES:** I dance better than my sister (does).

I can make friends more easily than she (does).

ACTIVITY 5: LISTENING/ SPEAKING

What does Richard like about London, England?

STEP **1** Listen to the tape and look at the list below. Check the things he thinks are good.

Richard likes . . .

1. _____ the people
2. _____ the hotel
3. _____ the buses
4. _____ the taxi drivers
5. _____ the subway
6. _____ English cooking
7. _____ the restaurants

STEP **2** Listen again and say why Richard likes or dislikes the things.

STEP **3** Tell the class about a place you visited. Use adverbs of comparison.

UNIT 24

SUPERLATIVES

UNIT GOALS:

- To understand the meaning of superlatives
- To know how to form regular and irregular superlatives
- To use the expression *one of the* + superlative + plural noun

▶ **O PENING TASK**

General Knowledge Quiz

STEP 1 Check the correct answer. Then compare your answers with your classmates'.

1. What is the largest ocean?
   a. Pacific   **b.** Atlantic   **c.** Indian

2. What's the most valuable painting in the world?
   a. Van Gogh's "Sunflowers"
   b. Leonardo da Vinci's "Mona Lisa"
   c. Rembrandt's "Self Portrait"

3. What's the most widely spoken language in the world?
   a. English   **b.** Spanish   **c.** Chinese

4. What's the hottest place in the world?
   a. Australia   **b.** Israel   **c.** Ethiopia

5. What's the tallest office building in the world?
   a. the Sears Tower, Chicago
   b. the World Trade Center, New York
   c. the Petronas Tower, Kuala Lumpur

6. What's the most crowded city in the world?
   a. Shanghai   **b.** Mexico City   **c.** Tokyo

7. What's the most expensive university in the United States?
   a. Harvard   **b.** Yale   **c.** M.I.T.

8. What's the wettest place in the world?
   a. Hawaii   **b.** India   **c.** Jamaica

9. What's the most nutritious fruit?
   a. banana   **b.** avocado   **c.** orange

10. What's the hardest gem?
    a. ruby   **b.** diamond   **c.** emerald

STEP 2 Now write similar questions. Quiz your classmates.

11. _____

12. _____

13. _____

14. _____

15. _____

▶ **S**uperlatives

EXAMPLES	EXPLANATIONS
(a) **The tallest** building in the world is the Petronas Tower. (b) **The least expensive** food on the menu is a hamburger. (c) Rosa writes **the most beautifully** of all.	Superlatives compare one thing or person to all the others in a group.
(d) Dr. Diaz is the most respected teacher **at the school.** (e) M.I.T. is the most expensive university **in the United States.** (f) Etsuko performs the best **of all the dancers.**	Use prepositional phrases after superlatives to identify the group.

EXERCISE 1

Go back to the Opening Task on page 393. Underline all the superlative forms in the questions.

▶ **EXAMPLE:** What is <u>the largest</u> ocean?

▶ **Regular and Irregular Superlative Forms**

Regular Forms

EXAMPLES	ADJECTIVE/ADVERB	SUPERLATIVE FORM	RULE
(a) The Sears Tower in Chicago is **the tallest** building in the United States.	*tall*	*the tallest*	One-syllable adjectives or adverbs: *the* + adjective/adverb + *-est*
(b) My grandfather worked **the hardest** of his three brothers.	*hard*	*the hardest*	
(c) Jupiter is **the largest** planet.	*large*	*the largest*	Adjectives/adverbs ending in *-e:* add *-st.*
(d) I get up **the latest** in my family	*late*	*the latest*	
(e) **The hottest** place in the world is Ethiopia.	*hot*	*the hottest*	One-syllable adjectives ending in consonant-vowel-consonant: double the final consonant, add *-est.*
(f) **The easiest** subject for me is geography.	*easy*	*the easiest*	Two-syllable adjectives/adverbs ending in *-y:* change *-y* to *-i:* add *-est.*
(g) She arrived **the earliest.**	*early*	*the earliest*	
(h) **The most nutritious** fruit is the avocado.	*nutritious*	*the most nutritious*	Adjectives/adverbs with two or more syllables: use *the* + *most/least.*
(i) **The least expensive** food on the menu is a hamburger.	*expensive*	*the least expensive*	
(j) Of all his friends, he drives **the most carefully.**	*carefully*	*the most carefully*	
(k) She danced **the least gracefully** of all the students.	*gracefully*	*the least gracefully*	

Irregular Forms

EXAMPLES	ADJECTIVE/ADVERB	ADVERB	SUPERLATIVE
(l) That college has **the best** professors.	good	well	the best
(m) That was **the worst** movie I saw last year.	bad	badly	the worst
(n) He ran **the farthest.**	far	far	the farthest

EXERCISE 2

Here are some interesting facts from the *Guinness Book of World Records*. Write the superlative form of the adjective/adverb in parentheses in the blanks.

▶ **EXAMPLE:** (cold) Antarctica is _____the coldest_____ place on earth.

1. _____ (large) cucumber weighed sixty-six pounds.

2. _____ (popular) tourist attraction in the United States is Disneyworld in Florida.

3. _____ (successful) pop group of all time was the Beatles.

4. _____ (heavy) baby at birth was a boy of twenty-two pounds eight ounces. He was born in Italy in 1955.

5. _____ (fat) person was a man in New York City. He weighed almost 1,200 pounds.

6. _____ (prolific) painter was Pablo Picasso. He produced about 13,500 paintings; 100,00 prints; 34,000 book illustrations; and 300 sculptures.

7. _____ (long) attack of hiccups lasted sixty-seven years.

8. _____ (big) omelet was made of 54,763 eggs with 531 pounds of cheese in Las Vegas, Nevada in 1986.

9. _____ (hot) city in the United States is Key West, Florida.

10. Mexico City is now the world's (fast)-growing _____ city.

EXERCISE 3

Fill in the name of a student in your class and the superlative form of each adverb.

	Name		Superlative	
1.	___Juan___	does the homework	_the most carefully_	(carefully).
2.	_____	writes	_____	(well).
3.	_____	arrives in class	_____	(early).
4.	_____	guesses new words	_____	(fast).
5.	_____	makes us laugh	_____	(often).
6.	_____	expresses opinions	_____	(open).
7.	_____	communicates in English	_____	(effectively).
8.	_____	participates in class	_____	(actively).

Add two statements of your own.

9. _____

10. _____

EXERCISE 4

Information Gap. Work with a partner. One person looks at Chart A on the next page, and the other person looks at Chart B on page A-21. Ask your partner questions to find out the missing information in your chart. Write the answers in the chart.

▶ **EXAMPLE:** **Student A:** What is the longest river in North America?

Student B: The Mississippi.

CHART A

	North America	South America	Asia	Europe	Africa	The World
long river		The Amazon		The Volga		The Nile
large country	Canada		The People's Republic of China		Sudan	
populated country		Brazil		Germany		The People's Republic of China
high mountain	Mt. McKinley		Mt. Everest		Mt. Kilimanjaro	
small country		French Guiana		Vatican City		Vatican City

EXERCISE 5

Play this modified Jeopardy game in two teams. Look at the gameboard on page 399. Team 1 chooses a category and a dollar amount. Choose one person in the class to read the questions under the CATEGORIES column aloud. Team 1 has one minute to choose an answer from the Answer Box. If the answer is correct, they "win" the money. If the answer is not correct, Team 2 answers the question and wins the money. The team with the most money at the end wins.

▶ **EXAMPLE:** **Team 1:** "Animals" for $20.

   Reader: What's the most dangerous animal?

   Team 1: Mosquitoes (They can give you malaria.)

GAMEBOARD

$$$	Planets	Animals	Other
$10			
$20			
$30			
$40			
$50			

CATEGORIES

Planets
$10	What is the largest planet in the solar system?
$20	What is the fastest planet?
$30	What is the hottest planet?
$40	What is the farthest planet from the sun?
$50	What is the closest planet to Earth?

Animals
$10	What is the tallest animal?
$20	What is the most dangerous animal?
$30	What is the fastest land animal?
$40	What is the most valuable animal?
$50	What is the largest and heaviest animal?

Other
$10	What is the hardest gem?
$20	What is the largest desert in the world?
$30	What is the highest court in the United States?
$40	What is the oldest country in the world?
$50	What is the shortest day of the year?

ANSWER BOX (Choose the answers to the questions from this box.)

Planets	Animals	Other
Pluto	mosquitoes	the Supreme Court
Mercury	the blue whale	the Sahara
Venus	giraffe	the winter solstice
Jupiter	cheetah	(first day of winter)
Mars	race horse	diamond
		Iraq

▶ **One Of The + Superlative + Plural Noun**

EXAMPLES	EXPLANATION
(a) Bach was **one of the greatest composers** of all time.	*One of the* + superlative + plural noun is common with the superlative form. Example (a) means that there are several composers we think of as the greatest composers of all time. Bach is one of them.
(b) He is **one of the least popular** students in the school.	

EXERCISE 6

Fill in the blanks with *one of the* + superlative + plural noun. Use the words in parentheses.

1. That's <u>**one of the most expensive cars**</u> you can buy. (expensive car)

2. In my opinion, wrestling is _____ you can play. (exciting sport)

3. Graduation was _____ of my life. (proud moment)

4. That was _____ in the city. (expensive hotel)

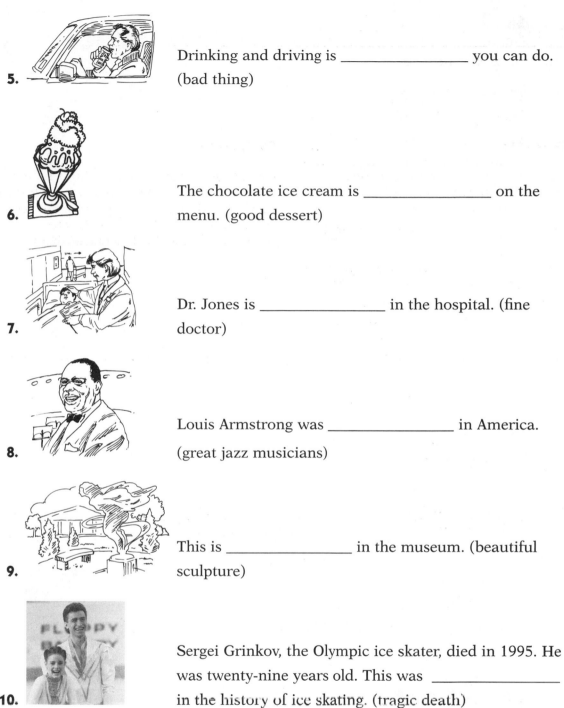

5. Drinking and driving is _____ you can do. (bad thing)

6. The chocolate ice cream is _____ on the menu. (good dessert)

7. Dr. Jones is _____ in the hospital. (fine doctor)

8. Louis Armstrong was _____ in America. (great jazz musicians)

9. This is _____ in the museum. (beautiful sculpture)

10. Sergei Grinkov, the Olympic ice skater, died in 1995. He was twenty-nine years old. This was _____ in the history of ice skating. (tragic death)

EXERCISE 7

Make sentences with *one of the* + superlative + plural noun. Compare your answers with your classmates'.

▶ **EXAMPLE:** 1. *Prague is one of the most beautiful cities in the world.*

1. a beautiful city in the world
2. an interesting place (in the city you are living in)
3. a good restaurant (in the city you are in)
4. a famous leader in the world today
5. a dangerous disease of our time
6. a serious problem in the world
7. a popular food (in the country you come from)
8. a funny show on television

Use Your English

ACTIVITY 1: WRITING/SPEAKING

Work in a group. Write five questions in the superlative form like the ones in the Opening Task on page 393. Then ask the class the questions.

▶ **EXAMPLES:** What's the most expensive car in the world?

What is the largest island?

ACTIVITY 2: WRITING/SPEAKING

Write ten questions to ask another student in the class about his or her home country or a country he or she knows. Use the superlative form of the words below or add your own.

▶ **EXAMPLES:** What's the most crowded city in . . . ?

What's the most popular sport in your country?

What's the most unusual food in your city?

crowded city	popular sport	popular food
polluted city	dangerous sport	unusual food
beautiful city	expensive sport	cheap food
important holiday	hot month	other
important monument	cold month	

ACTIVITY 3: SPEAKING

In groups, discuss the following statements. Say if you agree or disagree and why.

1. Money is the most important thing in life.
2. AIDS is the worst disease in the world today.
3. English is the most difficult language to learn.
4. Baseball is the most boring sport.
5. Democracy is the best form of government.

ACTIVITY 4: SPEAKING

Interview a partner about his or her life experience. Use the adjectives below to write questions with superlatives. Tell the class about the most interesting things you learned about your partner.

▶ **EXAMPLES:** What was the best experience you had this year?

What was the most embarrassing moment in your life?

Adjectives to describe experiences:

unusual	sad	exciting
embarrassing	interesting	frightening
happy	dangerous	beautiful
funny	good	bad

ACTIVITY 5: WRITING

Write a paragraph on one of the topics below:

a. The most embarrassing moment in my life.

b. The most frightening moment in my life.

c. The funniest moment in my life.

ACTIVITY 6: WRITING/ SPEAKING

STEP **1** Listen to the quiz show. Circle the letter of the correct answer.

Quiz Choices:

1. **a.** North America
2. **a.** the elephant
3. **a.** New York
4. **a.** Chinese
5. **a.** North America
6. **a.** The United States
7. **a.** Tokyo
8. **a.** The Himalayas
9. **a.** Spain
10. **a.** Islam/Muslim

b. Asia
b. the turtle
b. Los Angeles
b. French
b. Asia
b. China
b. Paris
b. The Andes
b. The United States
b. Christian

c. Africa
c. the bear
c. Chicago
c. English
c. Antarctica
c. Canada
c. Hong Kong
c. The Rockies
c. Italy
c. Hindu

STEP **2** Discuss your answers with your classmates.

UNIT 25

FACTUAL CONDITIONALS

If

UNIT GOALS:

- To use factual conditionals to express facts and habitual relationships
- To understand the order of clauses in factual conditionals

▶ OPENING TASK
That's Life

If you read a lot,
you learn a lot.

Find a match for each statement on the left. Write the letter in the blank next to the number.

_____ **1.** If you read a lot,

_____ **2.** If you play with fire,

_____ **3.** If you speak two languages,

_____ **4.** If you don't wash your hands,

_____ **5.** If you care about your health,

_____ **6.** If you eat too much,

_____ **7.** If you respect people,

_____ **8.** If you spend more money than you earn,

_____ **9.** If you work hard,

_____ **10.** If you speak well,

_____ **11.** If you think positively,

a. you get sick more often.

b. you don't smoke.

c. people respect you.

d. you have money problems.

e. you succeed.

f. you can communicate with more people.

g. people listen to you.

h. you live longer.

i. you gain weight.

j. you get burned.

k. you learn a lot.

Now make two similar true statements of your own.

12. _____

13. _____

▶ Expressing Facts

Factual conditionals tell about things that are always true and never change.

EXAMPLES		EXPLANATIONS
Clause 1 (*If* Clause)	**Clause 2** (Main Clause)	
(a) If you heat water to 212° (degrees) Fahrenheit,	it boils.	Use the simple present in both clauses.
(b) If you don't water a house plant,	it dies.	
(c) When (ever) you mix black and white,	you get gray.	You can use *when* or *whenever* in place of *if*.

EXERCISE 1

Test your knowledge. Circle the correct clause on the right. Discuss your answers with a partner.

1. If you put oil and water together,
   - **a.** the oil stays on top.
   - **b.** they mix.

2. If the temperature outside drops below 32° (degrees) Fahrenheit,
   - **a.** water freezes.
   - **b.** ice melts.

3. If you stay in the sun a lot,
   - **a.** your skin stays young and smooth.
   - **b.** your skin looks old.

4. If you smoke,
   - **a.** you have health problems.
   - **b.** you stay in good health.

5. If you don't refrigerate milk,
   - **a.** it stays fresh.
   - **b.** it goes bad.

6 If you fly west,
   - **a.** the time is earlier.
   - **b.** the time is later.

7. If you fly east,
   - **a.** the time is earlier
   - **b.** the time is later.

8. If your body temperature is 103° (degrees) Fahrenheit,
   - **a.** you are well.
   - **b.** you are sick.

EXERCISE 2

Think of the definitions of the words in italics. Find the definition on the right that completes each statement. Say your statements aloud.

1. If you live in a *democracy*, you can
2. If you're *patient*, you don't
3. If you're a *night owl*, you
4. If you're a *teenager*, you
5. If you're a *member of the faculty*, you
6. If you're a *pediatrician*, you
7. If you're a *blue-collar worker*, you may
8. If you're *broke*, you don't

a. want to be independent.
b. go to bed late.
c. teach in a school or college.
d. lose your temper.
e. work in a factory.
f. have any money.
g. treat sick children.
h. vote in elections.

FOCUS **2**

▶ **Expressing Habitual Relationships**

EXAMPLES		EXPLANATIONS
Clause 1 (*If* Clause)	**Clause 2** (Main Clause)	
(a) If I **cook,**	my husband **washes** the dishes.	Factual conditionals express present or past habitual relationships. Use the same tense in both clauses.
(b) If I **lied,**	my mother **punished** me.	
(c) When(ever) it **snowed,**	we **stayed** home from school.	You can use *when* or *whenever* in place of *if*.

EXERCISE 3

Make sentences with *if, when,* or *whenever* with the words below. Say your sentences aloud and compare your answers.

▶ **EXAMPLE:** I drive to school/take

If I drive to school, it takes about twenty minutes.

1. I drive to school/take
2. I take the bus to school/take
3. you have elderly parents/worry
4. you live with a roommate/share
5. you buy things on credit/pay
6. you take a vacation every year/feel
7. you never take a vacation/feel
8. exercise regularly/stay
9. someone sneezes/say
10. I don't want to cook/eat

EXERCISE 4

In some cultures, people say, "If you go out with wet hair, you get sick." We call these kinds of statements "old wives' tales." They are not always true, but people believe them and repeat them. Read the following "old wives' tales" and decide in your group if they are true or not.

1. If you go out with wet hair, you catch a cold.
2. If your ears are ringing, someone is talking about you.
3. If you eat chicken soup, your cold gets better.
4. If you hold your breath, your hiccups go away.
5. If you eat spinach, you get big and strong.

Now add a few old wives' tales from your home country and tell your group about them.

EXERCISE 5

Complete the *if* clauses with a statement of your own.

▶ **EXAMPLE:** If I feel very tired when I come home, I take a nap for ten minutes .

1. If I don't get enough sleep, _____.
2. If I get angry, _____.
3. If I get a headache, _____.

4. If I am late, _____.

5. If I gain weight, _____.

6. If I fail an exam, _____.

7. If I have money to spend, _____.

8. If I can't sleep at night, _____.

9. If I eat too much, _____.

10. If I get very worried, _____.

EXERCISE 6

Work with a partner. Ask each other questions about your childhood.

▶ **EXAMPLE:** When you were a child, what happened if/when you . . . told a lie?

If I told a lie, my mother yelled at me.

1. told a lie?

2. got sick?

3. disobeyed your parents?

4. did well in school?

5. got a bad grade on your report card?

6. came home very late?

7. had a serious personal problem?

8. fought with your brother or sister?

▶ **Order of Clauses in Factual Conditionals**

EXAMPLES	EXPLANATIONS
(a) If you study hard, you get good grades.	The *if* clause is usually first.
(b) How do you get an A in this class? You get an A **if you do all the work.**	When the *if* clause contains new information, the *if* clause can be second. When it is second, there is no comma between the two clauses.
(c) How do you get the color gray? You get gray **when(ever) you mix black and white.**	With *when* or *whenever,* you can also change the order of the clauses.

EXERCISE 7

Answer the questions below.

▶ **EXAMPLES:**   When do you feel nervous?

I feel nervous if I have many things to do and little time.

I feel nervous whenever I have a test.

1. When do you feel nervous?
2. When do you get a headache?
3. How do you catch a cold?
4. When do you have trouble sleeping?
5. When did your parents punish you?
6. When were your parents pleased with you?
7. When do you listen to music?
8. When do you get angry?
9. When do you feel happy?
10. How do you know if you're in love?

Use Your English

Psychologists say there are two personality types: A and B. "Type A" people worry, get nervous, and are under stress all the time. "Type B" people are calm and try to enjoy life.

STEP 1 Which personality type are you? Complete the statements.

1. Whenever there is a change in my life, I . . .
2. If I have a test, I . . .
3. When I get stuck in traffic, I . . .
4. When I enter a room with people I don't know, I . . .
5. When another driver on the road makes a mistake, I . . .
6. If a friend hurts my feelings, I . . .
7. If I don't hear from my family and friends, I . . .
8. When I have a lot of things to do in one day, I . . .
9. When I don't succeed at something, I . . .
10. When someone criticizes me, I . . .

STEP 2 Discuss your results in your group. Decide which students in the group are "Type A" personalities and which are "Type B." Explain why. Fill in the chart below.

Name	Type A Personality	Name	Type B Personality
Stefan	If he has a test, he worries a lot. When he doesn't succeed at something, he gets angry at himself.		

ACTIVITY 2: WRITING/SPEAKING

Do you have any special problems or unusual habits? Write down any habits you have. Share your statements with your group. Try to find the person with the most unusual habits.

▶ **EXAMPLES:** If I eat chocolate, I get a headache.

Whenever I feel anxious, I clean my apartment.

ACTIVITY 3: WRITING

Think about your childhood. Write five sentences with *if* clauses about past habits in your childhood.

▶ **EXAMPLES:** If my sister hit me, I hit her back.

If my mother yelled at me, I felt miserable.

ACTIVITY 4: SPEAKING

STEP 1 Compare habits in different countries. Write the name of a country in the left column and complete each *if/when(ever)* clause.

▶ **EXAMPLE:** In Canada, when you have dinner in a restaurant, you leave a tip.

Country	If/When(ever) Clause 1	Clause 2
Canada	you have dinner in a restaurant	you leave a tip
	someone gives you a compliment	
	someone gives you a gift	
	you greet an old friend	
	a baby is born	
	someone sneezes	
	someone invites you to dinner	
	you want to refuse someone's invitation	

STEP 2 Add two more habits to the list and make sentences about them.

ACTIVITY 5: LISTENING/ SPEAKING

Marcia and Eduardo are having a conversation about what they do if they can't sleep.

STEP 1 Listen to the conversation and then check the box if the statements below are true or false.

Read the statements. Check **True** or **False**.

	True	False
1. If Eduardo can't sleep, he takes a sleeping pill.		
2. If Marcia can't sleep, she drinks a glass of milk.		
3. If Eduardo can't sleep, he reads a boring book.		
4. If Eduardo drinks milk in the evening, he feels sick.		
5. If Marcia reads a boring book, she falls asleep.		

STEP 2 What conditions make people have problems with sleep? Tell the class.

Appendices

Appendix 1A   *Be: Present Tense*

I	am	
He She It	is	from Japan.
We You They	are	
There	is	a student from Japan in our class.
There	are	students from all over the world in this class.

Appendix 1B   *Be: Past Tense*

I He She It	was	
We You They	were	happy.
There	was	a party yesterday.
There	were	a lot of people there.

Appendix 1C   Simple Present

I You We They	work.
He She It	works.

Appendix 1D   Present Progressive

I	am	
He She It	is	working.
We You They	are	

Appendix 1E   Simple Past

I He She It We You They	worked	yesterday.

Appendix 1F   Future Tense with *Will*

I He She It We You They	will work	tomorrow.

Appendix 1G   Future Tense with *Be Going To*

I	am	
He She It	is	going to work in a few minutes.
We You They	are	

Appendix 1H   *Can/Might/May*

I He She It We You They	can might may	work.

Appendix 1I   *Be Able To*

I	am	
He She It	is	able to dance.
We You They	are	

Appendix 2A   Plural Nouns

Nouns	Singular	Plural
Regular	book table	books tables
Ends in vowel + *y*	toy	toys
Ends in vowel + *o*	radio	radios
Ends in consonant + *o*	potato tomato	potatoes tomatoes
Ends in −*y*	city	cities
Ends in *f, fe*	thief wife	thieves wives
(Except)	chief chef	chiefs chefs
Ends in *ss, ch, sh, x,* and *z*	class sandwich dish box	classes sandwiches dishes boxes
Irregular plural nouns	man woman child foot tooth mouse	men women children feet teeth mice
Plurals that stay the same	sheep deer fish	sheep deer fish
No singular form		scissors pants shorts pajamas glasses clothes

Appendix 2B   Simple Present: Third Person Singular

Rule	Example
1. Add -s to form the third person singular of most verbs.	My brother **sleeps** 8 hours a night.
2. Add -es to verbs ending in *sh, ch, x, z,* or *ss.*	She **watches** television every evening.
3. When the verb ends in a consonant + *y,* change the *y* to *i* and add -es.	He **hurries** to class every morning.
4. When the verb ends in a vowel + *y,* do not change the *y.* Add -s.	My sister **plays** the violin.
5. Irregular Forms: have go do	He **has** a good job. He **goes** to work every day. He **does** the laundry.

Appendix 2C   Present Progressive

1. Add -ing to the base of the verb.	talk study do agree	talking studying doing agreeing
2. If the verb ends in a single -e, drop the -e and add -ing.	drive	driving
3. If a one-syllable verb has a consonant, a vowel, and a consonant (c-v-c), double the last consonant and add -ing.	(c-v-c) s i t r u n	sitting running
Do not double the consonant if the verb ends in *w, x,* or *y.*	s h o w f i x p l a y	showing fixing playing
4. In two-sylllable verbs that end in a consonant, a vowel, and a consonant (c-v-c), double the last consonant only if the last syllable is stressed.	beGIN LISten	beginning listening
5. If the verb ends in -ie, drop the -ie, add -y and -ing.	lie die	lying dying

Appendix 2D Simple Past of Regular Verbs

1. Add -ed to most regular verbs.	start	started
2. If the verb ends in an -e, add -d.	like	liked
3. If the verb ends in a consonant + y, change the y to i and add -ed.	study	studied
4. If the verb ends in a vowel + y, don't change the y to i. Add -ed.	enjoy play	enjoyed played
5. If a one-syllable verb ends in a consonant, a vowel, and a consonant (c-v-c), double the last consonant and add -ed.	stop	stopped
Do not double the last consonant if it is w, x, or y.	show fix play	showed fixed played
6. If a two-syllable word ends in a consonant, a vowel, and a consonant (c-v-c), double the last consonant if the stress is on the last syllable.	ocCUR LISten	occurred listened

APPENDIX 3   Pronunciation Rules

Appendix 3A   Regular Plural Nouns

/s/	/z/		/ɪz/
After voiceless sounds (p, t, k, f, th)	After voiced sounds (b, d, g, v, m, n, l, r, ng) and vowel sounds		After s, z, sh, ch, ge/dge sounds. (This adds another syllable to the word.)
maps	jobs	pens	classes
pots	beds	schools	exercises
books	rugs	cars	dishes
cuffs	leaves	rings	sandwiches
months	rooms	days	colleges

Appendix 3B   Simple Present Tense: Third Person Singular

/s/	/z/	/ɪz/
After voiceless sounds (p, t, k, f)	After voiced final sounds (b, d, g, v, l, r, m, n, ng)	Verbs ending in sh, ch, z, s. (This adds another syllable to the word.)
He sleeps. She works.	She drives a car. He prepares dinner.	He teaches English. She rushes to class.

Appendix 3C   Simple Past Tense of Regular Verbs

/t/	/d/	/ɪd/
After voiceless sounds (p, k, f, s, sh, ch)	After voiced final sounds (b, g, v, l, r, m, n)	Verbs ending in t or d. (This adds another syllable to the word.)
He kissed her once. She asked a question.	We learned a song. They waved goodbye.	She painted a picture. The plane landed safely.

APPENDIX 4   Time Expressions

Appendix 4A   Simple Present

Adverbs of Frequency	Frequency Expressions	Time Expressions
always often frequently usually sometimes seldom rarely never	every { morning, afternoon, night, summer, winter, spring, fall, day, week, year } all the time once a week twice a month 3 times a year once in a while	in { 1997, October, the fall } on { Monday, Sundays, January 1st, the weekend } at { 6:00, noon, night, midnight }

Appendix 4B   Present Progressive

now	this semester
right now	this evening
at the moment	this week
today	this year
these days	
nowadays	

Appendix 4C   Past

yesterday	last	ago	in/on/at	
yesterday { morning, afternoon, evening }	last { night, week, month, year, summer }	{ an hour, two days, 6 months, a year } ago	in	{ 1988, June, the evening }
			on	{ Sunday, December 1, weekends }
			at	{ 6:00, night, midnight }

Appendix 4D   Future

this	next	tomorrow	other	in/on/at	
this { morning, afternoon, evening }	next { week, month, year, Sunday, weekend, summer }	tomorrow { morning, afternoon, evening, night }	soon, later, a week from today, tonight, for 3 days, until 3:00	in	{ 15 minutes, a few days, 2 weeks, March, 2005 }
				on	{ Tuesday, May 21 }
				at	{ 4:00, midnight }

Appendix 5A   Subject Pronouns

Subject Pronouns		
I	am	
You	are	
He		
She	is	
It		happy.
We		
You	are	
They		

Appendix 5B   Object Pronouns

		Object Pronouns
		me.
		you.
		him.
		her.
She	loves	it.
		us.
		you.
		them.

Appendix 5C   Demonstrative Pronouns

This That	is a list of subject pronouns.
These Those	are object pronouns.

Appendix 5D   Possessive Pronouns

This book is	mine. his. hers. * ours. yours. theirs.

* "It" does not have a possessive pronoun.

Appendix 5E   Reflexive Pronouns

I You We You They	love	myself. yourself. ourselves. yourselves. themselves.
He She It	loves	himself. herself. itself.

Appendix 5F   Reciprocal Pronoun

Friends help each other.

Appendix 6A   Possessive Nouns

Bob's Thomas' Thomas's The teacher's The students' The children's Bob and Andrea's	house is big.

Appendix 6B   Possessive Determiners (Adjectives)

My Your His Her Its Our Your Their	eyes are big.

Appendix 6C   Possessive Pronouns

The house is	mine. yours. his. hers. * ours. yours. theirs.

* "It" does not have a possessive pronoun.

Appendix 7A   Comparative Form (to compare two people, places, things or actions)

| Betsy | is | older
bigger
busier
later
more punctual
less talkative | than | Judy. |
| | plays the violin | faster
more beautifully
better | | |

Appendix 7B   Superlative Form (to compare one thing or person to all the others in a group)

| Betsy | is | the oldest
the biggest
the busiest
the most practical
the most punctual | of all her sisters. |
| | plays the violin | the fastest
more beautifully
the best | |

Appendix 7C   As...As (to say that two people, places, or things are the same)

| Betsy | is | as | old
big
busy
practical
punctual | as | Judy. |
| | plays the violin | | fast
beautifully
well | | |

Simple Form	Past-Tense Form	Past Participle	Simple Form	Past-Tense Form	Past Participle
be	was	been	leave	left	left
become	became	become	lend	lent	lent
begin	began	begun	let	let	let
bend	bent	bent	lose	lost	lost
bite	bit	bitten	make	made	made
blow	blew	blown	meet	met	met
break	broke	broken	pay	paid	paid
bring	brought	brought	put	put	put
build	built	built	quit	quit	quit
buy	bought	bought	read	read*	read*
catch	caught	caught	ride	rode	ridden
choose	chose	chosen	ring	rang	rung
come	came	come	run	ran	run
cost	cost	cost	say	said	said
cut	cut	cut	see	saw	seen
dig	dug	dug	sell	sold	sold
do	did	done	send	sent	sent
draw	drew	drawn	shake	shook	shaken
drink	drank	drunk	shoot	shot	shot
drive	drove	driven	shut	shut	shut
eat	ate	eaten	sing	sang	sung
fall	fell	fallen	sit	sat	sat
feed	fed	fed	sleep	slept	slept
feel	felt	felt	speak	spoke	spoken
fight	fought	fought	spend	spent	spent
find	found	found	stand	stood	stood
fly	flew	flown	steal	stole	stolen
forget	forgot	forgotten	swim	swam	swum
get	got	gotten	take	took	taken
give	gave	given	teach	taught	taught
go	went	gone	tear	tore	torn
grow	grew	grown	tell	told	told
hang	hung	hung	think	thought	thought
have	had	had	throw	threw	thrown
hear	heard	heard	understand	understood	understood
hide	hid	hidden	wake	woke	woken
hit	hit	hit	wear	wore	worn
hold	held	held	win	won	won
hurt	hurt	hurt	write	wrote	written
keep	kept	kept			
know	knew	known			
lead	led	led			

* Pronounce the base form: /rid/; pronounce the past-tense form and the past participle: red.

Exercises (second parts)

Unit 1

Exercise 5 (page 5)

List B

Men	Country	Nationality
1. Mario		Peruvian
2. Mohammed	Morocco	
3. Hideki and Yoshi		Japanese
4. Leonardo	The Dominican Republic	
5. Oumar		Senegalese
Women		
6. Lilik	Indonesia	
7. Krystyna		Polish
8. Liisa and Katja	Finland	
9. Belén		Spanish
10. Margarita and Dalia	Brazil	

Exercise 4 (page 18)

Example:

1.

2.

3.

4.

5.

6.

7.

8.

9.

10.

Exercise 6 (page 20)

Chart B

Name: Age:	Cindy 24	Shelly 30
1. Height		
tall		✔
average height		
short		
2. Weight		
thin		
average weight		✔
heavy		
3. Personality		
shy		✔
friendly		
quiet		✔
talkative		
neat		✔
messy		
funny		
serious		✔
nervous		
calm		✔

Exercise 6 (page 34)

MAP B

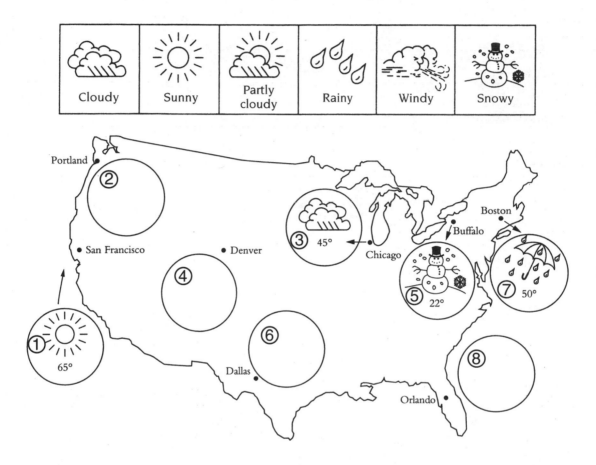

Exercise 7 (page 36)

Chart B

1. 11:30	**2.** 8:15	**3.** 7:35	**4.** 9:45
5. 1:55	**6.** 3:10	**7.** 2:40	**8.** 5:20

Exercise 10 (page 40)

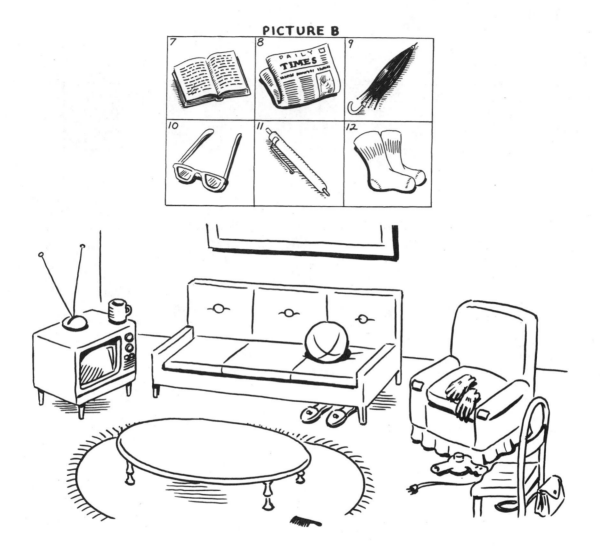

Exercise 2 (page 141)

Student B

	Nahal		Sang-Woo	
	Yes	**No**	**Yes**	**No**
1. like to learn English			✔	
2. want to meet English-speaking people	✔			
3. feel nervous when speaking English			✔	
4. like to work in groups	✔			
5. need grammar rules to learn English			✔	
6. learn by speaking and listening to English	✔			
7. learn by reading and writing English			✔	
8. learn slowly, step by step		✔		
9. try new ways of learning				✔

Answers to Exercise 15 (page 307)

Text B

1. Doina grew up in _____ (where).
2. She married a government official.
3. She was pregnant in 1976. She had _____ (what).
4. Doina was unhappy _____ (why).
5. She thought of ways to escape.
6. She taught her daughter _____ (what).
7. On October 9, 1988, she and her daughter swam across the Danube River to Serbia.
8. _____ caught them (who).
9. Doina and her daughter went to jail.
10. They tried to escape _____ from jail (when).
11. Finally, they left Romania on foot in the middle of the night.
12. They flew to _____ in 1989 (where).
13. Doina went to school to learn English.
14. She wrote _____ (what) in her ESL class.

Activity 2: Conclusion to Exercise 12 (page 304) and Activity 2 (page 309)

Activity 6: (page 311)

Only the Host looks at this game board.

GAME BOARD

$$$	Category 1 PEOPLE	Category 2 WH-QUESTIONS	Category 3 YES/NO QUESTIONS
$10	Ms. Ditto	a VCR	Yes, she did.
$20	Harry	on the first day of classes	Yes, he did.
$30	the Director	in the language lab	No, he didn't.
$40	Professor Brown	because he needed to pay for the ESL classes again this semester	No, he didn't.
$50	the students	she noticed grammar mistakes in the note	Yes, they did.

UNIT 24

Exercise 4 (page 397)

CHART B

	North America	Central and South America	Asia	Europe	Africa	The World
long river	The Mississippi		The Yangtze		The Nile	
large country		Brazil		France		The People's Republic of China
populated country	The United States		The People's Republic of China		Nigeria	
high mountain		Mt. Aconcagua		Mt. Elbrus		Mt. Everest
small country	Bermuda		Macao		the Seychelles	

Credits

Photo Credits

Page 1: Upper left, © The Stock Market/Julie Harrington; upper middle, © The Stock Market/Rob Lewine; upper right, © The Stock Market/Harvey Lloyd; lower left, © The Stock Market/Marco Cristofori; lower middle, © The Stock Market/Vince Streano; lower right, © The Stock Market/Roy Morsch. Page 9: (Top to bottom) © The Stock Market/Vivianne Holbrooke; © The Stock Market/Claudia Park. Page 11: © The Stock Market/Roy Morsch. Page 28: Upper left, © Corbis/Yannn Arthus-Bertrand; upper right, © The Stock Market/Ned Gillette; lower left, © The Stock Market/J. Messerschmidt; lower right, © Corbis/Vittoriano Rastelli. Page 46: © The Stock Market/Jeff Zaruba. Page 64: © Corbis/Richard A. Cooke. Page 65: Left, © Corbis/Michael T. Sedam; middle, © Corbis/Perry Conway; © Corbis/Wolfgang Kaehler. Page 69: Upper left, © The Stock Market/Frank P. Rossotto; upper right, © The Stock Market/Ray Shaw; lower left, © Corbis/David Turnley. Page 74: Top, © The Stock Market/Jon Feingersh. Page 107: © The Stock Market/Anne Heimann. Page 116: Left, © Heinle & Heinle, photograph by Jonathan Stark; right, © The Stock Market/David Pollack. Page 129 © Heinle & Heinle, photograph by Jonathan Stark. Page 130 © Heinle & Heinle, photograph by Jonathan Stark. Page 138: Left, © Heinle & Heinle, photograph by Jonathan Stark; right, © The Stock Market/John Henley. Page 153 © Heinle & Heinle, photograph by Jonathan Stark. Page 168 © Heinle & Heinle, photograph by Jonathan Stark. Page 172: © The Stock Market/Gabe Palmer. Page 188: © The Stock Market/David Woods. Page 198: Left, © The Stock Market/Chuck Savage; right, © The Stock Market/Jon Feingersh. Page 199: Top left, © The Stock Market/Peter Steiner; top middle, © The Stock Market/Jon Feingersh; middle left, © The Stock Market/David Frazier; middle middle, © Corbis/Gianni Orti; middle right, © The Stock Market/Michael Tamboririno; lower left, © The Stock Market/Chris Jones. Page 202: Left, © Heinle & Heinle, photograph by Jonathan Stark; middle, © The Stock Market/Peter Steiner; right, © The Stock Market/Rob & Sas. Page 228 © Heinle & Heinle, photograph by Jonathan Stark. Page 232: © The Stock Market/Gabe Palmer. Page 251: © The Stock Market/Nancy Ney. Page 258 © Heinle & Heinle, photograph by Jonathan Stark. Page 272: Top, © Corbis/Flip Schulke; middle, © Corbis/ Hulton-Deutsch Collection; bottom, © Corbis/Hulton-Deutsch Collection. Page 273: (Top to bottom) © Corbis/Hulton-Deutsch Collection; © Corbis/Underwood & Underwood; © Corbis/Robert Maass; © Corbis/Richard T. Nowitz. Page 283: photograph by Jonathan Stark. Page 286: © Corbis/Owen Franken. Page 288: © Corbis/Steve Chenn. Page 303 © Heinle & Heinle, photograph by Jonathan Stark Page 312: © Corbis/Roger Ressmeyer. Page 322: © Archive Photos/Curry. Page 347 © Heinle & Heinle, photograph by Jonathan Stark. Page 355 © Heinle & Heinle, photograph by Jonathan Stark. Page 362: Left, © Corbis/Michael Boys; right, © Corbis/Christpher Cormack. Page 378 © Heinle & Heinle, photograph by Jonathan Stark. Page 406: © Corbis/Laura Dwight.

Index

Use the Entire Grammar Dimensions Series

Grammar Dimensions Book 1, Platinum Edition
High Beginning
Student Text:	0-8384-0260-7
Workbook:	0-8384-0266-6
Audiocassette:	0-8384-0261-5
Teacher's Edition:	0-8384-0267-4

Grammar Dimensions Book 2, Platinum Edition
Intermediate
Student Text:	0-8384-0268-2
Workbook:	0-8384-0274-7
Audiocassette:	0-8384-0269-0
Teacher's Edition:	0-8384-0275-5

Grammar Dimensions Book 3, Platinum Edition
High Intermediate
Student Text:	0-8384-0277-1
Workbook:	0-8384-0284-4
Audiocassette:	0-8384-0278-X
Teacher's Edition:	0-8384-0285-2

Grammar Dimensions Book 4, Platinum Edition
Advanced
Student Text:	0-8384-0286-0
Workbook:	0-8384-0291-7
Audiocassette:	0-8384-0287-9
Teacher's Edition:	0-8384-0292-5

Read the Definitive Source for Grammar Reference and Teaching Guidance
The Grammar Book: An ESL/EFL Teacher's Course, Second Edition
Marianne Celce-Murcia and Diane Larsen-Freeman ISBN:0-8384-4725-2

For more information about ***Grammar Dimensions, Platinum Edition*** and
The Grammar Book, please contact your Heinle/Thomson Learning
representative or call (toll-free in the U.S.) 1-877-NEED-ESL